AIR CRASH INVESTIGATIONS

THE DEADLIEST SINGLE AIRCRAFT ACCIDENT IN AVIATION HISTORY

The Crash of Japan Airlines Flight 123

AIR CRASH INVESTIGATIONS

Over the last decades flying has become an every day event, there is nothing special about it anymore. Safety has increased tremendously, but unfortunately accidents still happen. Every accident is a source for improvement. It is therefore essential that the precise cause or probable cause of accidents is as widely known as possible. It can not only take away fear for flying but it can also make passengers aware of unusual things during a flight and so play a role in preventing accidents.

Air Crash Investigation Reports are published by official government entities and can in principle usually be down loaded from the websites of these entities. It is however not always easy, certainly not by foreign countries, to locate the report someone is looking for. Often the reports are accompanied by numerous extensive and very technical specifications and appendices and therefore not easy readable. In this series we have streamlined the reports of a number of important accidents in aviation without compromising in any way the content of the reports in order to make the issue at stake more easily accessible for a wider public.

Hans Griffioen, editor.

AIR CRASH INVESTIGATIONS

THE DEADLIEST SINGLE AIRCRAFT ACCIDENT IN AVIATION HISTORY

The Crash of Japan Airlines Flight 123

Hans Griffioen, editor

MABUHAY PUBLISHING

AIR CRASH INVESTIGATIONS

THE DEADLIEST SINGLE AIRCRAFT ACCIDENT IN AVIATION HISTORY

The Crash of Japan Airlines Flight 123

The details of the final Aircraft Accident Report of the Boeing 747 SR-100. JA8119, owned and operated by Japan Air Lines Co.. Ltd., that crashed in Gunma Prefecture, Japan on August 12, 1985, killing 520 people. Submitted by the Aircraft Accident Investigation Commission Ministry of Transport on June 19, 1987.

A Lulu.com imprint

ISBN: 978-1-257-83508-9

Contents:

281   ATTACHED PHOTOS

53. Scratches on vertical stabilizer front spar near FS445
54.   ,,   FS420
55.   ,,   FS220
56.   ,,   FS169
57.   ,,   FS143
58. Black substance adhering to right side skin of vertical stabilizer (1)
59.   ,,   ,,   (2)
60. Fractured left horizontal stabilizer leading edge
61. Fractured right horizontal leading edge
62. Fractured right horizontal stabilizer tip
63. Fractured left horizontal stabilizer tip
64. Aft pressure bulkhead   part 1 (pressurized side)
65.   ,,   part 1 (nonpressurized side)
66.   ,,   part 2 (pressurized side)
67.   ,,   part 2 (nonpressurized side)
68.   ,,   part 2A (pressurized side)
69.   ,,   part 2A (nonpressurized side0
70.   ,,   part 3 (pressurized side)
71.   ,,   part 3 (nonpressurized side)
72.   ,,   part 4 (pressurized side)
73.   ,,   part 5 (pressurized side)
74.   ,,   part 5 (nonpressurized side)
75.   ,,   part 6 (pressurized side)
76.   ,,   part 6 (nonpressurized side)
77. Buckling of aft pressure bulkhead (1)
78.   ,,   (2)
79.   ,,   (3)
80.   ,,   (4)
81.   ,,   (5)
82.   ,,   (6)
83.   ,,   (7)
84. Aft pressure bulkhead L18 splice - lower web edge
85.   ,,   - edge distance vicinity of rivet No. 29
86.   ,,   -   ,,   No. 84
87.   ,,   - adherence of tobacco nicotine in vicinity of rivet No. 21 to No. 24
88.   ,,   - adherence of tobacco nicotine in vicinity of rivet No. 39 to No. 45
89.   ,,   - adherence of tobacco nicotine in vicinity of rivet No. 49 to No. 55
90.   ,,   - adherence of tobacco nicotine in vicinity of rivet No. 70 to No. 72
91.   ,,   - adherence of tobacco nicotine in vicinity of rivet No. 75 to No. 78

92.   ,,   - adherence of tobacco nicotine in vicinity of rivet No. 41

93.   ,,   - adherence of tobacco nicotine in vicinity of rivet No. 50

94. Fuselage frame at fuselage to vertical fin joint (BS2436 – 2460)

95. Fuselage rupture at fuselage to vertical fin joint (BS2484)

96. Vertical stabilizer aft torque box – root of skin on left side

97. Central part of horizontal stabilizer center section

98. Insulation material adhering to fragments of ceiling of rearmost cabin lavatory (lavatory R)

99. Fracture of horizontal stabilizer jack screw (crash site)

100.   ,,   (condition before teardown)

101. Damage to magnetic tape of DFDR

102. Microstructure of upper web skin

103. Microstructure of lower web skin

104. Microstructure of tear strap

105. Microstructure of stiffener

106. Microstructure of rivet

107. Fracture surface of river hole No. 34 inboard

108.   ,,   (location 4.90 mm from hole edge)

109.   ,,   (location 0.28 mm from hole edge)

110.   ,,   (location 3.05 mm from hole edge)

111. Fracture surface of river hole No. 47 outboard (location 0.32 mm from hole edge)

112. Fracture surface of river hole No. 53 outboard (location 1.00 mm from hole edge)

113.   ,,   No. 66 outboard (location 0.80 mm from hole edge)

114.   ,,   No. 90 inboard   (location 2.60 mm from hole edge)

115. Fracture aspect of No. 1 strap

116.   ,,   No. 2 strap

117.   ,,   No. 3 strap

118.   ,,   No. 4 strap

119. Fracture aspect of stiffener L18, at rivet hole No. 30

120.   ,,   No. 83

121. Close up view of stiffener L18, revealing shear mode fracture, at rivet hole No. 30 outboard outboard

122.   ,,   No. 83 outboard

123. A part of failure line in lower web through rivet holes 84 – 89

124. The accident aircraft flying over Okutama

347   **ATTACHED ATTACHMENTS**

419   **IN THE AFTERMATH...**

13

SYNOPSIS

JA8119, a Boeing 747 SR-100 of Japan Air Lines Co., Ltd, during a flight from Tokyo to Osaka scheduled as flight 123 on August 12,1985, experienced an emergency at approximately 1825 hours when approaching east coast of Southern Izu Peninsula, and after a continued flight of about 30 minutes the aircraft crashed among mountains in Ueno Village, Tano Gun, Gunma Prefecture at approximately 1856 hours.

On board the aircraft were 509 passengers (including 12 infants) and a crew of 15; 524 persons in total, of which 520 persons (505 passengers and 15 crew-members) were killed, and 4 passengers seriously injured.

The aircraft was destroyed and fire occurred.

14

FACTUAL INFORMATION

CHAPTER 1

THE PROGRESS AND PROCESS OF THE AIRCRAFT ACCIDENT INVESTIGATIO

Summary of the Aircraft Accident

JA8119, a Boeing 747 SR-100 of Japan Air Lines Co., Ltd, during a flight from Tokyo to Osaka scheduled as flight 123 on August 12,1985, experienced an emergency at approximately 1825 hours when approaching east coast of Southern lzu Peninsula, and after a continued flight of about 30 minutes the aircraft crashed among mountains in Ueno Village, Tano Gun, Gunma Prefecture at approximately 1856 hours.

On board the aircraft were 509 passengers (including 12 infants) and a crew of 15; 524 persons in total, of which 520 persons (505 passengers and 15 crew-members) were killed, and 4 passengers seriously injured.

The aircraft was destroyed and fire occurred.

Outline of the Aircraft Accident Investigation

Notification and Organization

Upon receipt from Ministry of Transport of notification of the occurrence of the accident on August 12, 1985, the Aircraft Accident Investigation Commission (hereinafter referred to as "AAIC") appointed an investigator-in-charge and 15 investigators (including two medical officers of Air Self-Defense Force specialized in aviation medicine who had been assigned to AAIC) as a team in charge of the investigation of this accident. On April 6, 1986, two more investigators were appointed.

By request of AAIC, 6 personnel of Ministry of Transport participated in the fact finding investigation.

The following 13 technical advisers were appointed for the investigation of specialized matters with regard to the accident (titles are as of the date of appointment):

(1) For the investigation of damage to the airframe structure and related matters:

> **Junpei Shioiri:** Professor, Dept. of Technology. Hosei University

> **Kazuyuki Takeuchi:** Chief Research Engineer. 11/STOL Aircraft Research Group. National Aerospace Laboratory, Science and Technology Agency

> **Kouzaburo Yamane:** Chief. Flight Load Lab., First Airframe Division National Aerospace Laboratory, Science and Technology Agency

> **Hiroo Asada:** Chief, Full-Scale Test Lab., First Airframe Division, National Aerospace Laboratory, Science and Technology Agency

(2) For the investigation of fractured metal surfaces and related matters

> **Satoshi Nishijima:** Director, Fatigue Test Division, National

Research Institute for Metals, Science and Technology Agency

(3) For the analysis of flow-out phenomenon of pressurized air

Kazuaki Takeshima: Chief, two-dimensional Transonic Wind Tunnel Lab., Second Aerodynamics Division, National Aerospace Laboratory, Science and Technology Agency

(4) For the analysis of flight performance characteristics

Gorou Beppu: Director, Flight Research Division, National Aerospace Laboratory, Science and Technology Agency

Masaki Komoda: Chief, Flight Test Lab., Flight Research Division, National Aerospace Laboratory, Science and Technology Agency

Nagakatsu Kawahata: Chief, Flight Qualities Lab., Flight Research Division, National Aerospace Laboratory, Science and Technology Agency

(5) For the phonetic analysis of cockpit voice recorder

Osamu Fujiwara (until Jan. 1. 1986): Chief, Sensory Section, First Division, Aeromedical Laboratory, Air Self-Defense Force

Narisuke Utsuki: Sensory Section, First Division, Aeromedical Laboratory, Air Self-Defense Force

(6) For the acoustic analysis of cockpit voice recorder

Yoshio Yamasaki: Acoustic Section, Science and Engineering Research Laboratory. Waseda University

(7) For the analysis of photographic images

Toshihumi Sakata: Director, Tokai University Research and Information Center

For the purpose of study on relevant specialities, the Structural Investigation Group, Flight Performance Investigation Group and CYR (Cockpit Voice Recorder) Investigation Group were established.

Upon occurrence of the accident, chairman, members, investigator-in-charge, and investigators (including the assigned medical officers) were dispatched to the crash site, and at the same time an investigation team on the spot was organized. The team engaged in the investigation stayed at the site until October 13.

In carrying out the fact finding investigation, cooperation was given by a number of related organizations including Police Agency. Self-Defense Agency, Science and Technology Agency, Seismological Research Institute of Tokyo University, Maritime Safety Agency, Meteorological Agency, Gunma Prefecture, Ueno Village, local fire squadrons and related persons.

Cooperation was also rendered from Aeromedical Laboratory of Air Self-Defense Force, National Aerospace Laboratory, National Research Institute for Metals, and in the use of their installations and facilities in carrying out various tests and related matters.

Mr. George Seidlein (National Transportation Safety Board), Accredited Representative of the USA (the state of manufacture of the aircraft) and his advisers participated in the fact finding investigation

Implementation of Investigation

August 13 - Oct. 13, 1985   Investigation at crash site
Dec. 11 - 13. 1985   Investigation at crash site

April 17 - 20, 1986	Investigation at crash site
August 13 - Sept.17, 1985	Interview with passengers of the aircraft
August 15, 1985 - March 28, 1986	Interview with eye witnesses
August 15, 1985 - July 28, 1986	Decoding of records by Flight Date Recorder
August 15, 1985 - Sept. 30 1986	Decoding of records by Cockpit Voice Recorder
Nov. 1 - 20, 1985	Investigation of Bottom of Sagami Bay
Dec. 5, 1985-March 1. 1986	Restorative investigation of aft fuselage
Dec.8 - 10. 1985	Investigation of acoustic transmission characteristics, etc in airframe (by use of a Boeing 747)
Dec.16, 1985 - March 31, 1986,	Investigation of flight performance
July 1, 1986 and Feb.6, 1987	characteristics (including tests by flight simulator and variable stability and response airplane)
Dec.27, 1985 -March 31, 1986	Functional test and investigation of engines, equipment, etc.
Dec.27, 1985 --March 31, 1986	Investigation of alarm lights and switch lights
Jan.13, - March 28, 1986	Destructive tests of fasteners of vertical fin structure
March 23. - 30, 1986	Visit to USA of AAIC members and other personnel
April 17 - May 14, 1986	Investigation of areas below estimated flight path (by helicopter)
June 2 - 20, 1986	Test on structural elements of aft pressure bulkhead

June 10 – August 31, 1986	Investigation of air efflux
June 25 – July 10, 1986	Destructive test by inner pressure of vertical fin component structure
July 14, 1968	Experiments on depressurization inside fuselage and oxygen deficiency disease
August 28 – Nov. 30, 1986	Analysis of photographic images

Comments from Persons relevant to the Cause AAIC heard comments.

Hearing

AAIC published a draft of the report on factual investigation on March 28, 1986, and held a hearing on April 25 to hear the opinions of persons related to the accident as well as 11 men of learning and experience.

1. Date 10:02 — 16:13 hours, April 25, 1986
2. Place Large Assembly Ball, Ministry of Transport
3. Presider Hisaji Fujitomi, Director-General, Secretariat of AAIC
4. Witnesses (in order of witnesses)

- Mr. Hideo Hirasawa, Senior Vice President, Japan Air Lines Co., Ltd.

- Mr. Masayuki Ando, Co-pilot of B747, Japan Air Lines Co., Ltd. Vice President, Japan Air Lines' Flight Crew Union

- Capt. Ryuzou Yamada, Japan Air Lines Co., Ltd.Board Member, Japan Air Lines' Captain Association

- Dr. Hiroshi Nakaguchi, Opinions are asked by AAIC Professor Emeritus, Tokyo University Specialized in structural mechanics

- Dr. Shigeo Kobayashi Opinions are asked by AAICProfessor, Tokyo University Specialized in structural mechanics

- Mr. Hiroshi Ichikawa, Cabin Attendant, Japan Air Lines, Assistant General Secretary, Japan Air Lines Cabin Attendants Union

- Dr. Tsugihiko Sato, President, Osaka Institute of Technology Professor, Mechanical Engineering Dept.

- Capt. Hiroshi Fujimoto, Toa Domestic Airlines Co., Ltd. Chairman, Japan Federation of Civil Aviation Workers Unions for Air Safety

- Capt. Yoshimi Watari Toa Domestic Airlines Co., Ltd. President, Japan Flight Crew Unions Federation

- Mr. Yoshiyuki Funatsu Executive Vice President, All Nippon Airways Co., Ltd. Chairman, Safety Promotion Committee

- Dr. Keihachiro Shimizu Professor, International Budo University Professor Emeritus, Chiba University Former Member of Council for Civil Aviation

5. The contents of statements omitted (As described in the stenographic record of the hearing.)

Reporting and Publication

The progress and process of the investigation of the aircraft accident involving principal facts which become known by the factual investigation was reported to Minister for Transport and was published on August 19, August 27, September 14, December 19, 1985 and August 6,1986.

CHAPTER 2

THE FACTS

History of the Flight

On August 12 1985, the accident occurred, JA8119, a Boeing 747SR-100 of Japan Air Lines Co., Ltd. (hereinafter referred to as "JAL") was operated prior to this flight as scheduled flights 503, 504, 363, and 366 by crew other than the crew of the accident flight, except for the flight engineer (on duty on board flights 363 and 366).

The aircraft, as flight 366 (Fukuoka—Tokyo), landed at Tokyo International Airport 1712 hours, parked at Spot 18 at 1717 hours, and thereafter was inspected in preparation for operation as flight 123 (Tokyo-Osaka).

The aircraft's flight plan, which was submitted to Tokyo Airport Office of Tokyo Regional Civil Aviation Bureau, reads; IFR, cruising speed 467 knots (TAS) at cruising altitude 24,000 feet, destination Osaka International Airport, via Mihara Sagara, Seaperch, 1127, Kushimoto VORTAC, V55, Shinoda VOR/DME, and Osaka NDB, estimated flight hours 54 minutes up to Osaka NDB with fuel on board 3 hours and 15 minutes expressed in flight duration hour.

The aircraft, with the captain seated at the right-hand seat and the copilot on the left for the purpose of training the copilot for position as captain, started taxiing from Spot 18 at 1804 hours, and took off from Runway 15L at 1812 hours. (hereafter, refer to Attached Figure-1 and Attachment 5 and 6)

The aircraft requested to Tokyo Area Control Center (hereinafter referred to as "Tokyo Control"), approximately 1816:55 hours while climbing to 24,000 ft, for a direct route to Seaperch (A non-compulsory reporting point at 253° , 74NM from Oshima) from present position, and the request was approved at 1818:33 hours.

At 1824:35 hours just before the aircraft reached 24,000 feet, heading towards Seaperch and approaching east coast of South Izu Peninsula, the aircraft was brought into an abnormal situation which greatly affected continuation of the flight. At the same time, a loud noise like a "boom" was heard, immediately followed by an utterance of "squawk 77" (meaning emergency code number 7700 of ATC transponder) by both the captain and the copilot. Then, at 1825:21 the captain requested Tokyo Control clearance to descend to and maintain 22,000 feet, and to return to Haneda (Tokyo International Airport) on account of occurrence of such an abnormal situation. At 1825:40 the aircraft requested radar vector to Oshima. To this request, Tokyo Control inquired which was desired, right or left turn for change in heading for Haneda, and received the response from the pilot that he intended to make a right turn. Tokyo Control, accordingly, issued instructions to fly on a magnetic course of 90° after making a right turn for radar vector to Oshima, which was acknowledged by the aircraft at 1825:52.

Thereafter, the aircraft deviated from the course somewhat to the right near the middle of Southern Izu Peninsula, crossed the Peninsula heading WNW to cross over Suruga Bay. At about this time, unusual phugoid and dutch roll motions began, and these phenomena accompanied by large or small motions continued until just before the crash. At 1827:02 Tokyo Control confirmed the declaration of an emergency and then asked *"What is the nature of the emergency ?"* , but received no response from the aircraft. At 1828:31 Tokyo Control instructed again the aircraft to *"take a magnetic course of 90° for radar vector to Oshima"*, but the response now uncontrollable' was received from the aircraft at 1828:35.

The aircraft traversed Suruga Bay, passed over north of Yaizu City, Shizuoka Prefecture approximately 1830 hours, and then changed course to the right for a northbound flight approximately 1831 hours, about which time Tokyo Control asked the aircraft *"Can you descend?"*, to which the pilot responded *"Now descending"* at 1831:07, and then reported his altitude as 24,000 feet in response to the subsequent inquiry on current altitude. To a question made by Tokyo Control at 1831:14 *"Your present position is 72 NM from Nagoya Airport, Can you land at Nagoya?"*, the aircraft answered *"Request return to Haneda"*. At 1831:26 Tokyo Control suggested the use of Japanese to communicate thereafter, which was acknowledged by the aircraft.

At approximately 1835 hours, the aircraft turned to the right at a point about 35 kilometers west of Mt.Fuji for an eastward flight, and about 1838 hours turned the heading to the left at a point about 7 kilometers NNW of Mt.Fuji into a north-eastward flight, and at approximately 1841 hours the aircraft started a descent from altitude of about 21.000 feet over the vicinity of Otsuki City. Yamanashi Prefecture to an altitude of about 17,000 feet changing the heading about 360° to the right in about 3 minutes. Thereafter the aircraft continued flight descending rapidly eastward, transmitting *"aircraft uncontrollable"* at 1845 :46 hours, then turned left towards the north-east. At 1847:07 the aircraft requested radar vector to Haneda. to which Tokyo Control instructed the aircraft to *"maintain heading of 90° . Haneda's active runway 22"*, which was acknowledged by the aircraft. Then, in response to an inquiry *"Is the aircraft controllable?"* made by Tokyo Control at 1847:17, *"uncontrollable"* was answered. At approximately 1848 hours the aircraft turned to the left at an altitude of about 7,000 feet over the vicinity of Oku-Tama Town, Nishi-Tama Gun, Tokyo and flew WNW gradually climbing, and after reaching about 13,000 feet at about 1853 hours it started again a descent. and again transmitted *"uncontrollable"* at 1853: 31. At about 1854:19. the aircraft switched over communications to Tokyo Approach Control (hereinafter referred to as *"Tokyo Approach"*) at an altitude of 11,000 feet by an instruction of Tokyo Control. At 1854:25 the aircraft requested its position, to which Tokyo Approach gave *"55 nautical miles NW of Haneda and 25 nautical miles west of Kumagaya"*, which was acknowledged by the aircraft at 1854: 55. Then, at 1855:05 Tokyo Approach transmitted *"Both Haneda and Yokota are available"*, to which acknowledgement was made by the aircraft. After this, there was no response from the aircraft to calls of Tokyo Approach as well as Yokota Approach Control.

According to statements of eye-witnesses (4 persons) at points 3 to 4 kilometers SSW of the crash point, *"The aircraft flew in buzzing from Oku-Tama area located to the ESE at quite a low altitude and slow speed. slightly nose-up. The aircraft passed overhead, and made an abrupt right turn short of Mt.Sanpei (elevation 1,700 meters) situated to the NW and flew toward Mt. Mikuni (elevation 1,828 meters) located to the ENE. Then, about the time the aircraft would have passed Mt.Mikuni, the aircraft suddenly plunged into a dive banking to the left to NW direction,and went out of sight behind the mountain. Thereafter, smoke and flashing lights were seen emanating from behind the mountain,"*

The aircraft struck several trees on the ridge (elevation about 1,530 meters, location of the single larch on Attached Figure-13) located about 1.4 km NNW of Mt.Mikuni, then contacted the ridge (elevation 1,610 metres, location of the U-shaped ditch on Attached Figure-13) located 520 meters WNW of the previous ridge, and finally crashed on a ridge located further about 570 meters NW of the second ridge. The crash point was on the ridge (elevation 1,565 meters; 35° 59' 54N" . 138° 41' 49" E) about 2.5 km NNW of Mt.Mikuni located on boundaries of Gunma, Nagano and Saitama Prefectures.

The estimated time of the crash is at approximately 1856 hours.

Injuries to Persons

	Persons on board		Others
Injuries	Crew	Passengers	
Fatal	15	505	0
Serious	0	4	0
Minor	0	0	0
None	0	0	

Situation at Crash Site

The crash point of JA8119 was in a vicinity at an elevation of about 1,565 meters (76 Sector, State Forest. 3577 Aza Hontani, Ouaza Narahara, Ueno Village, Tano County, Gunma Prefecture) on a ridge extending east to west about 2.5 kilometers NNW of Mt. Mikuni. The area was a forested area of larch trees about 10 meters high, bushed thick with striped bamboo grass(see Photo-I).

The area is located about 26 kilometers SW of the hall of Ueno Village, where the Countermeasure Headquarters of the Accident was set up, and was accessible via Hontani Woodland Path along Kanna River upstream to the end of the road, and from there by climbing about 4 km, an elevation difference of about 600 meters. Although along Nagato Dale there was in part a truck path formerly used to transport lumber, the path was impassable at many points because of landslides. Also there was no climbing path in the vicinity of the crash site. The area was dangerous because of the risk of falling rocks.

A path climbing to the crash site was temporarily laid out within a few days after the accident by members of the local fire detachment and others. Two provisional heliports were established after the accident in the vicinity of the crash point for search and rescue purposes (see Attached Figure- 2).

A ditch tentatively called as the U-shaped ditch (hereinafter referred to as "the U-Ditch") located SE of the crash point and on a ridge extending north-east to south-west was separated from the crash point by a deep valley where the main stream of Sugeno Dale runs the area between bushed thick with striped bamboo grass (see Photo-3).

Meanwhile, the area from the U-Ditch to a single larch tree located further about 520 meters to south-east on a ridge extending north-east to south-west (hereinafter referred to *"the single larch tree"*) was on a slope with planted and natural forests mingled together. The area on the south side of the ridge where the single larch tree was located was covered entirely with an natural forest (see Photo-2 and Attached Figure-19).

Damage to Aircraft

Extent of Damage

The aircraft was destroyed

Damage to Aircraft by part

Fuselage (see Attached Figure-4 and --5)

1. Sections 41 and 42 (BS90-1000) near the nose were substantially damaged and subjected to fire. The cockpit was nearly gutted by fire.

   A portion on the copilot side of P5 overhead panel, a portion of P4 panel for flight engineer, and some of instruments were substantially damaged, but were free of fire.

   The upper deck was broken into two main blocks.

2. Section 44 (BS1000-1480) in and around mid fuselage was destroyed and the original form undiscernible for the wreckage was scattered widely.,

3. Section 46 (BS1480-2360) in and around aft fuselage was

destroyed, except that the left side fuselage and a portion of the floor panel of BS1800 to near BS2360 bore slight resemblance to their original form (see Photo--4 and

4. Section 48 (BS2360-2792) of the aft most fuselage, where the vertical stabilizer is mounted, had a portion below the fixture of the horizontal stabilizer separated and scattered. The tail cone portion aft of BS2658 was not recovered (see Attached Figure--25 and --26).

The APO fire wall in BS2658 was not recovered except for a small portion remaining attached to the fuselage frame.

Wings (see Attached Figure-6)

1. The left wing retained its linear shape as a whole from root to tip, but its leading edge flap and trailing edge flap were both damaged and separated from the wing. Pylon positions of No.1 and No.2 engines were gutted by fire.

2. The right wing, including the leading and the trailing edge flap, was shattered to such an extent that it retained no .resemblance to the original form. Their main wreckage of outer wing was recovered between the single larch tree and the crash point.

The structural portions recovered between the single larch tree and Sugeno Dale were slender and wrinkled fragments, long along the spar and short along the longitudinal axis of the aircraft. The fragments of the wing's under-surface were significant in scratches due to impact with the ground, and much smaller as compared with those of the wing upper-surface.

Attached figure-29 was made based on recovered parts.

Empennage (see Attached Figure – 7)

1. A portion of the leading edge of the vertical fin was broken into four parts, and separated from the airframe. The foremost dorsal fin of the stabilizer was also separated. A slight portion of the right side skin of the torque box and stringers were fractured and separated, but other parts were not recovered from the accident site.

2. A small portion of the vertical fin torque box base attached to the fuselage remained on the fuselage structure. A portion of left rear skin and a stringer of the torque box were found on the surface beneath the flight path of the aircraft.

3. The tie-rod link connecting the leading edge of the vertical fin to the fuselage, only the head portion of the eye bolt near the attachment to the fuselage was recovered (see Photo-11).

4. The horizontal plane was separated from the fuselage, and the left outside elevator was torn off from the stabilizer. A portion of the leading edge of the root of the stabilizer was fractured and separated.

   The left leading edge of the horizontal stabilizer's center section and up to the vicinity of SS165.73 was damaged (see Photo-6).

5. The horizontal stabilizer's upper gimbal was fractured and separated from the stabilizer and recovered on a slope about 80 meters south of the spot the stabilizer was recovered.

6. Part of the aft most lavatory's entry ceiling panel and fragments of the passenger cabin interior material were recovered at the spot where the horizontal stabilizer's upper gimbal fell.

Engines

1. No.1 engine was heavily damaged in its right lower portion and the core engine cases were disconnected at some flanges. The spinner, most of fan blades, fan case, engine mounts, gear box, cowling. and thrust reverser were torn off and separated from the engine. The rotor and fan blades remained connected to the shaft, but were separated from front compressor stage 2--4 and the turbine assembly.

   No.2 rotor jammed into the stator and was damaged to a large extent (see Photo-7).

2. No.2 engine was heavily damaged in its left lower portion and the core engine cases were disconnected at some flanges. The spinner, fan blades, fan case, gear box and engine mounts were torn off and separated from the engine. The rotor and fan blade remained connected to the shaft but was separated from front compressor stage 2-4 and the turbine assembly.

   No.2 rotor jammed into the stator, and was damaged to a large extent together with the compressor turbine (see Photo-8).

3. No.3 engine was damaged in its upper portion, where part of the rear compressor case was cracked, but the original form almost preserved up to the turbine assembly.

   The spinner, fan blades, fan case, and a portion of thrust reverser were torn off and separated from the engine (see Photo-9).

4. The fan section and core of No.4 engine were destroyed, the fan and the high pressure compressor shaft being severed, and broken into two in the vicinity of stage 9 of the high pressure compressor. The spinner, fan blades, fan case, thrust reverser, engine mounts, gear boxes, combustion

chamber, high and low pressure turbine blades, turbine sleeve and plug were torn off and separated (see Photo-10).

The thrust reverser screw jack was broken and separated from the engine. As to the thrust reverser pneumatic drive unit. only a part of its motor was recovered.

The fan front case was broken in its almost directly below portion, and damage to its lower portion left of the engine body was significant.

No.4 engine nose cowl was severed in the upper half (about 150 degrees) as well as in the right side (about 1/4 of the circumference), and the left side portion was destroyed, retaining no resemblance to its original form.

Others

1. All landing gears were torn off at their fittings and separated from the fuselage. The front gear was subjected to fire.

2. The digital flight data recorder and the cockpit voice recorder were both found among the wreckage in the third branch of Sugeno Dale, part of their outer case being collapsed.

3. The attach screw on the lowest portion of the lining of the engine fan exit case and fragments of the cascade vane were found imbedded in the severed section (about 14 meters height from the ground) of the single larch tree.

4. The portion of the hydraulic lines for the elevator control system running along the rear spar of the horizontal stabilizer was not damaged.

    The lines for other hydraulic systems were severely damaged, and it was impossible to specify its locations and damaged conditions.

5. With regard to the APU systems, the pneumatic duct,

battery, and wiring, etc installed forward of the fire wall were recovered in a damaged state, but for the portion of aft of the fire wall (APU compartment) only the air intake duct was recovered from Sagami Bay. The APU and other portions have not been discovered.

6. A portion of P2, P4. P5 and P6 panel. installed in the cockpit were recovered (see Attached Figure-12).

Distribution of Wreckage. etc. (see Attached Figure-13 to --19)

> On a slope, about 1.565 meters in elevation, south of the range extending east and west from the crash point (the location of the provisional heliport) earth was exposed about 40 meters long and about 10 meters wide, around which the left and the right landing gear support beam, skin from the right wing and flap trucks, etc were found buried.

> The nose, left wing, nose wheels and main wheels of the aircraft were scattered for about 110 meters west of the crash point, most of which were burnt. Nearby trees were cut off, brought down, or scorched.

> The fuselage portion from the upper deck cabin to the vicinity of the upper part of the wing was split in two and scattered for about 200 meters NNW of the crash point, while the portion adjacent to the nose was gutted by fire. Nearby trees were cut off, brought down, or scorched.

> Trees within an area extending about 244 meters NNW of the crash pointwith a width of about 35 meters were cut off or brought down, where a part of the right wing, aft fuselage, etc. were scattered. Most of the aft fuselage wreckage was lying in a heap in the third branch of Sugeno Dale.

- ➢ In the U-Ditch located about 570 meters SE of the crash point, trees on the range were scratched about 40 meters long and about 2--10 meters wide in a V-shape, where parts on the right wing tip, wing skin and others lay scattered about.

- ➢ Trees on a slope located about 140 meters SE of the U-Ditch were cut off or brought down in an area about 40 meters long by 18 meters wide, where Parts of No.4 engine lay scattered about.

- ➢ The single larch tree on a range of about 1,530 meters elevation, and about 520 meters ESE of the U-Ditch were cut off at a height of about 14 meters from the ground. The tip of five trees out of the densely grown hemlock spruce located about•meters west of the single larch tree were cut off about two meters higher than the single larch tree was cut off. Lying scattered in the vicinity were the right main wing trailing flap, No.8 track rod end fitting, the leading edge flap, flap track fairing, turbine blades, etc.

- ➢ No.4 engine and its parts, and parts in the right wing leading edge, etc were lying widely scattered between the single larch tree and the U-Ditch.

- ➢ Part of the leading edge of the vertical fin and others were lying scattered at a spot about 60 meters SE of the U-Ditch.

- ➢ The right wing skin, part of the horizontal stabilizer, etc were lying widely scattered on the NW side slope of the U-Ditch.

- ➢ The horizontal stabilizer was recovered almost whole at a spot about 510 meters east of the crash point (see Photo--6).

- ➢ Trees were cut off or brought down in an area extending about 75 meters NNW of the point about 50 meters E of

> the crash point with a width of about 10 meters, around which parts of No.2 engine and others were lying scattered.

> No.1 and No.2 engines were found in the third branch of Sugeno Dale, while No.3 engine was in the 4th branch of Sugeno Dale (see Photo--7,--8 and 9)

> Part of the aft fuselage structure near the fitting of the horizontal stabilizer was found scattered in the main stream of Sugeno Dale and near the 4th branch of Sugeno Dale.

Recovery of wreckage floating on the water and others

> *Status of recovery of floating wreckage.* A total of 53 pieces of floating wreckage, mostly debris of honeycomb of the vertical fin, were recovered from Sagami Bay and other locations (see Attached Figure--20, and Photo-14, --15 and --16).
> Discovered first was "CD upper half of the leading edge of the vertical stabilizer", which were recovered at approximately 1855 hours, August 13, 1965.

> *Investigation on wreckage on the bottom of the sea.* During the period of November 11 to 20, 1985, an investigation was carried out on the wreckage which may have sunk to the bottom of Sagami BaY in accordance with the following, using a survey vessel of Maritime Safety Agency as well as a submarine work and experiment vessel of the Oceanic Science and Technology Center. There was, however, nothing found which may be regarded as/ the wreckage of the the aircraft.

1. *Investigation area.* An area in which part of the wreckage of the aircraft might have sunk, judging from the status of the aircraft, wind direction and speed, status of recovery of floating wreckage on the water, ocean currents and tides, etc at the estimated time the

abnormal situation occurred (see Attached Figure--21).

2. *Investigation method.* Taking the isobath of 200 meters as the division line, a part of the above area of which depth is less than 200 meters was investigated by a side scan sonar (type SMS960) of Maritime Safety Agency, while the other part of the area whose depth is more than 200 meters was by a side scan sonar (type NE 157) of the Oceanic Science and Technology Center.

The result of the sonar investigation indicated 17 spots as possible locations where non-natural substances existed (see Attached Figure-21). On these spots a follow-up investigation was made for the substances using a towing type deep-sea camera and a video tape recorder of the Oceanic Science and Technology Center.

Wreckage discovered on Flight Course

Besides the flotsam recovered on Sagami Bay, five pieces of wreckages had been discovered up to July 2,1986 (see Attached Figure-22 and -27, and Photo-17,-18,-19 and -20).

Other Damage

About 3,300 trees in the larch grove of about 3.22 hectares in the state forest located in Hontani, Narahara, Ueno Village, Tano County, Gunma Prefecture were brought down, cut off, or burnt down.

Crew Information

Flight Crew

Captain: Male 49 years old.
- Joined JAL December 1, 1966;
- Acquired Airline Transport Pilot License No.1125 July 4. 1969

- Ratings and Limitations Boeing 747 July 1, 1975
  land single, land multiple, YS-11, B-727, and DC 8;
- Qualified as captain who may authorize his copilot to fly aircraft from the left-hand seat (*) June 16, 1977;
- Holds Class 1 Medical Certificate No.12810242 valid until January 18, 1986;
- Total Flying Hours:12,423 hours 41 minutes
- Flying Hours on Boeing 747:4,842 hours 22 minutes
- Flying Hours last 30 days: 53 hours 46 minutes
- Latest Training received:
  - for rescue: March 19. 1985
  - on the ground (in study room): January 30 & March 26 1985
  - by flight: simulator June 27,1985
- Latest Checks received:
  - Proficiency: June 28, 1985
  - Route: February 5, 1985

Copilot: Male 39 years old
- Joined JAL April 18, 1970;
- Acquired Airline Transport: Pilot License No.2834 June 20, 1984
- Ratings and Limitations: Boeing 747 May 23, 1979
  land single, land multiple, and DC 8;
- Qualified as left-seat copilot (*): June 4, 1984;
- Holds Class 1 Medical Certificate No.12553779 valid until November 11. 1985:
- Total Flying Hours: 3,963 hours 34.minutes
- Flying Hours on Boeing 747: 2,665 hours 30 minutes
- Flying Hours last 30 days: 46 hours 47 minutes
- Latest Training received:
  - for rescue: April 5, 1985
  - on the ground (in study room): April 8 & 16. 1985
  - by flight simulator: May 5, 1985
- Latest Checks received:
  - Route: July 19, 1985

(Note) In an ordinary flight, the captain flies the plane from the left-hand seat, and the copilot assists the captain in the right-hand seat. However, Director of Operation Crew Department for each type of aircraft may, pursuant to a provision of company regulations, for the purpose of training the copilot for captainship or other reasons, approve the copilot to fly the aircraft from the left-hand seat as left-seat copilot, provided he has completed an established course of training, and that a captain experienced to a certain level is seated in the right-hand seat and supervises the copilot as captain capable of permitting the copilot to fly the plane from the left-hand seat.

Flight Engineer: Male 46 years old
- Joined JAL: April 1, 1957;
- Acquired Flight Engineer License No.266 September 8, 1965
- Ratings and Limitations: Boeing 747 November 7, 1972 DC-6, B-727, and DC 8;
- Holds Class 2 Medical Certificate No.22552133 valid until Novembei 13, 1985;
- Total Flying Hours   9,831 hours 03 minutes
- Flying Hours on Boeing 747: 3,846 hours 31 minutes
- Flying Hours last 30 days: 41 hours 26 minutes
- Latest training received:
  - for rescue: November 14, 1984
  - on the ground (in study room): October 5 & November 28, 1984
  - by flight simulator: February 10, 1985
- Latest Checks received:
  - Route: August 27, 1984

Cabin Attendants

Chief Purser: Male 39 years old (seated A1)
- Joined:JAL October 18, 1969
- Total flight hours: 10,225 hours 33 minutes
- Latest rescue training: December 6. 1984

Assistant Purser: Female 30 years old (seated A)

- Joined JAL: January 22, 1974
- Total flight hours: 5,704 hours 55 minutes
- Latest rescue training: June 25, 1985

Female 31 years old (seated Cl)
- Joined JAL: January 17, 1975
- Total flight hours: 4,815 hours 43 minutes
- Latest training: June 25, 1985

Female 28 Years old (seated A2)
- Joined JAL: September 1. 1977
- Total flight hours: 4.432 hours 13 minutes
- Latest rescue training June 25. 1985

Female 30 years old (seated D2)
- Joined JAL: December 1, 1977
- Total flight hours: 3.161 hours 23 minutes
- Latest rescue training: June 25. 1985

Female 29 years old (seated El)
- Joined JAL: January 5. 1978
- Total flight hours: 4.227 hours 03 minutes
- Latest rescue training: June 4, 1984

Female 27 years old (seated B1)
- Joined JAL: January 5, 1978
- Total flight hours: 4.165 hours 54 minutes
- Latest rescue training: January 9, 1985

Female 28 years old (seated DI)
- Joined JAL: January 10, 1979
- Total flight hours: 3,541 hours 01 minutes
- Latest rescue training: June 21. 1984

Stewardess

Female 25 years old (seated C2)
- Joined JAL: November 24, 1981
- Total flight hours: 2,179 hours 44 minutes
- Latest rescue training: June 25. 1985

Female 26 years old (seated E2)
- Joined JAL: May 20. 1982
- Total flight hours: 1,610 hours 37 minutes
- Latest rescue training: June 6. 1984

Female 24 years old (seated B2)
- Joined JAL: January 12. 1984
- Total flight hours: 549 hours 19 minutes
- Latest rescue training: June 25, 1b85

Female 24 years old (seated D2)
- Joined JAL: June 19. 1984
- Total flight hours: 363 hours 41 minutes
- Latest rescue training: December 27, 1984

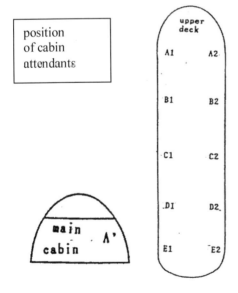

Aircraft Information

Aircraft

1. Nationality and Registration Mark   JA8119
2. Type   Boeing 747SR-100
3. Date of Manufacture   January 30, 1974
   Serial Number   No.20783
4. Certificate of Airworthiness   No.48-028
   Validity   As far as the aircraft is subjected to the JCAB approved Maintenance Manuals (JAL)
5. Total Flying Hours   25,030 hours 18 minutes

   Total Landings   18,835
   Flying Hours and Landings after Periodic Inspection
   After "A" Maintenance(*) conducted on July 21, 1985
        Flying Hours   181 hours 18 minutes
        Landings   122
   After "C" Maintenance(*) conducted on November 20 to December 5, 1984
        Flying Hours   1,700 hours 31 minutes
        Landings   1,240
   Flying Hours and Landings after repairs made in relation to the accident at Osaka International Airport in June 1978
        Flying Hours   16,195 hours 59 minutes
        Landings   12,319

(Remarks) "A" Maintenance is a prescribed maintenance for every 250 flying hours, while "C" Maintenance is the maintenance for every 3,000 hours.

6. Repairs related to the accident at Osaka International Airport in June 1978.
   On June 2, 1978, JA8119, during a landing roll at Osaka International Airport struck its aft fuselage on the runway and the airframe was substantially damaged.

The aircraft was ferried to Tokyo International Airport after provisional repairs made by JAL at Osaka International Airport for June 7 to 14, 1978. The regular repairs were carried out by a Boeing AOG (Aircraft on Ground) repair team dispatched from the company at Tokyo International Airport between June 17 and July 11, 1978. Required parts were sent from the Boeing Company, and the lower structures of the aft fuselage were refitted and repaired.

Prior to the repairs, an application for the repairs and modification inspection was submitted to Tokyo Regional Civil Aviation Bureau, and the aircraft passed said inspection on July 12, 1978.

The details are described in Attachment 1

Engines

The aircraft was equipped with four Pratt and Whitney JT9D-7A engines.

Engine No.	Serial No.	Total Run Hours
1	685792	33,795 hours 43 minutes
2	685764	32,762 hours 08 minutes
3	686046	29,623 hours 35 Minutes
4	685929	33,841 hours 58 minutes

Weight and Center of Gravity

The gross weight of the aircraft at take-off is calculated as 527,333 pounds and the center of gravity as 22.8% MAC, and both were within the prescribed limits(the maximum take-off weight is 570,000 pounds; the center of gravity corresponding to the take-off weight is 14.496-33.0% MAC).

Fuel and Lubrication Oil

The fuel on board was JET--A/40 and engine lubrication oil

was Mobile JET OIL-2, both being regular products.

Meteorological Information

Synoptic Weather Conditions

Synoptic weather conditions for the time zone related to the accident in Kanto and Koushin Districts and Shizuoka Prefecture, according to Meteorological Agency, were as follows:

On the day of the accident, Honshu Island and its vicinity were covered by a Pacific High, but the atmosphere in these areas was somewhat unstable, and thunder-clouds were formed in afternoon hours in Tokyo Metropolis and the western part of Saitama Prefecture, and the northern part of Gunma Prefecture. Heavy rain accompanied by the thunderclouds was observed, as much as 38 mm at Banba in Gunma Prefecture, and 30 mm at Ogouchi of Tokyo Metropolis for one hour from 1600 to 1700 hours.

The thunderclouds over the western part of Saitama Prefecture developed as high as 13,000 meters at maximum at about 1700 hours, and a heavy rainfall of 58 mm was observed at Chichibu City for one hour from 1700 to 1800 hours. However, the thunderclouds declined thereafter, decreasing their height to 6,000 meters at 1800 hours, and further weakened at 1900 hours. The rain at Chichibu City ceased to fall, and rainfall in some parts of Gunma, Saitama and Nagano Prefectures was limited to several millimeters for an hour from 1800 to 1900 hours.

The Thunderstorm over the northern part of Gunma Prefecture developed after dark, but it had almost died out by 2200 hours.

Between Izu Oshima Island and Izu Peninsula, weak cumulus was scattered over, locally with middle stratum clouds and upper stratum clouds. The wind was about 5 m/s from the south.

Observations at related Airports

Meteorological Observations at Tokyo International Airport, Yokota Airport, Nagoya Airport, and Shizuhama Airport in the time zone related to the accident were as follows:

Observed Location	Tokyo International Airport				Yokota Airport	
Observed Hour	1700	1800	1830	1900	1800	1900
Wind (degree/knot)	210/18	220/17	210/15	220/13	Calm	Calm
Visibility (km)	40	40	40	40	50	50
Present Weather					showers	
Cloud Amount	1/8	1/8	1/8	5/8	2/8	6/8
Cloud Form	Cb	Cu	Cu	Ac	Cb	Ac
Ceiling (feet)	2,000	3,000	3,000	9,000	3,500	12,000
"	7/8	3/8	3/8	7/8	2/8	6/8
	Ci	Ac	Ac	Ci	Cu	Ci
	—	9,000	9,000	—	3,500	20,000
"		7/8	7/8		5/8	
		Ci	Ci		Ac	
		—	—		12,000	
"					6/8	
					Ci	
					20,000	
Temperature (°C)	29	29	29	28	28	28
Dew Point (°C)	21	21	21	21	23	23
QNH (inch/Hg)	29.91	29.93	29.93	29.94	29.96	29.97
Remarks	Cb 50 km NW				Cb 14 NM NW, moving NE	

Observed Location	Nagoya Airport				Shizuhama Airport	
Observed Hour	1700	1800	1830	1900	1800	1900
Wind (degree/knot)	180/7	210/4	220/10	Calm	240/5	250/5
Visibility (km)	10	10	10	10	60	40
Present Weather	showers					
Cloud Amount	2/8	2/8	1/8	1/8	1/8	1/8
Cloud Form	Cu	Cu	Cu	Cu	Cu	Cu
Ceiling (feet)	1,300	1,500	1,000	1,000	2,500	2,500
"	1/8	5/8	3/8	5/8	1/8	1/8
	Cb	Sc	Cu	Cu	St	St
	2,500	4,000	2,000	2,000	3,500	3,500
"	6/8	7/8	7/8	7/8	2/8	3/8
	Sc	Ac	Ac	Ac	Ac	Ac
	5,000	12,000	12,000	10,000	10,000	10,000
"					7/8	7/8
					Ci	Ci
					25,000	25,000
Temperature (°C)	25	26	26	26	29	28
Dew Point (°C)	23	24	24	23	25	24
QNH (inch/Hg)	29.98	29.99	30.00	30.00	29.98	29.99
記事	Cb NE					

Note:

Tokyo International Airport, Yokota Airport and Nagoya Airport are located about 109 km ESE, about 66 km ESE and about 180 km WSW, respectively of the crash site.

Sizuhama Airport (Oigawa-Cho, Shita-Gun, Shizuoka Prefecture) is situated about 10 km south of the flight course of the aircraft at approximately 1831 hours.

Radar Sketch Chart

Tokyo Radar Sketch Charts(1800 hours and 1900 hours) by Meteorological Agency are shown in Attached Figure 23 and -24.

Briefing to Flight Crew

The following are a summary of the weather information which was briefed to the crew of JAL Flight 123 by a JAL dispatcher:

- The meteorological synopsis is such that while a Pacific High is covering Japan proper and its vicinity, Typhoon 9 was located south of Okinawa with an indication of moving north gradually, causing a warm and moist air mass to flow in from the south so that the atmospheric condition is becoming unstable in western Japan and towards the south, and favorable to formation of cumulus type clouds. Although weather is cloudy or drizzly in western Japan, it is fine in Kanto Area.

- The current and forecast weather of Tokyo International Airport (the destination airport and the alternate airport) and Osaka International Airport (the destination airport):

    Tokyo International Airport. 1630 hours, wind 200° at 18 knots, visibility more than 10 km, 1/8 cumulus, 2,000 ft, 7/8 cirrus, temperature 30°C, dew point 21°C, QNH 2990 inch Hg

Forecast for 1500 hours to 1500 hours of the following day, wind 200° at 20 knots, visibility more than 10 km, 3/8 cumulus 1,400 ft, 4/8 altocumulus 11,000 ft 5/8 cirrus 21,000 ft

Temporary change for 1600 to 2100 hours, visibility 7 km, shower, 6/8 cumulus 1,300 ft, 1/8 cumulonimbus 1,700 ft, 8/8 altocumulus 9,000 ft

Osaka International Airport, 1630 hours, wind variable 4 knots, visibility more than 10 km, shower, 1/8 cumulus 2,000 ft, 3/8 cumulus 3,500 ft. 6/8 stratocumulus 6,000 ft, temperature 28°C, dew point 25°C, QNH 29.92 inch Hg

Forecast for 1500 hours to 1500 hours of the following day, wind 090° at 7 knots; visibility more than 10 km, 2/8 cumulus 3,000 ft, 7/8 altocumulus 10,000 ft

Temporary change for 1500 hours to 2100 hours, visibility 7 km, shower, 1/8 cumulus 2,000 ft, 5/8 cumulus 2,000 ft, 5/8 cumulus 3,000 ft, 7/8 altocumulus 10,000 ft.

On the day of the accident, the western Japan was covered by rain clouds from the early morning, and there was a well-developed cumulonimbus in the vicinity of Kowa, Aichi Prefecture, where JAL Flight 151 (New Tokyo International Airport 0745 hours-Osaka International Airport 0850 hours) encountered severe turbulence. To avoid it, subsequent scheduled flight of JAL flew a route (Zama-Nagoya) deviated to the north from the regular route (Yokosuka-Hamamatsu-Kowa). JAL Flight 121 (Tokyo International Airport 1700 hours--Osaka International Airport 1800 hours), however took the regular route because the radar echo was judged as decreasing thereafter.

Briefing of meteorological conditions en route was also

given to the flight crew of Flight 123 by the dispatcher. The captain desired a flight plan on a route detoured to south than is normal (refer to History of the Flight) for the reason that the radar echo near Kowa had not been cleared up and that almost no radar echo was found over the sea further south, and it was acknowledged by the dispatcher.

Others

According to a witness who was of the captain of a Lockheed L-1011 (on a flight for Komatsu via Zama departing Tokyo International Airport 1831 hours) and who saw the accident aircraft turning over the vicinity of Otsuki, Mt. Fuji above about its 8th station was visible, and there were no clouds at altitudes 10,000-25.000 ft on the course including over the vicinity of Otsuki.

Sunset at the crash site was about 1840 hours.

Aids to Navigation

Functions and operational conditions of the aids to navigation related to the flight of the aircraft were normal during the related hours.

Communications

The aircraft was communicating with Tokyo Aerodrome Control, Tokyo Terminal Control, Tokyo Area Control, Tokyo Approach Control, and Flight Operations Department of Tokyo Airport Branch of JAL. According to communication records contact with the aircraft was maintained up to approximately 1 minute and 30 seconds before the crash, during which time the aircraft failed to respond several times and there were some cases that the other aircraft used the same frequency.

Contents of the communications with the aircraft which are not included in the records of the cockpit voice recorder are attached as Attachment 3 "Communication Records with ATC Facilities" and Attachment 4 "Communication Records with Company"

Flight Recorders

The aircraft was equipped with a Sundstrand Model 573A Flight Data Recorder (hereinafter referred to as DFDR). Serial No.3413 and a Collins Model 642C-1 Cockpit Voice Recorder (hereinafter referred to as CVR). Serial No.2579.

The DFDR was recovered, part of its outer case being crushed, and the 28 meters of magnetic tape on which the digital signals of the flight was recorded was broken at spots shown in (1) and (2) of Photo-101, and for about 1 meter before and after the broken spot was found damage such as many small folds and wrinkles (see Photo-101). The flight records deciphered are attached as *"Attachment 5 DFDR Record"*.

The CVR was also recovered. Although its outer case was crushed in part the voice-recording magnetic tape was kept intact. The voice records deciphered are attached as *"Attachment 6 CYR Record"*.

Responsive Actions of Cabin Attendants

Responsive actions taken by the cabin attendants after the occurrence of the abnormal situation are summarized as follows, based on the CVR record and statement of survivors:

Guidance by cabin attendants on how to put on and use the oxygen mask was given to passengers without delay immediately after the abnormal situation occurred with the sound like "bang". This responsive action was continued up to about 1847 hours when the aircraft descended to about 10,000 feet, during which time passengers were briefed on the flight information, etc, and the flight crew in the cockpit was kept informed of the status in the passenger cabin, and in the aft portion of the passenger cabin, cabin attendants were moving around checking the status passengers were using the oxygen mask, taking oxygen for themselves from empty oxygen masks in the cabin, not relying upon the portable oxygen bottle.

After 1847 hours, guidance was provided on how to wear the life jacket as well as shock-buffering attitude to be taken in preparation for an emergency landing (or an alighting on the water).

Medical information

Injuries to Survivors

Out of a total of 524 persons on board consisting of 509 passengers and a crew of 15. only four passengers (all female) survived, all being seated at the left side or near the center of seat row number 54 to 60 of aft fuselage (see Attached Figure-5).

Medical inspection at hospital upon their rescue indicated that all four survivors were seriously injured with bone fractures at parts different for each due to strong impact from the crash, and subjected more or less to a traumatic shock, which would require 2 to 6 months to recover completely.

Recovery of Bodies

For convenience's sake in describing the conditions in which bodies were recovered, seating is divided into the following five sections by seat row number (see Attached Figure-5).

A : The upper deck seats and No.1--No.8(8 row)
B : No.10--No.18(9 row)
C : No.19--No.31(13 row)
D : No.32--No.42(11 row)
E : No.43--No.60(18 row)

Bodies in A and B sections were recovered mainly at the

crash point as well as in its vicinity, while bodies in C sections were near the top of the ridge because C section turned over B section subsequent to crash of the damaged airframe. Bodies in D section were recovered in an extensive area right of the right forward slope of the ridge. Bodies in E section which fell down to the dale together with the damaged airframe were recovered concentrated within a narrow area with relatively less damage. The four survivors were also rescued from this section.

Damage to the Bodies

Damage to the bodies in section A to D sections by severance, fire burn and carbonization was remarkable because they were subjected to severe shock from breakage of the airframe, and heat of fire.

On the bodies of passengers in E section, there was found comparatively little cosmetic damage, but autopsy indicated almost all of them suffered from total bruise, brain damage or bursting of internal organs, resulting in instantaneous or near-instantaneous death except for the four survivors.

Survival Aspects

Search and Rescue Activities

The Rescue Coordination Center of Tokyo Airport Office of Tokyo Regional Civil Aviation Bureau (hereinafter referred to as the Coordination Center) began to gather information with close coordination with Tokyo Area Control Center and JAL, upon receipt of a report that an emergency occurred to JAL Flight 123 from the Area Control Center at 1826 hours, August 12, 1985.

The Coordination Center, upon receipt of a report at 1859 hours from the Tokyo Approach Control that the target of the aircraft disappeared from radar screen at a point 59 nautical miles on a magnetic bearing of 308° from Haneda at 1857 hours, forwarded the said information to the Police Agency, Iruma Rescue Coordination Center of Air Self-Defence Force, and Maritime Safety Agency, while Administrator of the Tokyo Airport Office requested Commander of Central District Air Corps of Air Self-Defence Force as well as Superintendent General of East District Corps of Ground Self-Defence Force to dispatch their troops for calamity relief at 2033 and 2130 hours, respectively.

Furthermore, the Rescue Coordination Center received approximately 1915 hours via Yokota Approach Control the information from a US Air Force aircraft (C-130) to the effect that a fire was found at a point 35 nautical miles on 305 radial of Yokota TACAN.

The Government, upon occurrence of the accident on August 12, established The JAL Aircraft Accident Countermeasure Headquarters, of which the chief was Minister of Transport, with the intent of making every possible effort toward rescue of survivors and recovery of remains with close coordination maintained between related organisations.

Within Ministry of Transport, too, its accident countermeasure head-quarters was established, assigning the permanent vice-minister as its chief, immediately after the accident occurred.

The Police Agency, establishing *"August 12 JAL Crash Accident Countermeasure Headquarters"* within the agency immediately after the accident occurred, ordered the prefectural polices of Gunma, Nagano, Yamanashi, and Saitama Prefectures within whose jurisdiction the crash spot might be located, to carry out confirmation of the crash site, search, and information collection, and instructed Tokyo Metropolitan Police Board, Saitama and Shizuoka Prefectural Polices and others to provide supporting by their task force and helicopter fleet. In response to the orders, each prefectural police established their commanding system in an early stage, and developed, all night August 12 to 13 activities for confirmation of the crash site, search, and information collection. As a result of the searching activities focused on areas on the boundary between Gunma and Nagano Prefectures by helicopters, wreckage of the JAL aircraft was found by a helicopter of Nagano Prefectural Police at approximately 0537 hours, August 13, and the crash site was confirmed.

The Gunma Prefectural Police, carried out search and rescue for survivors, with the support of task forces, rescue units, helicopters from Tokyo Metropolitan Police Board, and Saitama and Nagano Prefectural Polices.

The number of police-related personnel and equipment engaged in search and rescue August 12 to 13 were asfollows:

	August 12	August 13
Personnel	about 2,500	about 3,500
Vehicles	about 250	about 400
Aircraft		7

The Self-Defence Agency, upon receipt of information from the Coordination Center to the effect that the target of JAL Flight 123 disappeared from the radar screen, judged the situation as an emergency, dispatched at 1901 hours two jets in wait on the ground originally for the scramble mission. The aircraft had a flare in sight at a location which seemed to be the accident site. For more accurate confirmation of the location, the Agency dispatched 1954 hours a helicopter, who arrived over the site 2042 hours. The Agency instructed its Air Self-Defence Force and Ground Self-Defence Force to locate the crash spot and to prepare for movement to the calamity area, and to collect information.

Based on the instruction above as well as the request of Administrator of Tokyo Airport Office to dispatch troops for calamity relief, Central District Air Corps of Air Self-Defence Force, and Eastern District Corps of Ground Self-Defence Force developed, all night from August 12 to 13, movement of their party to the estimated crash site, confirmation of the crash point by helicopters, search, and collection of information.

As a result of their research activities, wreckage of the JAL aircraft was found 0439 hours, August 13, and the crash site was confirmed.

The Self-Defense Agency carried out search and rescue of survivors on the surface as well as from the air, using members of Ground Self-Defence Force and Air Self-Defence Force.

The number of persons of the Agency engaged in the search and rescue and equipment used August 12 to 13 were as follows:

	August 12	August 13
Personnel	about 1,000	about 3,200
Vehicles	about 180	about 480
Aircraft	about 10	about 10

The Maritime Safety Agency received from the Coordination Center on August 12 information to the effect that the target of JAL Flight 123 disappeared from the radar screen.

Since they also received from the Coordination Center approximately 0230 hours August 13 the information that there was a possibility of passengers being sucked out due to the pressure difference in and outside the cabin should the door have been broken open, the Agency immediately ordered their patrol boats out; and furthermore, from 0710 hours, dispatched their aircraft for search over the Suruga Bay and Sea of Sagami.

The number of personnel and equipment of the Maritime Safety Agency engaged in the search on August 13 were as follows:

Personnel	161
Ships	6
Aircraft	3

The Fire Fighting Headquarters of the Tano Fujioka Extensive Municipal Zone Redevelopment Association (hereinafter referred to as *"Tano Fujioka Extensive Fire Fighting Headquarters"*), instructed, about 1955 hours August 12, Ueno Village Fire Sub-station and Oku Tano Fire Branch in whose jurisdiction the JAL aircraft might have crashed, to carry out information gathering and search activities; and set up the Fire Fighting Center for missing JAL Aircraft about 0230 hours August 13. Based on the above instruction, the initial search was conducted on the area including Nakanosawa, Budou Pass and Ryouginyama using three vehicles; and after the crash site was confirmed in the early morning, an advance troop of 7 was headed for the crash site from Mototani Woodland Path Terminal and engaged in search and rescue of survivors.

The Tano Fujioka Extensive Fire Fighting Headquarters arranged ambulances for carriage of survivors one at Ueno Village General Ground, and three (one of them belonging to a private hospital) at Fujioka First Primary School's Ground.

The Gunma Prefecture Chapter of Japan Red Cross Society, after the JAL aircraft accident occurred August 12, endeavored to gather information in close coordination with the Fire Fighting and Calamity-Preventive Section of Gunma Prefectural Government and Gunma Prefectural Police, and ordered their three relief squads to be on stand-by alert.

Thereafter, the chief of the red cross chapter (Governor of Gunma Prefecture) ordered the relief squad out, based on the information that the JAL aircraft crashed.

The relief squads departed for Ueno Village. and upon arrival at the Ueno Village Hall, it was brought under the command of Chief of the Counter measure headquarters at Site for JAL Aircraft Crash Accident of Gunma Prefectural Police (Director of Gunma Prefectural Police), and set up a first aid station at the side of Ueno Village General Ground.

The above headquarters at the site, after the presence of survivors was confirmed, requested the Relief Squad to dispatch 2 doctors and 2 nurses.

The relief team flew over the site by a helicopter of Tokyo Metropolitan Police Board and descended to the ground by a hoist. They administered first aid treatment to the four survivors at the site, treatment at Ueno Village General Ground, and intravenous drip injection during the airlift from the Ground to Fujioka City First Primary School's Ground, etc. Persons called out of the relief squad on August 13 totaled 20.

Gunma Prefecture municipalities including Fujioka City and Ueno Village together coordinated extensive search and rescue measures.

Ueno Village Fire Corps issued a standby order to its 6th, 7th and 8th team about 2305 hours August 12, because the JAL aircraft was estimated to have crashed in the vicinity of Ueno Village. and thereafter extended the standby order to all teams in the early morning of August 13.

About 0600 hours August 13. all teams were ordered to rally at Ueno Village Middle School, and about 0630 hours, all teams, approximately 160 persons were headed for the crash site in two groups.

Upon arrival at the crash site, all teams were engaged in search and rescue for survivors.

Ueno Village Hunters Association was requested by Gunma Prefectural Police, slightly before 2100 hours August 12, to provide guidance service for the mountainous search. Members rallied at Ueno Village Hall waiting for the arrival of a task force of the Prefectural Police, and upon its arrival, they guided the task force to the site taking two different routes.

After arrival at the crash site, they were engaged in search and rescue of survivors. Members called up of the Association totaled 11.

Situation from Discovery of Survivors up to their Rescue and Accommodation

Various reports by the related units and personnel are synthesized as follows:

After the crash site was confirmed, comprehensive search and rescue activities were energetically extended throughout the crash site in a steep mountainous region by Police, Self-Defense Forces, Ueno Village Fire Corps, Ueno Village Hunters Association, Tano Fujioka Extensive Fire Fighting Headquarters, etc.

As a result of these activities, at approximately 1045 hours August 13, survivors were discovered on the third branch of Sugeno Dale where wreckage was widely scattered, and four survivors were rescued up to 1140 hours from among wreckage scattered about 4 meters x 4 meters by cooperative actions of search teams of the above-mentioned organizations. All the survivors left the accident site at 1329 hours on board a large helicopter of Ground Self-Defense Force to Ueno Village General Ground, where they were given first aid treatment, and from there they were carried to Fujioka City First Primary School's Ground by the above helicopter and a helicopter of Tokyo Metropolitan Fire Fighting Board with two on board each.

Thereafter, they were carried by two ambulances to a hospital in Fujioka City at 1413 and 1417 hours.

CHAPTER 3

VERIFYING THE FACTS

Investigation of Damage to Aft Airframe

Reconstruction was conducted on the airframe wreckage aft of the vicinity of BS2200 in the investigation of wreckage of the aircraft, on the assumption that an irregularity occurred in the aft airframe during the flight, from the fact that the vertical fin and a portion of the aft fuselage were discovered from Sagami Bay as well as from the records of DFDR and CYR.

The reconstruction was carried out mainly on wreckage of the structure, and functional components, passenger cabin interior materials, flooring and seating, etc were not reinstated. Recovered wreckage was restored as much as possible, but some of the fragment was unidentifiable because of substantial damage.

The reconstruction was conducted separately for aft fuselage, vertical fin, horizontal fin, and aft pressure bulkhead.

The aft fuselage was reconstructed by assembling the wreckage three-dimensionally (see Photo-21 and -22).

The vertical fin was reconstructed by spreading the wreckage, mainly of the forward torque box, on a stand(see Photo-23). The rudder was not reconstructed because the wreckage recovered was insufficient.

As to the horizontal fin, for convenience of transport, the elevators had been removed, and the horizontal stabilizer separated into eight parts. Each elevator was spread on a stand, and the divided horizontal stabilizer was spread, enclosed in a wooden framework.

The aft pressure bulkhead was reconstructed by assembling its wreckage separately from the fuselage (see Photo-24).

1. Damage to the aft fuselage is shown on Attached Figure--25 and -26.
2. Damage to the vertical fin is shown on Attached Figure--27 and -28.
3. Damage to the horizontal stabilizer is shown on Attached Figure-30 and 31
4. Damage to the .aft pressure bulkhead is shown on Attached Figure-32.

Investigation of Damage to Aft Fuselage

1. The aft fuselage was substantially damaged in the structures on the right side surface and the under surface. The damage was especially significant below R5 door and between FS2360 (to which the aft pressure bulkhead is attached) and BS2484, and there were many small pieces of wreckage whose location could not be specified from restoration.

2. The fuselage structure (including the APU fire wall) aft of BS2658 (to which APU fire wall is attached) was not found in the recovered debris. It is noted that the APU air intake duct attached to this part of structure was recovered from Sagami Bay.

3. In BS2360. the ringform chord of a Y-section (hereinafter referred to as "Y" chord, see Figure-1) retained on the whole its original circular form although partly bent.

Figure 1. Cross Section of Joint of Y Chord and Fuselage

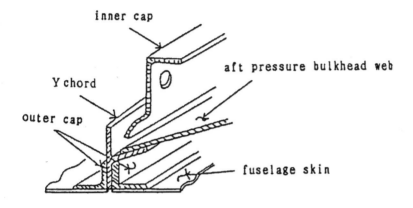

4. A major part of the inner cap (a ringform angle of L-section lightening holes) attached inside of, and along the Y chord was fractured and separated from the Y chord, and the rivets connecting the inner cap with Y chord were sheared off by forces at right angles to their shanks.

5. Fractures along the circumference of BS2658 (where APU fire wall is attached) were as follows:

(see Figure-2 for fuselage stringer numbers at BS2658 ; see Figure-3 for cross section of the joint of APU fire wall and fuselage)

Figure 2. Cross Section of BS2658 where APU Fire Wall is attached (as viewed from the rear)

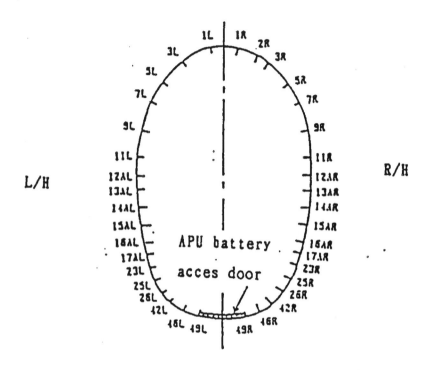

Figure-3 Cross Section of Joint of APU Fire Wall and Fuselage.

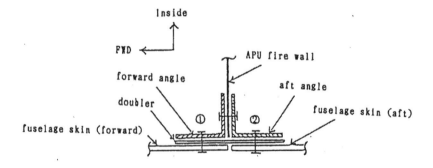

a. Between fuselage stringer IL (hereinafter stringers are represented by abbreviation only, where L indicates left side, and R right side) and IR, the forward angle, doubler, and forward fuselage skin were all fractured on fastener row (1) (see Photo-33).

b. Between 2R and 7R, both angles were partially fractured at the L section's corner (hereinafter referred to as "corner"), but the hinge support channel of the APU air intake duct remained attached.

   The hinge support channel originally fixed in parallel to the APU fire wall (at right angles to the fuselage skin) were bent backward at the joint with the doubler (see Photo-34).

   In the vicinity of 7R, a few fragments of the APU fire wall, remained attached.

c. The portion Near 9R remained, the cross section shown in Figure-3 being kept unchanged. From 11R through 15AR a fracture was found on fastener row (2), only the doubler remaining in the rear. The doubler was fractured on fastener row (2) by tension (see Photo-35).

d. In the vicinity of 15AR there was a slight portion where the forward angle, doubler and forward fuselage skin were all fractured on fastener row (1), but from there to 23R the cross section as shown in Figure-3 was kept unchanged, and fragments of the APU fire wall, although few, were remaining.

e. From 23R to 49R, the forward angle was fractured at the corner, and aft thereof only the doubler was remaining.

   Many of fastener holes in the doubler were elongated in the longitudinal direction, and bending of the doubler itself outward of the fuselage was observed (see Photo-37 and -38).

f.   Near 3L, all other than the doubler were fractured at the corner of the forward angle. Fasteners remained on the doubler (see Photo-39).

g.   From the middle of 4L and 5L to 7L, the cross section as shown in Figure -3 was unchanged and part of APU fire wall was remaining.

h.   From 9L to 16AL, all except the doubler were fractured at the corner of the forward angle. Fasteners remained on the doubler (see Photo-40).

i.   From 17AL up to 42L., the forward angle, doubler, and forward fuselage skin were all fractured on fastener row 1 (see Photo-41).

j.   From 46L up to 49L, except than the doubler were fractured at the corner of the forward angle. Many fastener holes were elongated in the longitudinal direction.
     Bending of the doubler outward of the fuselage was observed (see Photo -42).

Investigation of Damage to Vertical Fin

1.   *Vertical Fin Forward Torque Box*
     a.   In that part of the vertical fin forward torque box above FS395 recovered from Sagami Bay, part of the skin of the honeycomb structure was peeled off and the apex was damaged, but there was little damage to the front apex chord and web, and on the whole the box structure was retained.
          The portion below FS395 was broken into five large parts including the dorsal fin, and most of the front spar web was fractured and separated from the spar chord. Most of the ribs were also fractured and separated from the forward torque box skin.

b. In most part of the left side front spar chord of the forward torque box above FS395, the skin of the vertical fin's aft torque box was fractured immediately aft of the spar chord, leaving some skin on the spar chord side. The skin which remained on the spar chord side was bent outward (see Figure-4a and the arrow in Photo-44): Above the vicinity of FS545, there was part where the head of rivets connecting the aft torque box skin and the spar chord was broken o.f by a force applied in its shank direction, and the skin was separated (see Figure-0 and the arrow in Photo-45).

c. The right side front spar chord .of the forward torque box above FS395 was fractured for almost half of its entire length in the same state as shown in Figure-4b(see the arrow in Photo-46). A very small number of rivets near FS 545 were found sheared off by force at right angle to their shanks (see Figure -4c and the arrow in Photo-47). Near FS495, the aft torque box's skin was torn off and fractured, and there were parts where fragments remained connected to the spar chord (see Figure-4d and an arrow in Photo-48).

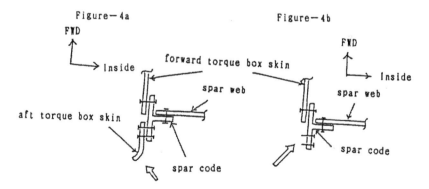

Figure—4a

Figure—4b

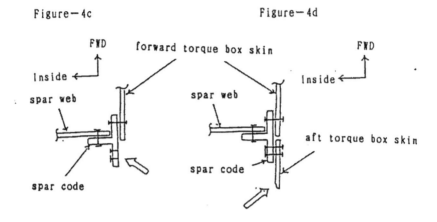

Figure—4c   Figure—4d

d. The end fitting at the fuselage side of the tie rod link connecting the vertical fin's auxiliary span with the fuselage was fractured at the neck of an eye bolt, but no evidence of fatigue fracture was recognized on the fracture surface, and the fracture would have been caused by tension. Its end fitting on the auxiliary spar side, including the attaching bracket, was fractured and separated, and has not been recovered.

2. *Vertical Fin Front Spar*

   a. The following parts of the vertical fin front spar chord were remaining: (see Attached Figure--34)

   Left Side: The part FS295 TO FS420 was connected to the forward torque box. out of which the portion about 30 cm above FS295 to FS395 retained the T-section form.

   Right Side: The part from FS169 to FS220 was connected to the skin of the aft torque box (separated from the forward torque box). The portion from FS245 to FS395 retained the T-section form, and was connected to the forward torque box.

b. As to rib angles on the front spar side of the ribs between the front spar and the rear spar, the parts as shown in Attached Figure-34 were recovered in a state of being connected to the front spar web. These rib angles were, except for those connected to FS545, FS445 and FS195 (refer to Photo-49, -53 and -56), all fractured at the L-section corner (see Photo-50,-52,-54 and -57).

A macroscopic observation of these fracture surfaces indicated that the fracture would have developed as a whole starboard to port.

c. At the following locations on the rear surface of the front spar web (the surface to which the rib angles are attached) were found abrasions which would have been caused at the time the rib angle was fractured:

(see Attached Figure-34)

1. above FS445 (see Photo-53)
2. above FS420 (see Photo-54)
3. above FS220 (see Photo-55)
4. above FS169 (see Photo-56)
5. above FS143 (see Photo-57)

3. *Vertical Fin Aft Torque Box*

a. The skin attached to the rear spar was not recovered except for the lower skin which was recovered attached to the fuselage structure (see Attached Figure-27 and -28).

b. An observation by the electron microscope with the replica method of fracture surfaces of the lower skin and stringers recovered connected to the fuselage structure revealed no fatigue fracture on them. Also, a macroscopic observation of the stringer surface indicated that the fractures would have developed from inside to outside.

c.   A part of the skin (to which some of stringers of 2L to 5L are attached), recovered from beneath the flight path, of the vertical fin aft torque box was bent to the outside both longitudinally and laterally. A macroscopic observation of the fracture surface of the skin and stringers indicated that the fracture would have developed from inside to outside.

Investigation of Damage to Horizontal Stabilizer

1.   The horizontal stabilizer, for both the right and the left side, were not subjected to significant damage except for damage to the leading edge near its base to the fuselage, forward torque box and the tips.

  The left hand outboard elevator and the some portion of the both forward torque box (including the fairing) near the base to the fuselage were fractured and separated from the horizontal stabilizer, but these were otherwise intact.

2.   Left Leading Edge and Forward Torque Box
  The portion from near SS195.25 to near SS310 was crushed by a force from the front (see Photo-60).

3.   Right Leading Edge and Forward Torque Box
  The portion from near SS167.73 to near SS285 was crushed by a force from the front (see Photo-61).

4.   The right stabilizer tip portion between SS510 and the tip was crushed by a force from the front, but there was no significant damage to the left stabilizer tip portion except that a part of. the honeycomb structure at the upper surface was missing (see Photo-62 and -63).

Investigation of Damage to Aft Pressure Bulkhead

1.   Structure of Aft Pressure Bulkhead

The aft pressure bulkhead is a semi-spheric structure about 4,560 mm in diameter 2,560 mm in radius of curvature, and 1,390 mm in height of dome.

The main structure of the aft pressure bulkhead is such that 18 webs (fan-shaped) are assembled in a dome shape, and thereon are arranged 4 straps (strip-shaped) concentrically, 36 full-length stiffeners (for reinforcement) radially, further arrayed therein short-length stiffeners, all these elements being riveted down to form a single body.

In this report, the following numbers are given to the structural components for identification as viewed the aft pressure bulkhead from the rear:

Setting 12 O'clock and 6 O'clock as 0 and 36, respectively. stiffeners are named clockwise Zero, Rl. R2, R3, • • • , and counter-clockwise Ll, L2, L3, • •

The stiffener portion where the fan-shaped web is connected is designated as joint, and the stiffener portion between joints as reinforcement, being prefixed by the stiffener number. (Examples: L18 joint, L20 reinforcement)

In L18 joint, the upper side fan-shaped web and the lower side fan-shaped web are referred to as the upper web and the lower web, respectively; web portions sectioned by each strap and stiffeners were designated sequentially as Bay 1, Bay 2, Bay 3, Bay 4, and Bay 5 from the outer margin of the bulkhead to the center. Rivets fastened on the joint are also named sequentially as No.1, No.2, No.2• • • from the outer margin toward the center.

Straps are designated sequentially No.1, No.2. No.3, and No.4 from the outer margin of the bulkhead toward the center.

2. The aft pressure bulkhead, as see shown in the damage

chart (Attached Figure--32), was broken into six main parts, with much complex damage to lower Parts. The damage to each part was as follows:

(a) Part 1 (see Photo-64 and -5)

R6 joint, L2 joint and outer margin of the webs (fractured at No.2 rivet row in the connecting section with the Y chord) were all in such a state as the fracture would have been caused by tension. The portion between the second and the third strap was bent towards the non-pressurized side.

Some of structure from the fourth strap to the center side was not recovered, but the fracture surface was in such a state as the fracture would have been caused by tearing.

(b) Part 2 (see Photo-66 and -67)

Web margins were all fractured at No.2 rivet row in such a state as the fracture is estimated to have been caused by tension. The web's fracture surfaces on the center side were also in a fractured state estimated to have been caused by tension. Between the second and the third strap, there was a large bend leading to the damage in Part 1. The portion outside of the first strap and surrounded by L16 reinforcement and L18 joint (Part 2A) was fractured and separated (see Photo-68 and 69). This part contains the passage the bundle of electrical wires.

Refer to "(7)Investigation on Fractured Surface of Aft Pressure Bulkhead" for the state of fracture of L18 joint.

(c) Part 3 (see Photo--70 and —71)

The fractured surface of webs along R34 joint. R30 joint and R32 reinforcement were in such a state that the fracture is estimated to have been caused by peel-off or tear-off. Webs   near   the   hydraulic   piping   pas (between L30 and L32) and the APU high pressure air duct passage were fractured and separated by tear-off. Most of the web's outer margins were fractured at No.2 rivet row, but the portion from L18 joint to L22 joint was in a fractured state estimated to have been caused by tear-off. The portion from L32 reinforcement to R33 reinforcement was buckled by a force from below.

(d) Part 4 (see Photo-72)

From R18 joint through to R33 reinforcement, webs were united to the fuselage by the Y chord, but were fractured on a circumference near the Y chord.

(e) Part 5 (see Photo*-73 and -74)

This is the part leading to the center side of Part 4. Each fracture surface was in such a state that the fracture was estimated to have been caused by tearing or peeling.

(f) Part 6 (see Photo--75 and --76)

The fracture at R6 joint was caused by tension at the rivet row, but fractures at R12 reinforcement and the lower portion were estimated to have been caused by tear-off. The outer margins were connected to the fuselage skin by the Y chord (Photographed is the fuselage skin cut off for convenience of transport).

3. Breaking and Bending of Aft Pressure Bulkhead

a. The aft pressure bulkhead was broken and bent to a large degree toward the non-pressurized side between the second strap and the third strap. The breaking and bending extended archwise from R5 reinforcement anticlockwise to L10 joint, viewing the bulkhead from the rear. The web was broken open between LID joint and L12 reinforcement. From this opening along L10 joint up to the third strap the web was fractured and again along the third strap it was broken and bent toward the non-pressurized side up to L18 joint. Furthermore, there were shallow contact scars on the web surface from L12 reinforcement to L16 reinforcement almost on an extended line of the former breaking and bending (see Photo-77 to —83).

b. A measurement of the distance along the spherical surface of the above breaking and bending from the web's outer margin (fractured at No.2 rivet row) showed that it was 1,350 mm at R5 reinforcement, 1,300 mm at 0 reinforcement, and 1,200 mm at L10 joint.

4. Appearance of Lower Web Edge at L18 Joint

At L18 joint the lower web edge had been cut off between the first and the third strap about 1,050 mm along the web edge with a width of about 20 mm at right angles thereto (see Attached Figure--36 and Photo-84). The cut-off portion expressed in rivet numbers was from No.30 to No.83.

In the cut-off position, an aluminum filler about 0.9 mm in thickness had been inserted and riveted to the stiffener together with the upper web. The cutoff of the lower web edge was made in the repair work related to the accident which occurred to the aircraft June 2, 1978.

5. Rivet Row at L18 Joint
    a. At the lower web edge of L18 joint, the edge distance of the rivet hole gradually decreased from the outer margin toward rivet No.29 as well as from the center toward rivet No.84. The edge distance near portion where the web edge had been cut off were as follows:
    (see Photo-85 and -86)

(Remarks) In this Report, the edge distance is defined as the shortest distance from the edge of the rivet hole to the edge of the web.

Rivet No.	Edge Distance(mm)
No.25	3.0
No.26	3.6
No.27	unable to measure due to fracture
No.28	"
No.29	"
No.84	3.5
No.85	2.9
No.86	4.6
No.87	3.5
No.88	4.9

b. Edge distances at the upper web edge of L18 joint were all more than 6 mm except for rivets Nos.28, No.29, No.47, No.63, No.107 and No.120 (excludes the rivet holes for which the measurement was impossible due to fracture or other reasons).

c. Most of rivet holes along the line of the fracture in the upper web were fractured by tension load, and the holes were transformed into an elliptical shape. The major axes were measured as follows:

Rivet No.	Average Major Axes (mm)	Standard Deviation(mm)	Max. Major Axes (mm)
No. 2 – No. 30	5.05	0.38	5.9
No.31 – No. 82	4.78	0.26	5.4
No.83 – No.136	4.75	0.25	5.5

Out of the above, sections between the following rivet holes were in such a state that the fracture was estimated to have been caused by heavy tension

Rivet No.	Average Major Axes (mm)	Standard Deviation(mm)	Max. Major Axes (mm)
No. 14 – No. 27	5.3	0.25	5.9
No.123 – No.136	5.0	0.25	5.5

d. The diameter of the rivet holes of the lower web along the line of the fracture in the upper web were measured as follows:

Rivet No.	Average Major Axes (mm)	Standard Deviation(mm)	Max. Major Axes (mm)
No. 2 — No. 30	4.95	0.42	5.5
No. 31 — No. 82	4.68	0.16	5.1
No. 83 — No.136	4.63	0.18	4.9

e. The riveting was, on the whole, found somewhat irregular

6. Investigation on Qualities of Structural Materials of the Aft Pressure Bulkhead

An investigation was carried out on conformity of webs, stiffeners, straps and rivets composing the structure of the aft pressure bulkhead to the aircraft manufacturer's specifications for materials   and the materials standards. Specifications for the structural materials are as follows:

- Upper Web…Aluminum Alloy 2024-142 clad, about 0.8mm thick
- Lower Web…Aluminum Alloy 2024-142 clad, about 0.9mm thick
- Straps………..Aluminum Alloy 2024-13 clad, about 1.0mm thick -
- Stiffeners, full-length type Aluminum Alloy 2024-142, about
2.4mm thick Z-shaped Section
- Stiffeners, short-length type Aluminum Alloy 2024-142, about 1.0
mm thick, L/Z-shaped Section
- Rivet………..Aluminum Alloy 2017-13, BACR15BB D

Investigated items were chemical analysis, metallurgical structure inspection, mechanical properties test, etc. As for the clad materials, its core material was subjected to investigation.

Samples was made as follows:

Samples	Taken From
upper webs	near L17 stiffener
lower webs	near R27 stiffener
straps	No.2 strap
stiffeners	L18 stiffener
rivet	location No.29 on L18 stiffener

a. *Chemical Analysis*

Fe, Cu, Mn, Mg, Si, Cr, Zn and Ti were quantified by atomic absorption spectrometry as well as by emission Petrochemical analysis.

For rivets, quantification was made only by atomic absorption spectrometry.

Results of the chemical analysis are shown in Table 1.

As shown in Table—1, the upper and the lower webs, straps, and stiffeners are verified as normal 2024 aluminum alloy, and rivets as normal 2017 aluminum alloy.

The results in Table-1 met also specifications for materials prescribed by the aircraft manufacturer and the materials standards.

b. *Inspection on Microstructure*

Microstructures were inspected by optical microscope for the upper and the lower webs, straps and stiffeners on three cross sections perpendicular with each other: parallel to the plane, and vertical to and parallel to the direction of roll; and of the rivets on the longitudinal cross section.

Micrographs of the sections for these materials are shown in Photo--102 to —106.

As evidenced by these photographs, there were no abnormalities recognized on microstructures of the upper and lower webs, straps, stiffeners and rivets.

c.   *Hardness Test*

Vickers hardness was measured for the upper and lower webs, straps and stiffeners on a cross section parallel to the plane surface.

Vickers hardness was also measured for the rivets on the longitudinal section.

Results of the hardness test are shown on Table--2 and Figure-5.

d.   *Tension Test*

A tension test was conducted at room temperature for the upper and lower webs, with standard test pieces, three for each, whose axis is vertical to the rolling direction.

Results of the tension test are shown on Table--2.
The test results met specifications of the aircraft manufacturer of the materials as well as the materials standards, and said materials were verified as normal, without any 'contradiction in the trend between properties of the above materials.

e.   *Investigation on Material Quality by Measurement of Conductivity*

Electric conductivity of each structural materials of the upper and lower webs, straps and stiffeners was measured for the purpose of determining suitability of heat treatment in the manufacturing stage as well as investigation of subsequent thermal history.

Results of the measurement are shown in table 3.

The results on the stiffener included one measurement which did not fall within the allowance with a slight deviation. But no problem in the heat treatment process was recognized with regard to said material, judging from the results of measurement at other points of the same structural material.

Based on the results of the conductivity

measurement, combined with the results of the hardness test in item (c) above, it is estimated that normal heat treatment had been given to the structural materials of the aft pressure bulkhead. It is hard to presume that inappropriate heat treatment was accorded such as to exert a bad influence on the structural strength of the aft pressure bulkhead materials in the working process.

It is also estimated from these results of measurement that it had had no subsequent thermal history, such as from a fire.

Table-1. Chemical Composition (weight ratio in %)

Structural Materials	Si	Fe	Cu	Mn	Mg	Cr	Zn	Ti	Al
upper web	0.19	0.32	4.39	0.69	1.26	0.018	0.077	0.043	Balance
lower web	0.21	0.28	4.39	0.56	1.35	0.017	0.061	0.031	Balance
straps	0.18	0.30	4.83	0.63	1.36	0.025	0.180	0.034	Balance
Aircraft Manufacturer's Specifications QQ-A-250/5	Max. 0.50	Max. 0.50	3.8 thru. 4.9	0.30 thru. 0.9	1.2 thru. 1.8	Max. 0.10	Max. 0.25	Max. 0.15	Balance
Equivalent to ALUMINUM ALLOY ALCLAD 2024 (CORE), JIS A2024PC (CORE)									
Stiffener	0.21	0.31	4.57	0.61	1.44	0.024	0.160	0.041	Balance
Aircraft Manufacturer's Specifications QQ-A-200/3	Max. 0.50	Max. 0.50	3.8 thru. 4.9	0.30 thru. 0.9	1.2 thru. 1.8	Max. 0.10	Max. 0.25	Max. 0.15	Balance
Equivalent to ALUMINUM ALLOY 2024, JIS A2024P									
rivet	0.30	0.50	3.90	0.55	0.49	0.024	0.048	0.022	Balance
Aircraft Manufacturer's Specifications QQ-A-430	0.20 thru. 0.8	Max. 0.7	3.5 thru. 4.5	0.40 thru. 1.0	0.4 thru. 0.8	Max. 0.10	Max. 0.25	Max. 0.15	Balance
Equivalent to ALUMINUM ALLOY 2017, JIS A2017W									

Table—2 Mechanical Properties

Structure	0.2% Stress MPa(ksi)	Tensile Strengh MPa(ksi)	Elongation %	Vickers Hardness	Remarks
upper web					
Average	269(39.0)	403(58.4)	17.4	134	0.82mm thick
test piece—1	266	405	18.6		Clad
test piece—2	276	406	—		0.052mm thick
test piece—3	265	399	16.2		(6.4%)
lower web					
Average	293(42.5)	423(61.4)	18.5	141	0.90mm thick
test piece—1	294	425	17.8		Clad
test piece—2	292	419	19.9		0.058mm thick
test piece—3	292	425	17.8		(6.4%)
Strap				143	1.03mm thick Clad 0.045mm thick (4.4%)
Aircraft Mnfctrs Specifications QQ—A—250/5 BAC 5946	Min. 234(34.0)	Min. 393(57.0)	Min. 15	*126—163	For 0.53—1.58mm thickplate,Clad thickness required is Min. 4%.
ALUMINUM ALLOY ALCLAD 2024 (CORE), equivalent to JIS A2024PC (CORE)					
Stiffener				140	板厚 2.50mm
Aircraft Mnfctrs Specifications QQ—A—200/3				*126—163	
ALUMINUM ALLOY 2024, equivalent to JIS A2024P					
Rivet				see Chart—5	
Aircraft Mnfctrs Specifications QQ—A—430					
ALUMINUM ALLOY 2017, equivalent to JIS A2017W					

* The Vickers hardness 126—163 are converted from HRB 70.0—83.5.

Table—3 Measurements of Conductivity (%IACS)

Structural Parts	Measured Points					Allowances
	A	B	C	D	E	
Upper Web (2024-T42 clad)	31.0	31.2	31.2	30.6	31.1	29.4—34.4
Lower Web (2024-T42 clad)	32.5	32.3	31.8	32.2	32.3	30.7—35.2
Strap (2024-T3 clad)	30.9	31.0	31.0	31.2	31.1	30.9—34.8
Stiffener (2024-T42)	29.0	29.3	28.8	29.3	29.2	29.0—32.0

%IACS : PERCENT INTERNATIONAL ANNEALED COPPER STANDARDS
being in accordance with Processing Specification of Aircraft
Manufacturer: BAC 5946

Figure 5. Hardness Distribution of L18 Stiffener in No. 29 Rivet
BACR15BB – D Aluminum Alloy 2017-T3

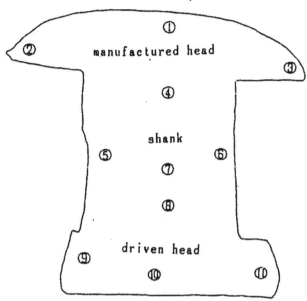

Measured Points	Micro Vickers Hardness
	HV(500g)
①	144
②	134
③	142
④	154
⑤	137
⑥	156
⑦	149
⑧	154
⑨	166
⑩	179
⑪	170

Based on the results of the testing including the chemical. analysis, microstructure inspection, and mechanical properties test above, it is verified that qualities of the structural materials used in the aft pressure bulkhead met specifications for materials of the aircraft manufacturer, and materials standards.

7. *Investigation on Fracture Surfaces of the Aft Pressure Bulkhead*

The aft pressure bulkhead was broken, as shown in Figure-6, into 6 principal blocks. An electron-microscopic observation was carried out by use of the reprica•method on fracture surfaces of the major fracture lines which seem to he straight (including the peripheral portion).

Especially along the fracture line of 1.18 splice, the fracture surface analysis was conducted for overall length directly by scanning electron microscope.

Figure-6. Major Fracture Lines Major fracture lines, indicate points observed by electron microscope, as viewed from aft of the pressure bulkhead.

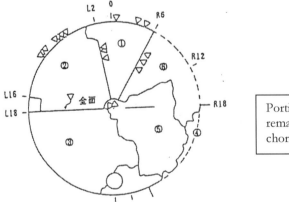

Portion not fractured and remained intact with Y chord (see Figure - D

a.   Fracture of webs along L18 stiffener

Fracture of the aft pressure bulkhead along L18 stiffener is as shown in Attached Figure-37.

The major fracture lines along L18 stiffener run through rivet holes of the 2nd to the 29th rivet juncture and through the 84th to the 132nd rivet juncture, counted from the peripheral end, in the second row from the lower edge of the upper web. The structure :Joss section, excluding the strap fixture is as shown in Attached Figure-38(a).

Meanwhile, between the 30th to 83rd rivet the main fracture line runs through the first rivet line from the lower edge of the upper web. Structure cross section of the portion strengthened by the doubler plate between the first strap and the second strap, and between the second strap and the third strap are shown in Attached Figure-38 (b).

Fracture along L18 stiffener of the lower web runs only between the 64th and the 89th rivet hole on the first row from the upper edge of the lower web. The fracture line almost coincides with the fracture line of the upper web riveted together.

With regard to the fracture aspect of the upper and the lower web, fractures through rivet holes on the second row from the lower edge of the upper web shown in Attached Figure--38(a) are mostly of the type shown in Attached Figure --38(c), while fractures through rivet holes on the first row from the lower edge of the upper web as shown in Attached Figure--38(b) are almost of the type of Attached Figure-38(d) with some exceptions as in Attached Figure--38(e).

b. *Microscopic Observation of Fracture Surface on Upper Web along L18 Stiffener*

As shown in Photo--107 to Photo--114, traces of fatigue failure originating from the rivet hole were observed in several locations.

No abnormality such as corrosions and defects in materials was recognized from microscopic point of view.

It is noted that in each attached photograph, the pressurized side is brought "up", non-pressurized side "down", the outboard side to the left, and inboard side to the right.

c. *Distribution of Fatigue Failure of the Upper ieb along L18 Stiffener*

(i) Distribution of Fatigue Failure
Dimensions of fatigue cracks, widths between hole edges, and others verified on the fracture surface of the upper web are shown in Table—4 below.

Table-4 Distribution of Fatigue Failure

Bay No. (Rivet No)	Length L (mm)	Width between Hole Edge in total × (mm)	Lengths of Fatigue Cracks in total f (mm)	Number of Holes N	Number of Holes with Fatigue Crack Nf	Fatigue Failure Ratio	
						f/x %	Nf/N %
1 (2～ 30)	531.26	396.23	4.98	28	6	1	21
2 (31～ 56)	481.09	366.24	205.55	25	21	56	84
3 (57～ 82)	496.03	382.32	53.78	25	10	14	40
4 (83～108)	478.50	363.41	13.80	25	16	4	64
5 (109～132)	433.25	324.27	1.46	23	4	0.5	17

(ii) Distribution of Fatigue Failure Ratios between Hole Edges

Ratios of fatigue failure between the hole edges, when shown in a bar
chart, are varying along stiffener L18 as in Figure-7 below.

Figure-7   Distribution of Fatigue Failure Ratios between Hole Edges

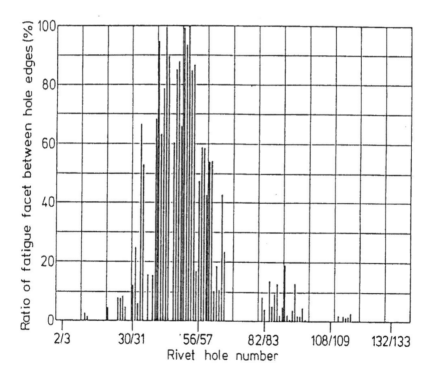

Distribution of Striation Spacing

Relationship between the distance from the hole center (a) and the striation spacing (s) is shown in Figure-8, taking as an example rivet hole 53 where striation was clearly observed from a scanning electron microscopic observation on the fatigue fracture surface.

It is noted that "striation" is defined as a striped pattern created by repeated stress on a fatigue fracture surface.

Figure-8. Variation in Striation Intervals (53rd rivet)

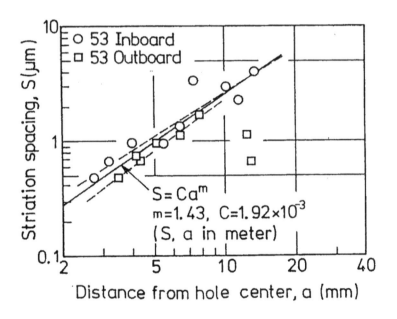

In Table-5 are shown the striation spacing(s) at the distance (a) of 2.5 mm from the hole center, the exponent (m) indicative of relation between (s) and (a), the correlation coefficient (r) indicating the degree to which data are arranged linearly when plotted on the graph as in Figure-8, and the number of striation (N) calculated thereon.

Table-5 Relationship between Distance (a) from Rivet Hole Center and Striation spacing (s), and Number(N) of Striations calculated from them

Rivet Hole		Number	Exponent m	s (μm) at a = 2.5mm	Correlation Coefficient r	Distance from Hole Center Edge of Fatigue Crack		Number of Striations N
						Initial	Terminal	
32	Inboard	3	8.280	0.068	0.878	2.39	3.44	6586
34	"Average	9	2.288	0.203	0.939	2.23	7.46	8803
41	of	10	1.718	0.232	0.953	2.60	12.15	9788
44	both	13	0.815	0.557	0.549	2.52	15.84	9849
48	sides"	12	2.475	0.171	0.927	2.19	10.39	10818
49	"	8	2.676	0.179	0.928	2.44	7.00	7181
50	"	9	2.087	0.299	0.914	2.32	9.39	6521
51	"	6	1.188	0.779	0.918	2.36	7.15	3246
52	"	10	2.283	0.179	0.825	2.32	9.19	9930
53	"	15	1.430	0.363	0.930	2.48	14.24	8497
54	Inboard	4	2.896	0.190	0.912	2.18	7.38	8127
56	Outboard	4	2.371	0.444	0.844	1.78	6.06	5320
57	Inboard	5	2.096	0.182	0.872	2.23	7.68	10529
59	"Average of	7	4.143	0.076	0.939	2.28	6.98	13615
61	both side"	9	2.149	0.141	0.773	2.32	8.37	12999
62	Outboard	5	3.339	0.130	0.831	2.22	4.60	8850
66	Outboard	5	2.514	0.290	0.929	1.77	5.68	7973

(iv) *Fracture of Four Straps attached at Right Angles to L18 Stiffener*

The fracture line of the four straps attached at right angles to L18 stiffener almost coincides with the fracture line of the web riveted together therewith.

As shown in enlarged views in Photo--112 to Photo--115, the fracture surface of the straps is inclined about 45 degrees in the direction of thickness and the fracture is considered as resulting from tension due to overload.

No problem was found such as corrosion and defects in materials.

Coating was flaked off in part near the fracture surface because of severe plastic deformation.

(v) *Fracture of L18 Stiffener*

L18 Stiffener was fractured, as shown in Photo-119 and Photo-120, at rivet hole 30 and rivet hole 83.

Fractures, as evidenced also by the state of fracture of the web described earlier, were caused at rivet hole 30 to 83 in such a manner that the stiffener portion involving rivet hole 30 to 83 was pulled upward relative to the remaining right and left side portions.

The former rivet hole remained attached to the upper side fragment, while the latter to the lower side fragment.

The fracture surface of the stiffener had an aspect characteristic of the fracture due to shear as shown in Photo-121 and -122.

In this case too, neither corrosion nor other defects in the materials were found, and the fracture was recognized as resulting simply from overload.

(vi) Fracture of other parts

Excluding fractures visually recognized as resulting from tension, the fracture surface analysis was carried out by electron microscope with the replica method on the fracture line (including outer margin portions)which looks macroscopically linear as shown in Figure-6. The analysis indicated the fractures were all due to overload.

The fracture of the outer margin portion left and downward of L18 stiffener is of a type as shown in Figure-38(e), and is recognized as due to overload.

The sole fracture through rivet hole 84 to 89 of the lower web along L18 stiffener is also recognized as due to tension by overload as can be seen in Photo-123.

Investigation of Engines, Equipment, etc and Function Tests

Engines

Visual inspections were made on engines.

1. The variable stators in the forward compressor of No.1 Engine were at the closed position, and the actuator was off the set position, about 6 mm from the retracted position (forward thrust position).

    As to the thrust reverser, only the left upper screw jack and carriage were recovered intact in the fan exit rear case. The recovered screw jack was at the retracted position.

2. The variable stator of No.2 and No.3 engine were at the closed position, and the actuators were at the retracted position. Although thrust reverser of No.2 engine was not identified, the engine was estimated to have been at the forward thrust position, since the yellow mark of retracted position was recognized in the recovered pneumatic drive unit.

3. The thrust reverser of No.3 engine was approximately at the forward thrust position, while the pneumatic drive unit at the retracted position.

4. The variable stators of No.4 engine were at the open, or closed position on a random basis. The thrust reverser screw jack of the engine was at the extended position (reverse position). It was impossible to determine the position of the thrust reverser from the motor assembly of the pneumatic drive unit.

Function Tests of Equipment

1. Function tests and disassembly check were carried out on the following equipment:

    a. Elevator Power Control Package (Note)(two each for inboard and outboard) (Note) the power control package is hereinafter referred to as "PCP")

Equivalent angles. calculated from the distance between the actuator body edge surface and the eye end center before the function test were as follows:

Location	Equivalent. Angle
right inboard	about 20° nose up
right outboard	about 15° "
left inboard	about 18° "
left outboard	about 15° "

Results of the function test revealed that some of the functions deviates somewhat from prescribed values, but to a degree that would not cause any practical problem, except for the right inboard PCP.

No irregularities were recognized from results of disassembly check.

b. Elevator Position Transmitter (one each for left and right) There were no irregularities in functions. No irregularities were recognized from results of disassembly check.

c. Flight Spoiler PCP (one for outboard, set position unknown)

The position before the disassembly was the retracted position, and there were no irregularities in functions. No irregularities were recognized from results of disassembly check.

d. Right Stabilizer Control Module (one)

Only a partial function test could be carried out since the motor, pressure switch, and others were missing, and the arming and the manual control lever of the control valve were bent.

The manual arm valve was at the neutral, and the hydraulic fluid leaked from the valve down position, releasing the brake from action. The disassembly check did not clarify the reason for this irregular function.

e. Upper Rudder Ratio Changer Control Unit (one)
Fractures and dents were found, and the linearity was somewhat off the prescribed value in some position.
No irregularities were recognized from results of disassembly check.

f. Lower Rudder Ratio Changer Control Unit (one)
No irregularities were recognized from results of the functional test and disassembly check.

g. Rudder Ratio Changer Comparater No irregularities were recognized from results of the functional test and disassembly check.

h. Left and Right Stabilizer Control Brake (one each)
No irregularities were recognized from results of the functional test and disassembly check.

i. Trailing Edge Flap Flow Control Module (one, set position unknown)
In a test of the pressure setting value of the priority valve, it became functional at 1.470 psi. The disassembly check revealed that a crack extended for about one half the circumference of the priority valve flange, and the poppet stop had fractured.

j. Outboard Aileron PCP (one, set position unknown)
A function test was conducted at 1,500 psi. one half the regular actuating pressure, since the piston rod was transformed, and the servo valve fixing screws had come loose. From the test, it was estimated that there were no irregularities in functions. Some portions of the unit which were unable to disassemble due to transformation were cut away. From results of disassembly check, no

irregularities were estimated.

2. For the following equipment, only the disassembly check was conducted because the damage was severe:

    a. Flap Control Modular (two, one outboard, the other set position unknown)

        The two bypath valves were at the bypath position, and the control valves were at the neutral and the up-select position.

    b. Hydraulic Return Module (two, set position unknown)

        There was no clog in either the primary and the secondary element. About 90 cc's of malodorous liquid was recovered from one of return modules. All filter elements were damaged.

    c. Constant Speed Driv6 (two, set position unknown)

        Although the outside was one of return modules. All filter elements were damaged.damaged, no irregularities were found in the internal structure.

    d. Trailing Edge Flap Hydraulic Motor (one each for inboard and outboard)

        Although the outside was damaged, no irregularities were found in the internal structure.

    e. Hydraulic Pressure Module (three. set position unknown)

        One was subjected to substantial external damage. The filter element of a module free of external damage was out of joint. There was no clog in the filter element for any of the modules. The recovered hydraulic fluid was discolored to light brown, but not malodorous.

    f. Engine Driven Pumps (two) and Pneumatic Pumps (four)

Unit	Hyd.system	Conditions
Engine-Driven Pump	No.2	Evidence of dry run. Cylinder block discolored. Residue of gellatinized hydraulic fluid about 5 cc
"	No.4	No evidence of dry run. There is external damage.
Pneumatic-driven Pump	No.1	No evidence of dry run. External damage, but internal structure in excellent conditions. Residue of hydraulic fluid about 70 cc
"	No.2	Clear evidence of dry run. Internal damage significant. No residue of hydraulic fluid.
"	No.3	Evidence of dry run. External damage. Cylinder block discolored.
"	No.4	Evidence of dry run is most significant. A lot of grated metal present. No residue of hydraulic fluid.

(Note) No.1 and No.3 engine-driven pumps were not recovered.

g. Case Drain Module (two, set position unknown)The AP Pop-up Indicator on System A (EDP's case line) of one module popped up and was dented. Results of disassembly check indicated no clog in the filter. The hydraulic fluid remained about 28 cc, but discolored. In the filter bowl on EDP side of the other module, there was an earthy foreign material, but there was no clog in the filter.

h. Flight Spoiler PCP (five)

Unit	Set Position	Conditions
Outboard Flight Spoiler	No.3	Actuator and input lever were in full retracted position. Results of disassembly revealed no irregularities.Residue of hydraulic fluid about 250 cc
"	unknown	Actuator was in full retracted position. It was impossible to determine existence of irregularities due to total severe burn-out. No residue of hydraulic fluid.
"	unknown	Actuator in a position extended 4 mm from full retracted position. Other conditions the same as above.
"	unknown	Actuator was in full retracted position. Other conditions the same as above.
Inboard Flight Spoiler PCP	unknown	Damaged. Actuator position unknown. There was grated metal which seems foreign, but no irregularities in structural components.

(Note) The other 5 units were not recovered.

i. Inboard Flight Spoiler Ratio Chan^{g}er Actuator (one, set position unknown) The actuator was approximately in the full retracted position, and no irregularities were recognized from results of disassembly check.

(Note) The fact that the actuator was in the full retracted position indicates that the speed brake was in the down position or in the in-flight speed brake position.

j. Flight Control Shut-off Valve (four)

Set Position	Conditions
unknown	Lever was in the open position. Although it was damaged, no irregularities were recognized from results of disassembly check.
unknown	Lever was broken. A test conducted by running hydraulic fluid revealed the valve was in the closed position. The disassembly check revealed that it was rusted and corroded.
unknown	Lever was in the closed position. Although it was damaged, no irregularities were recognized from results of disassembly check. Residue of hydraulic fluid about 2 cc.
unknown	Lever was in the open position. The electric circuit operated normally with DC20V and 27V. Between pin 2—4 (Valve open indicator circuit), poor connection was occasionally indicated. There were no irregularities from results of disassembly check.

k. Elevator Feel Computer (one)

It was impossible to specify the position of the lever since the stabilizer input lever was not fixed. It was also impossible to estimate the Position of the stabilizer input lever from dents, scars, etc. The system feel pressure transducer electric receptacle was torn off from its mount, but a circuit still connected circuit of electric pin 1 and pin 5. (This indicates there was less than 2596 difference between the feel pressure of the two systems). No irregularities were recognized from results of disassembly check.

l. Stabilizer Control Module (one, left side)

Although the arming nose-up solenoid and the manual control lever were missing and the motor-operated valve electric plug was fractured, the manual input lever in the neutral position, and the lever moved smooth and was made sprung back to the neutral position.

There were no irregularities recognized from results of disassembly check except that water and the hydraulic fluid had been mixed into the pneumatic housing. Hydraulic fluid remained about 20 cc.

m. Stabilizer Trim Drive Mechanism (one)

The jack screw was fractured at a point about 655 mm from the upper end stopper. About one third of the circumference of the gear housing was missing. Cracks were found on the upper cover housing umbrella.

Residue of the hydraulic fluid was about 2,800 cc.

The primary brake was manually operable at both the horizontal and the vertical position. The left and the right hydromotor were in a good working condition', and no irregularities were recognized from results of disassembly check.

The horizontal stabilizer angle corresponding to the position of the stabilizer ball screw and nut is 3.54 units.

(Note) The "unit" approximately equals "degree". The neutral position of the horizontal stabilizer is 3 units. The operable range of the manual lever in the cockpit is 1/4 unit (nose-down side) to 13-3/4 units (nose-up side).

n. Elevator Feel Actuator (one)

The piston on one side was at the full retracted position, the position of the piston on the other side was extended 10 mm.

Although somewhat damaged, it was in a good condition, and no irregularities were recognized from results of disassembly check.

o. Reserver Pressure Module (two, set position unknown)

One module bore evidence of the inside being flooded with water, and the metallic filter element on the inlet side was rusted. Three valves operated smoothly.

The other unit was damaged substantially throughout, and a slight clog was found in the paper filter element. Two valves were operable by finger, but the other was not.

p. Wing Gear Door Actuator (one, set position unknown)

It was substantially damaged throughout, dented in the middle of the cylinder, and was bent about 5° . The actuator was at the full retracted position (position the gear door is opening).

q. Nose Gear Door Operated Sequence Valve (one, nose gear)

It sustained substantial fire damage throughout. The distance from the eye end center to the body edge surface was 57 mm. A check of the hydraulic paths indicated that the hydraulic path between "L" and "DN" and the path between "R" and "C" were clear and that "UP" and "0" were in the closed position.(The valve position above indicate that the nose gear was unlocked and in the middle position.

3. Visual checks were conducted on instruments and others of which the disassembly check was impractical due to severe damage. Their indication or state clarified by the visual check were as follows:

Unit	Set Position or Systems	Indication or Condition
Air Cycle Machine Exit Temperature Indicator	unknown	12°F
Compressor Discharge Temperature Indicator	unknown	off scale below 0
Turbine By-path Valve Position Indicator	unknown	Full cool
Inlet Door Position Indicator	unknown	Full cool
Exhaust Door Position Indicator	unknown	Full hot
Out Flow Valve Position Indicator	right side	full closed position
"	left side	about 25% open
CSD Oil Temperature Indicator	unknown	142°C
KW/KVAR Meter	---	-3KW/KVAR(Note)
DC Ammeter	unknown	+50 amperes
Total Air Tem/Indctr	---	36.1°C
Total Weight/Total Fuel Weight Indicator	P4 panel	Total Weight 496.0(×1,000 lb) Total Fuel Weight 049.3(×1,000 lb)
Consumed Fuel Indctr	No.1	6,750 lb
"	No.2	7,790 lb
"	No.3	6,610 lb
"	No.4	6,690 lb
Fuel Quantity Indicator(main tank)	No.2	Pointer 10,000 lb Counter 12,750 lb
" (reserve tank)	No.1	Pointer 2,400 lb Counter 3,250 lb
" (reserve tank)	No.4	Pointer 550 lb Counter 3,250 lb
Fuel Pressure Gauge	No.1 or No.2	Inlet Pointer 1.2(×10psi) First Stage Pointer 10.2(×10psi) DIFF Pointer 9 (×10psi)
"	No.4	Inlet Pointer off scale First Stage Pointer 14.8(×10psi) DIFF Pointer 14.3(×10psi)

(Note) Since KW/KVAR is read by switching one another, it is unknown which is indicated.

Unit	Set Position or Systems	Indication or Condition
Fuel Pressure Indctr	No.3	unknown
Fuel Temp/Indicator	unknown	−56°C
Hydraulic Fluid Pressure Indicator	unknown	1.2 (×1,000psi)
	unknown	0.35(×1,000psi)
Hydraulic Quantity Indicator	unknown	16USgal
	unknown	0.3USgal
	unknown	off scale belwo 0
	unknown	off scale belwo 0
N_2 Tachometer	No.1	Pointer 6% Counter 999 Red Pointer 101%
	No.2	Pointer 47% Counter between 55 and 56 Red Pointer lacking
	No.3	Pointer 3% Counter 00 Red Pointer lacking
	No.4	Pointer 0% Counter 988 Red Pointer 111%
Engine Oil Temperature Indicator	No.1 or 2	−22°C
	No.1 or 2	−35°C
	No.4	unknown
Engine Vibration Indicator	No.1	unknown
	No.2	0 but pointer transformed
	No.3	2
	No.4	unknown
Oxygen Pressure Indicator	− − −	Crew Pointer lacking Passenger Pointer 0 psi
Frequency Meter	− − −	386 Hz
AC Voltmeter	unknow	105.5V
APU Tachometer	− − −	32%
APU Oil Qty Indicator	− − −	0.3 USgal
Engine Oil Quantity Indicator	No.2	unknown
	No.3	unknown
	No.4	unknown

(4) Inspection of Flap Positions

Flap units, estimated from the ball screw position of the trailing edge flap jack screw recovered from the crash site, were as follows:

Item	Position	Flap Unit (Note 1)
Inboard Jack Screw	unknown	11.6
"	unknown	12.2
"	unknown	13.3
"	unknown	unknown
Outboard Jack Screw	outboard	5.6
"	inboard	6.1
"	inboard	5.7
"	outboard	(Note 2)

(Note 1) The "unit" equals nearly "degree".
(Note 2) Unmeasurable due to a breakage in the middle.

The leading edge flap is estimated to have been at extended position from an investigation on four leading edge flap rotary actuators (set position unknown for all).

Investigation of Warning Lights, Switch Lights, etc

It was very difficult to identify systems or to judge on their operational status, because the wiring, electric bulbs, switches and circuit breakers equipped to P2, P4, P5 and P6 were severely damaged or contaminated (see Attached Figure-12).

Warning Lights and Switch Lights

As for electric bulbs, their condition of "on" or "off" at the time of crash were studied by inspecting the status of filaments visually or by microscope. The number of inspected electric bulbs totaled 373, out of which 56 are estimated to have beern lit, 251 (including 105 whose filament was not broken down) to have been off, and 66 were unknown due to damage.

It was impossible to determine the operational status of each generator at the time of crash from the lighting status of electric bulbs of the generator system which could be specified.

Visual inspection and functional test were conducted on switches and circuit breakers.

The number of inspected switches totaled 138, out of which 4 were "on", 115 were "off", and 19 were unknown due to damage. A total of 132 circuit breakers were inspected, and they are all damaged except one.

From these inspections, it was impossible to obtain sufficient information to estimate the state of the aircraft.

Other Necessary Matters

Investigation of Adhesion of Thermal Insulation to Structure of Non-pressurized Area of the Aft Fuselage

Extensive adhesion of thermal insulation material(*Note) installed inside the pressurized cabin wall for thermal and acoustical insulation in the aircraft was found in non-pressurized area aft of the aft pressure bulkhead.

Distinctive features of the adhesion of the insulating material are as follows:

Note: Fiberglass material installed inside the wall of the pressurized cabin for thermal and acoustic insulation. (Thermal Acoustical Fiberglass Insulation)

1. *Fuselage*

    The insulation material was found in a mass between fuselage frames to which the vertical fin is attached as well as in the vicinity of the root of the aft torque box (see Photo-94 and -95).

2. *Vertical Fin*

    Fragments of the film cover of the insulator were found on the VOR antenna cable of the vertical fin aft torque box, and others (see Photo-96).

3.   Horizontal Fin

Such adhesion of the insulation material as it would have been sprayed aftward was found on the elevator control cable inside the horizontal stabilizer's center section (see Photo-97).

4.   From the vicinity of stringer 2R through to the vicinity of 8R at BS2638, a portion of the fastener connecting the fuselage skin with the frame was fractured with the result that the fuselage skin was suspended. On some of the fastener holes on the suspended portion of the fuselage skin was observed adhesion of the insulation material which would have been blown out from inside the fuselage (see Photo-43).

5.   A large amount of insulation material was found on the exposed inner side of a fragment (70 cm x 53 cm) of the ceiling of the aft lavatory (Lavatory R) of the passenger cabin referred to in Item 7 of Para.2.4.2.3 (see Photo-98).

Investigation of Black Marks on Wreckage

On a portion of the right side skin of the vertical fin aft torque box (the skin connected portion from the vicinity of FS245 to the vicinity of FS345 of the front spar in Attached Figure-28) were found black marks which had blown out in stripes through the edge of the head of the rivets connecting the skin to the stringer. The black marks were significant in the vicinity of FS200 through to the vicinity of FS295 on the rivet row along the stringer (see Photo-58 and —59).

The analysis of the marks revealed that the main component was aluminum alloy powder, mingled with hydraulic fluid, grease and sand dust.

Chemical analysis was conducted on adhesions collected

from, several portions inside the aft torque box of the vertical fin, several portions on the left side skin of the vertical fin recovered from a forest on a mountain under the flight course (in Nippara, Okutama-City), several portions inside the fuselage in the vicinity of BS2436, and fragments of the cabin interior material as referred to in para.2.4.2.3(7), which results revealed components of the hydraulic liquid on all the specimens.

Investigation of Contact Marks on Upper Surface of the Lower Rudder

On the upper surface of the lower rudder, there were found striped contact marks which would have been caused by contact with gum seal installed on the under surface of the upper rudder. The state of the contact marks are shown in Figure-9.

These marks are estimated to have been caused by difference in rudder angle between the upper rudder and the lower rudder.

On Boeing 747 aircraft, the upper rudder is operated by No.I and No.3 hydraulic system, and the lower rudder by No.2 and No.4 hydraulic system.

During flight, almost no difference is caused in rudder angle between both rudders because they are operated in concert. During maintenance, however. inspection is conducted by operating each hydraulic system separately, thus causing a difference in rudder angle between rudders.

An investigation made on several aircraft of the same type in current operation revealed the same marks on them as the mark "A" as shown in Figure--9. Therefore, the mark "A" is estimated to have been caused during the maintenance work.

Marks "B" and "C" in Figure-9 are estimated to be marks caused by adhesion of the gum seal installed under the surface of the upper rudder strongly compressed between the two rudders.

Such severe compression to the gum seal does not occur during operation. The adhesion may therefore be estimated to have resulted from severe compression applied to the gum seal by the upper rudder when it was torn off. It was. however, impossible to clarify the process by which marks B and C were caused, because a little was recovered of the wreckage of the rudder.

Figure-9 Stripped Contact Marks on Upper Surface of Lower Rudder

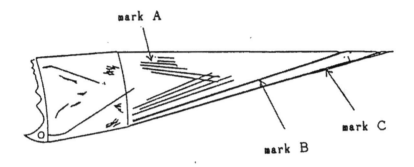

Investigation of Adhesion of Tobacco Nicotine

At 18L joint of the aft pressure bulkhead, there was adhesion of tobacco nicotine on the surface mutually overlapped among the tower web, the upper web and the splice plate near the following rivets:

1. near Rivet No.21--No.24 (see Photo-87)
2. near Rivet No.39--No.45 (see Photo-88)
3. near Rivet No.49--No.55 (see Photo-89)
4. near Rivet No.70--No.72 (see Photo-90)
5. near Rivet No.75--No.78 (see Photo-91)

Out of the above, in the vicinity of rivets No.41 and No.56. a slight gap came to separate the lower web and the spliced plate, through which a very small amount of tobacco nicotine would have been blown out towards the non-pressurized side (see Photo--92 and --93).

In L18 joint, all fatigue failures occurred on the upper web. Except for (1) of the preceding paragraph, every adhesion of tobacco nicotine was found on the joint surface of the lower web and the splice plate.

As to (1) of the preceding paragraph, adhesion of tobacco nicotine was found on the joint surface of the upper web and the lower web, but no fatigue failures were recognized between rivets No.21 to No.24. (No splice plate is applied tothis section.)

No adhesion of tobacco nicotine was found in R18 joint where its joint work had been conducted at the same time as repair work to the aft pressure bulkhead carried out in relation to the accident of June 2, 1978.

Investigation of Stabilizer Jack Screw Access Door

1. The stabilizer jack screw access door (hereinafter referred to as "Pressure relief door") is an access door to the stabilizer jack screw in the aft fuselage, and it also functions to release pressure from within the aft fuselage to prevent structural damage in case the pressure increases and reaches a certain value for some reason or other. (*Note)

    *(Note) As a cause for the increased pressure, rupture of APU high pressure air duct or the aft pressure bulkhead is conceivable.

    The pressure relief door is a plug type door having an area of 0.485 square meter, opening outward using the front as a hinge.

2. The pressure relief door has a springed latch mechanism, and the mechanism in accordance with manufacturing specifications is set so as to unlatch (the door opens) when the pressure differential between inside of the aft fuselage

and the outside air rises to between 1.0 psi to 1.5 psi. The specifications further prescribe that in test and adjustment at the time of manufacture the latch should be unlatched when loads of 199.6 kg(440 1b)$\pm$ 18.1 kg(40 lb) are applied on the center line of the roller of the latch mechanism.

3. The stay brace which keeps the pressure relief door in a full open position while on the ground was fractured at the portion where it is fixed to the pressure relief door. and the pressure relief door was separated from the stay brace. There was found, on the edge of the skin of the pressure relief door near the hinge, a indentation which was estimated to have been caused by overswing of the pressure relief door to the opening direction. There was no other damage to the pressure relief door (see Photo--25 to --29).

4. The length of springs of the door latch mechanism were as follows:
(see Photo-32)

Before Disassembly
      Left Side Spring 69.8 mm
      Right Side Spring   71.5 mm

After Disassembly (free length)
      Left Side Spring 73.2 mm
      Right Side Spring   73.4 mm

5. A disassembly check of the latch mechanism revealed scratches on the surface of the shoulder nut caused by scraping against the trunnion (see Photo --30 and --31). The scraping of the shoulder nut against the trunnion does not occur when the pressure relief door is manually operated. It does occur only when the pressure relief door is made open from the closed position by a force other than manual force (see Attached Figure-33). However, AS was described in para.2.16.5.2, the latch mechanism had been tested and

adjusted in the manufacture stage, where the scratches could also have been brought into existence on the shoulder nut due to scraping against the trunnion.

It was impossible to determine whether the scratches recognized on the shoulder nut were all caused at the test in the manufacturing stage or they involve scratches which would have come into being when the latch released during the flight of the aircraft.

6. As a result of a functional test of the pressure relief door carried out in accordance with the procedures set forth by the manufacturer of the latch mechanism, it was found that the door opened under a load of about 110 kg (average of three times of testing) instead of the prescribed 199.6 kg(440 lb).

7. Relationship between the load applied on the center line of the roller of the latch mechanism and the pressure the door is subject to by the pressure differential with the outer air is as follows:

load on roller center line	pressure differential
199.6 kg	about 1.2 psi
110 kg	about 0.7 psi

8. During the flight, the pressure differential before the occurrence of the irregular situation between the pressure cabin and the outer air is estimated to have been about 8.7 psi. Therefore, the door is estimated to have opened if the aft fuselage had been pressurized in flight by the pressurized air in the Passenger cabin.

Investigation of Horizontal Stabilizer Body Seal Door

1. The horizontal stabilizer body seal door assembly (hereinafter referred to as "body seal") consists of sliding blade seals and seal door.

Sliding blade seal is directly attached to the horizontal stabilizer and seal doors are coupled to the stabilizer through the drive mechanism.

2. The body seals have the function to shut the openings of the fuselage in coordination with the operation (pitch trim) of the horizontal stabilizer.

    Therefore, when the non-pressurized area aft of the aft pressure bulkhead is pressurized, the body seals are also subjected to pressure.

3. The status of damage to the body seal is shown in Attached Figure--35.

4. Relationship between the position of the seal door and the operative angle of the horizontal stabilizer is shown in Figure--10.

    Since the position of the horizontal stabilizer when the irregular sound occurred during flight over Sagami Bay is estimated to have been about --1° it is estimated that the lower seal doors rose to seal the lower openings of the fuselage together with the sliding blade seals as shown in Figure-10 and Figure-11.

5. Under the above condition, it is estimated that the lower openings of the fuselage would have a area large than the upper openings and that the lower sliding blade seals were more vulnerable to the inner pressure.

6. As seen from Attached Figure-35. damage to the lower sliding blade seals was slight. There were fragments, other than the wreckage shown in Attached Figure-35. whose location was difficult to specify. In view of the fact that they were recovered from the crash site, it is estimated that the horizontal stabilizer body seal doors were not damaged to such an extent that they constituted a large opening during flight.

Figure-10. Relationship between Seal Door and Operative Angle of Horizontal Stabilizer

Stab position at abnormal situation in flight
(APP.-1°)

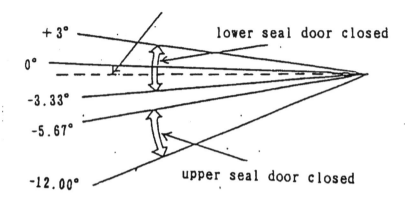

lower seal door closed

upper seal door closed

Note "door closed" means the situation that the seal. doors closed the fuselage openings

Figure-11.Functional Sketch of Horizontal Stabilizer Body Seal Door

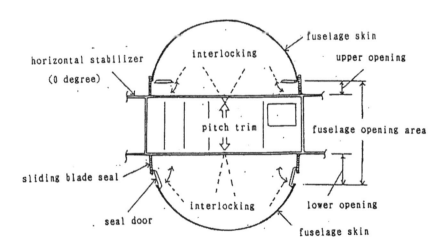

Investigation of Explosives and Others

Inspection was made on about 160 pieces of specimen taken from cabin interior material, lavatory interior material, aft pressure bulkhead, vertical fin fixture and horizontal fin fixture, etc, out of the aircraft wreckage recovered from the crash site. Sagami Bay. etc for any possibility of inclusion of gunpowder, explosives. etc. In the investigation, no inorganic substances such as ammonium or chlorine, nor nitroglycerin or trinitrotoluen (organic substances) were detected from any of these specimens. There were no traces found from the wreckage of the subjection to explosion blasts.

Investigation of Radioactive Substances

1. On board the aircraft were loaded radioactive substances. 93 in number of package and 13 of nuclear kind (an radioactive amount of 161.7729 millicuries) for use mainly in medicine.

    The radioactive substance was found to meet the criteria for air transport in packaging configuration, storage limit, loading procedures, etc.

2. On August 13, 1985. a radioactive substance transport accident countermeasure meeting was held by Ministry of Transport, and Science and Technology Agency as main members.

3. During August 14. to 16. 1985, specialists in radioactive substance and officers-in-charge of related ministries and agencies were sent to the crash site, and the recovery work and investigation on site was carried out. By this work, 64.896, in radioactive amount, of the loaded radioactive substance was recovered. Measurement of the radioactive amount rate on the ground at the crash site indicated that radioactivity was at such a level as to exert no influence to the human body.

4. On October 11, 1985. search at the crash site as well as

5. investigation on radioactive pollution were again carried out, and it was confirmed that there was no radioactive influence to the environment.

CHAPTER 4

TESTS AND RESEACH

Tests and Research for Analysis

Tests and research conducted for the analysis are described below. For reference materials, refer to Addenda separately bound.

Tests and Research for Analysis of Rupture of Aft Pressure Bulkhead (Reference Material - Addendum 1)

Along L18 splice of BS2360 aft pressure bulkhead, fatigue cracks emanating from a number of rivet holes were recognized by electron microscopic observation, as shown in Table--4. Analysis and test were conducted for the purpose of studying the behavior of propagation of such multiple fatigue cracks, and also evaluating the residual strength of the pressure bulkhead having such fatigue cracks.

Analysis of Propagation of Multiple Fatigue Cracks

L18 splice is the portion where the new and the old components of the pressure bulkhead were spliced together in the repair work following the accident at Osaka International Airport.

The splice portion was, as shown in Attached Figure-38(a) and (b), composed of 2 different types of splice: splice by two-row riveting and splice by one-row riveting.

The facts as listed below were confirmed by an analytical, comparative study made on propagation of multiple fatigue cracks in cases of the two different joint types. In this analysis the loads were calculated by the finite element method on the assumption that 8.9 psi a maximum operating differential pressure is applied once per flight, and the propagation of the fatigue cracks was calculated by estimating the stress intensity factor, taking into account whether there were initial flaws or not at the edge of rivet holes.

1. With regard to the propagation of fatigue cracks, the crack propagation rate for a one-row riveted splice has been calculated to be more than twice as fast as the rate for a two-row riveted splice when using the method in para.2 of Addendum 1. This analysis assumes that the method is valid at any distance away from the rivet.

2. The doublers applied to bay 2 and bay 3 of the accident aircraft as shown in Figure-12 have little effect on the stress distribution along L18 splice, and therefore have little effect on the propagation of fatigue cracks

3. The number of pressure cycles (number of flights) required for fatigue cracks to propagate to the length they were in the accident aircraft is calculated to be more than 10 thousand.

4. If 6.9 psi, the maximum operating differential pressure of the pressurization control is selected, the number of pressure cycles required for fatigue cracks to propagate to the length they were in the accident aircraft is calculated in the order of 30 thousand.

Evaluation of Residual Strength

In order to evaluate the residual strength of a fatigue cracked thin plate lapped splice with rivets, two methods are conceivable: i.e., the method based on the fracture toughness, and the one based on the condition of the net section yielding (the condition in which average stress applied to the gross section minus fatigue crack area and section area of rivet hole becomes equal to yield stress). To determine which of the evaluation methods mentioned above is appropriate in the case of the accident aircraft, residual strength test was carried out on the thin plates lapped splice with rivets of 400 mm wide and 1,100--1,200 mm long (including single thin plates with rivet holes only) which have flaws at the edge of rivet holes simulating various fatigue cracks, machined as test pieces.

The test result indicated that in case of the same material and the same crack size as the accident aircraft, the residual strength obtained by the test was not more than 23% higher than that evaluated under the condition of the net section yielding. Meanwhile, the residual strength obtained by the fracture toughness was as much as 1.4 to 2.5 times the value obtained by the test. Therefore, it was decided that the residual strength of the accident aircraft be evaluated under the condition of the net section yielding.

In the case of the accident aircraft, the net section area of bay 2 excluding the fatigue crack surface is much smaller than that of other bays. Therefore, when the residual strength of bay 2 is evaluated as 1.2 times the stress under the condition of the net section yielding, the calculation showed that the bay will be fractured by a differential pressure of 6.9 to 9.4 psi. From comparison of these figures with the estimated cabin differential pressure of 8.66 psi(*) at 1824:35 hours when the abnormal situation occurred, it is conceivable that rupture of the bulkhead started from bay 2.

*(Remarks) The cabin differential pressure when abnormal situation occurred at about 1824:35 was calculated from DFDR records and others as follows:

Flight altitude 24,000ft ....pressure of standard atmosphere 5.70 psi
Cabin altitude 650ft........pressure of standard atmosphere 14.36 psi
Cabin differential pressure 14.36 -5.70 = 8.66 psi

When bay 2 is fractured, the load applied to bay 2 has to be shared by other parts, with the result that firstly load on bay 3 exceeds its residual strength. When bay 3 is fractured in succession, the load on the 2nd strap exceeds its residual strength. In the same manner, loads shared on bay 4 and bay 1, the 1st strap and the 3rd strap and L18 stiffener exceed successively their own residual strengths, respectively.

The estimated strengths of parts are summarized in Table-6 below. It is noted that values in the table are strength calculated on the assumption that parts which have been fractured do not share any load in each step considered.

Table-6 Estimated Strength of Parts of L18 Splice

Condition of calculation	The weakest part	Estimated strength (psi)
ALL parts not fractured (Fatigue cracks the same as accident aircraft)	bay 2	6.9 — 9.4
bay 2 fractured	bay 3	6.7 — 9.0
bay 2 and bay 3 both fractured	2nd strap	6.0 — 6.5
bay 2, bay 3 and 2nd strap fractured	bay 4	6.2 — 8.4
	bay 1	6.9 — 9.4
bay 2, bay 3, 2nd strap, bay 4 and bay 1 fractured	3rd strap and L18 stiffener	5.6 — 5.8
	1st strap and L18 stiffener	5.9 — 6.1

When L18 splice is broken into two portions, upper and lower, the stress of bay 5 connected with a collector ring increase. This indicates a possibility that the connection of the web and the ring is then ruptured towards a series of succeeding ruptures.

Figure-12 Vicinity of L18 Splice of the Aft Pressure Bulkhead

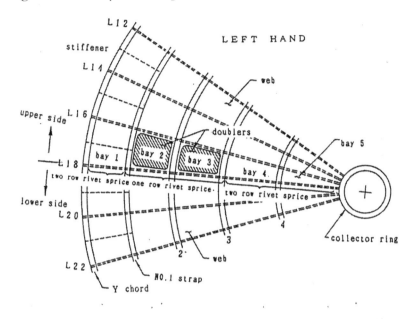

From the analysis of propagation of fatigue cracks, the analysis on the residual strength and its test results, and the aspects of destruction of the wreckage, the sequence of rupture in L18 splice of the aft pressure bulkhead is estimated as follows:

1. Since bay 2 and bay 3 were of one-row riveting, the stress on the hole edge was high, and judging from the behavior of fatigue cracks existent at hole edges, the fatigue crack was initiated and propagated on the rivet hole in a comparatively early period after the repair was made for the accident at Osaka International Airport. Fatigue cracks were initiated also on rivet holes of the webs overlapping with the 1st strap, the 2nd strap and the 3rd strap.

2. Following the propagation of fatigue cracks from rivet holes in bay 2 and bay 3, fatigue cracks were initiated and propagated on the upper side rivet hole edges (subjected to higher stress than lower side rivet hole edges) located above the two-row riveting on both bay 1 and bay 4 which are of the two-row riveting structure.

3. Bay 2 having fatigue cracks was fractured by a estimated cabin differential pressure of 8.66 psi.

4. In bay 3, fracture started from the outboard portion where fatigue cracks concentrated, ending in total fracture.

5. The 2nd strap fractured, then bay 1 and bay 4 fractured, being followed by fracture of the 1st strap, the 3rd strap, the 4th strap, bay 5 and L18 stiffener, resulting in overall fracture of L18 splice.

6. After L18 splice was separated into upper and lower parts, the web above its portion connected with collector ring was fractured, and the fracture progressed along R6 stiffener and L2 stiffener.

    On the other hand, the web above the portion connected with Y chord on the outboard side was also fractured, with the result that an opening was brought into being in the upper portion of the aft pressure bulkhead.

Test and Research for Analysis of Rupture of Vertical Fin (Reference Material — Addendum 2)

The vertical fin is ordinarily not designed as to withstand an excessive internal pressure. In this accident, the possibility would be high that part of pressurized cabin air, which flowed out due to rupture of the aft pressure bulkhead, rushed into the vertical fin, and the excessive internal pressure ruptured the aft torque box structure. A study was made then on the possibility of the vertical fin being ruptured by the internal pressure as well as on the sequence of rupture, by calculating the strength of the vertical fin structure against the internal pressure, and by conducting, for the corroboration purpose, a fracture test of component structures of the vertical fin by internal pressure and a fracture test on fasteners.

Strength of Fixture between Stringer and Rib Chord

The skin of aft torque box of the vertical fin, as shown in Figure--13, is connected to the rib through the stringers. The calculation indicated that when the internal pressure is applied to the vertical fin of such a structure,

1. at a differential pressure of about 4.8-5.4 psi, the fixture between the stringer and rib chord is damaged and detached at a location in the vicinity of PS520--570, and the connection there is lost; and

2. the fracture mentioned above induces the similar fracture of neighboring fixtures between the stringer and the rib chord, expanding the area of such fracture, and causing at the same time expansion of the fracture of connecting rivets between the rib's shear tie and the skin toward the rib chord direction.

The calculation results were confirmed by the fracture tests of component structures of the vertical fin by internal pressure.

Furthermore. calculation of the external aerodynamic force being applied to the vertical fin in the flight condition immediately before the abnormal situation occurred at about 1824:35 indicates that a differential pressure not exceeding 0.5 psi at the maximum is applied to the skin of the aft torque box from inside to outside.

It is conceivable that the fixture between the stringer and the rib chord is fractured when the internal pressure increases as much as about 4 psi, if the calculation and test results above as well as such factors as the external aerodynamic force to the vertical fin, manufacture allowances, play in structures, and accuracy of the analysis and test are all taken into account.

Strength of Fixture between Skin and Spar Chord

The calculation revealed that when fixture between the stringer and the rib chord is disconnected, the skin of the aft torque box inflates in a pillow shape due to a differential pressure, causing the rib to buckle, with the result that the skin inflates further causing a peel fracture (so as to peel off the skin) at the fixture between the skin and the spar chord in the vicinity of FS295-450 at a differential pressure of about 2.0-4.5 psi.

The fixture between the front spar chord and the skin would be fractured earlier than the fixture between the rear spar chord and the skin due to effects of the external aerodynamic force, the rigidity of the forward torque box, etc., even if the internal pressure loads are of the same degree.

Other Strength

Calculation indicated that the fin tip and its fixture on the tip of the vertical fin have a higher strength against internal pressure than the fixture between the stringer and the rib chord.

Estimation of Sequence of Rupture

From results of the study up to the previous paragraph on the strength of each component structure, it is conceivable that the vertical fin may be ruptured when part of the pressurized cabin air, which flows out due to rupture of the aft pressure bulkhead, rushes into the vertical fin, resulting in a rise of about 4 psi in the internal pressure.

It would be difficult to determine details of the sequence of rupture due to the fact that the calculations made on the strength of the vertical fin were all carried out with a static analysis method and that the recovery of wreckage of the vertical fin was partial. However, based on the analysis and test results, and also taking into account the locations where the wreckage was recovered (2.4.3) and the damage to the aircraft (2.4.2 and 2.15.3), the following would be considered as the most probable sequence rupture:

1. Part of the pressurized cabin air, which flows out due to rupture of the aft pressure bulkhead, rushes into the vertical fin, causing internal pressure rise there.

2. When the internal pressure rises about 4 psi, the fixture between the stringer and the rib chord near the top of the aft torque box is fractured.

3. When one fixture between the stringer and the rib chord is fractured, it induces the similar fracture of neighboring fixtures between the stringer and the rib chord, expanding the area of such fracture, and causing at the same time' expansion of the fracture of connecting rivets between the rib's shear tie and the skin toward the rib chord direction.

4. When the stringer and the rib chord are disconnected, the skin of the aft torque box inflates in a pillow shape due to a pressure differential between the outside and inside, causing the rib to buckle, with a result that the skin inflates further and a peel fracture is caused at the fixture between the skin and the spar chord.

5. When such peel fracture occurs at a location, the skin starts to be peeled off for a considerably wide range, aided by aerodynamic force of the external air flow.

6. The aft torque box loses its function as a major structural component, giving rise to collapse of the rear spar, and to separation of the rudder supported by the spar, as well as to damage of the rudder-related control cable system and the rudder-related hydraulic lines.

Study on Flutter and Divergence

A study was made on the possibility that flutter or divergence of the vertical fin might have contributed to the rupture of the vertical stabilizer and the rudder.

It was confirmed in the analysis and test conducted at the development stage of B-747 aircraft that neither flutter nor divergence occurs in relation to the vertical fin including the rudder, not only in case the structure and functions are normal, but also in case the hydraulic system pressure drops, or in case the rudder and the control actuator are disconnected. It has been also confirmed that neither flutter nor divergence occurs at a speed up to 1.2 V_D, with a reduction in basis stiffness of 2596 of the vertical stabilizer.

Based on the above confirmation the sequence of rupture under the assumption that flutter or divergence contributed to the fracture of the vertical fin including the rudder would be as follows:

1. Part of the pressurized cabin air, which flows out due to rupture of the aft pressure bulkhead, rushes into the vertical fin, causing internal pressure rise there.

2. When the internal pressure rises about 4 PSi, the fixture between the stringer and the rib chord near the top of the aft torque box is fractured.

3. When one fixture between the stringer and the rib chord is fractured it induces the similar fracture of neighboring fixtures between the stringer and the rib chord, expanding the area of such fracture, and causing at the same time expansion of fracture of connecting rivets between the rib's shear tie and the skin toward the rib chord direction.

4. Since connection between the stringer and the rib chord has weakened stiffness of the aft torque box decreases considerably, and flutter related to the vertical fin involving

rudder, or divergence of the vertical fin occurs, with the result of rupture of the vertical fin, and separation of the rudder.

5. In these processes is conceivable the contribution of buckling of the rib. Peel fracture of the fixture of the skin, local collapse of the skin, etc.

Such a process of the rupture may be possible, but no evidence was found of occurrence of flutter nor divergence from records of the three-axis accelerometer of DFDR or from the state of damage of the recovered wreckage.

Figure-13 Fixture between Stringer and Rib Chord
(Cross section of vertical fin)

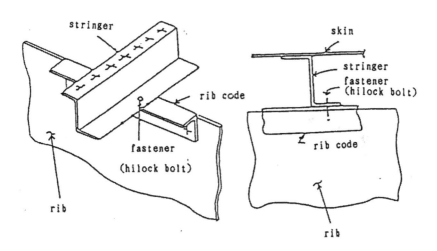

(Details of "A" section)

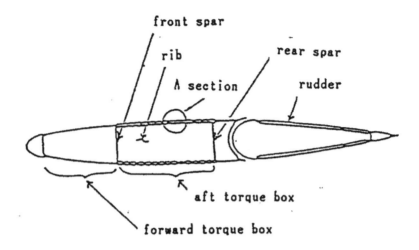

Study on Structural Strength in the Vicinity of APU Firewall (Reference Material — Addendum 3)

In order to study how structures in the vicinity of the APU firewall may be damaged in case the air in the cabin flows out by rupture of the aft pressure bulkhead (BS2360) and effects as a pressure on the APU firewall, analysis and calculation were made on the strength of each structure in the vicinity.

Outlines of the calculation as well as estimated sequence of rupture based thereon are as in the following paragraphs.

Estimated Strength of Each Structural Parts

Calculation showed that in case the APU fire wall is subjected to a pressure and all the structural parts are normal, the wall is the weakest in lateral beams ① and ⑥ shown in Figure-14, and they buckle under a pressure of 2.2 to 2.5 psi. When lateral beams ① and ⑥ are fractured, lateral beams C, ③, ⑤ and ⑦ are also estimated to be easily fractured.

The calculation also indicated that in case lateral beams, except lateral beams ② and ④ supporting the support struts, are all fractured, the lower part of the peripheral frame is fractured under a pressure of 2.1 to 3.5 psi, in which case the support struts are also fractured under a pressure of 4.4. to 4.8 psi. These are summarized in Table-7.

Estimation of Sequence of Rupture

Based on the estimated anti-pressure strength of the structural parts above as well as the state of damage of the recovered airframe, the sequence of rupture of the APU firewall is estimated as follows:

1. First of all, lateral beams of the upper and the lower portion except for ② and ④ buckle under a pressure of about 2.2 to 3.5 psi.

2. Then, fracture of the lower part of the peripheral frame (under a pressure of about 2.1 to 2.5 psi), as well as buckling (under a pressure of about 3.1 to 3.9 psi) and fracture of the lateral beams supported by the support struts, occurs almost simultaneously, causing the air to flow rearward.

3. The air pressure which caused the APU firewall to be ruptured is estimated to have been of the order of 3 to 4 psi.

4. Following the complicated rupture of the firewall and structures in the neighborhood, the support struts were also fractured, with the result that the APU is separated together with structures aft of BS 2658 firewall.

5. The time required for the pressure to the APU firewall to reach about 4 psi is estimated to be extremely short, and

122

therefore the rupture would have been momentary and impulsive. However, the actual process of destruction would have been more complicated than that estimated in the above calculation which based on static analysis.

Figure- 14. Outline of APU firewall Structure

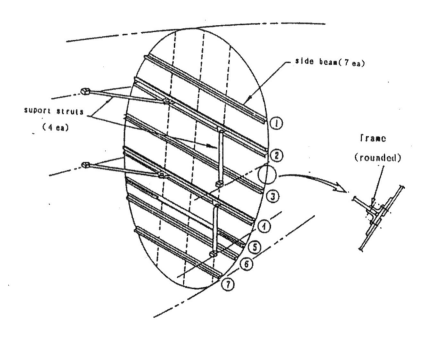

Table-7 Estimated Strength of Structural Parts of APU Firewall (in psi)

Calculation model / Parts	In case all parts normal	In case lateral beams except ② & ④ are fractured	In case lateral beams except ②&④& lower portion of peripheral frame are fractured
Lateral beam	2.2~2.5	3.1~3.9	
Peripheral frame		2.1~3.5	
Support strut	6.5	6.3	4.4~4.8

Study by Numerical Calculation on Discharge of Pressurized Air from Aft Pressure Bulkhead (Reference Material - Addendum 4)

A study was made on the relationship between the facts listed below and the phenomena which could occur if part of the aft pressure bulkhead ruptures to make an opening, and air in a pressurized compartment discharges into the empennage.

1. Fog formation in the passenger cabin (based on witness)
2. Depressurization alert (based on CVR record)
3. Start of automatic play of pre-recorded announcement and drop-out of oxygen masks (based on CVR record and witness)
4. Rupture of the APU firewall and the vertical fin (based on wreckage investigation)

All above are closely related to the pressure or temperature at some parts of the internal fuselage. Therefore, analysis and calculation was conducted using a quasi-static method wherein the space within the airplane was divided into eight compartments, and time history of pressure and temperature was estimated from the movement of air resulting from differential pressure among compartments.

The study was made assuming a wide variety of change for conditions which would affect critical results of the calculation, such as the area of the opening in the aft pressure bulkhead, and release pressure of the vertical fin and the APU firewall. (As to the release pressure, the calculation was carried out for a range of $\pm.30\%6$ of 4.75 psi and 4.00 psi for the vertical fin and the APU firewall, respectively, based on results of fracture test of component structures of the vertical fin by internal pressure etc).

From wreckage investigation, the area of opening of the aft pressure bulkhead is estimated as of the order of 2-3 square meters. The calculation indicates when the area of opening of the aft pressure bulkhead is varied from 1.5 to 3.5 square meters, the following times are required before the phenomena occur after the rupture of the bulkhead:

- The time the release pressure of
  APU firewall is reached
  (rupture begins)   0.09--0.04 second

- The time the release pressure of
  vertical fin is reached
  (rupture begins)   not ruptured 0.29 second

- The time relative humidity
  reaches 100 %   1.73--1.21 seconds

- The time the pressure
  equivalent to cabin altitude
  10,000 ft is reached (alert
  detector functions)   2.21--1.56 seconds

- The time the pressure
  equivalent to cabin altitude
  14,000 ft is reached (oxygen
  masks drop out, and detector
  functions for pre-recorded
  announcement)   3.37--2.40 seconds

provided that the release pressure of the APU firewall and the vertical fin are taken as 4.00 and 4.75 psi, respectively, and that the rupture of the APU firewall and the vertical fin by internal pressure is momentary, and further that the pressure relief door can open, but the upper and lower body seals are not damaged.

Detailed results which are arrived at, when the release pressure of the APU firewall and the vertical fin and other conditions are varied, are shown in Addendum 4.

From these calculations, it was found that rupture starts earlier at the APU firewall than at the vertical fin, and fog is formed about 2 seconds after the rupture of the aft pressure bulkhead. Furthermore, the decompression speed of the pressurized compartment is of such an order that the pressure equivalent to cabin altitude 14,000 feet is reached within several seconds after the rupture of the aft pressure bulkhead. There are slight differential pressure among the passenger cabin, cockpit and cargo compartment which are all pressurized, but they are negligible. In addition, when the release pressure are changed to the value in the estimation of rupture of the APU firewall, the time up to occurrence of phenomena varies about 0.01- 0.03 seconds compared with the figures above, both in the time the release pressure of the APU firewall is reached and the time the release pressure of the vertical fin is reached.

A study was also made on possible cases where decompression speed of the pressurized compartment becomes slow. The most contributive to the decompression speed rate of the pressurized compartment is the area of the opening in the aft pressure bulkhead. Irrespective of the afore-mentioned estimation of rupture, cases where decompression speed of the pressurized compartment becomes slow were sought for from among various combinations of conditions. And as an example, the case is obtained where the opening area of the aft pressure bulkhead is 0.6 square meters, the release pressure of APU firewall is 4.00 psi, and the release pressure of the vertical fin is 3.33 psi, in which case the times required before the phenomena occur are as follows:

The time the release pressure of APU
firewall is reached (rupture begins)   0.42 second

The time the release pressure of
vertical fin is reached (rupture begins)   0.41 second

The time relative humidity reaches 100 %   3,97 second

The time the pressure equivalent to

cabin altitude 10,000 ft is reached
(alert detector functions)   5.02 second

The time the pressure equivalent
to cabin altitude 14,000 ft is
reached (oxygen masks drop out,
and detector functions for pre-recorded
announcement)   7.51 second

The APU firewall and the vertical fin rupture almost simultaneously, although the latter is slightly earlier, and the fog formation is about 4 seconds after, and the reaching to the pressure equivalent to cabin altitude 14,000 feet is about 7.5 seconds after. The smaller the area of the opening in the aft pressure bulkhead, the slower the decompression speed of the pressurized compartment. However, pressure condition that causes the APU firewall and the vertical fin both to rupture becomes unsatisfied.

A study was also made on the situation after the aft pressure bulkhead was opened. Immediately after the aft pressure bulkhead is opened, the pressurized air discharges to the non-pressurized compartment side, and a shock wave is generated in the front. It is, however, inconceivable that the shock wave progresses one-dimensionally to hit the APU firewall without loss of the strength, in light of the facts that the cross section of the fuselage aft of the aft pressure bulkhead is much larger than the opening area of the aft pressure bulkhead, that the horizontal stabilizer structure runs through inside of the fuselage, and that many obstacles including fuselage frames exist along the flow path. In this study loads applied on the APU firewall were sought for with two cases where all obstacles on the flow path except those in the flow-in portion of the APU firewall are disregarded and either reflection of the shock wave or stagnation of the jet stream are taken into account.

The study result indicated that in the two cases the average differential pressure were 2.74 psi and 2.88 psi, respectively. From this, it is inconceivable that the APU firewall will be ruptured by the transitional phenomena caused immediately after the opening of the aft pressure bulkhead, because these values, although they are values taken to the larger side, are smaller than the estimated values for the rupture of the APU firewall of 3-4 psi.

Displayed Time on Various Records

Time Display of CYR

Since time is not recorded on CVR, its estimation was made by the method below.

The time scale on CVR was estimated by collating, as precisely as possible using a sound spectro-analyzer and others, contents of the communication with air traffic controllers recorded on CVR tape with contents of the same voice portion of the communications recorded on the ATC communication tape on which the time signal of the Japan Standard Time is recorded.

However, an error may be involved to some extent except for the aforementioned portions which have been collated with the ATC tape, because the running speed of CVR tape cannot be kept always uniform due to limited characteristics of the equipment.

Time Display of DFDR

On DFDR is recorded the time of the intra-aircraft clock whose display is on the captain's seat. Since the time of the clock is not always accurate, the following adjustment was necessary.

On DFDR is recorded the keying time at the communication with Air Traffic Control, while on ATC communication record tape is recorded the time signal of the Japan Standard Time. Collation made of DFDR keying times with the recorded Japan Standard Time indicated a delay of about 6 seconds in DFDR recorded time. Therefore, the DFDR time is described by adding 6 seconds.

There may be an error not exceeding one second in the time display of DFDR collated with ATC communication record tape on which the time signal of Japan Standard Time is recorded, because on DFDR the keying signal is recorded with a delay of less than one second after a keying is done.

Error Correction in DFDR Record (Reference Material - Addendum 5)

1. Outline of DFDR Record

The DFDR record is a digital recording system in which data is recorded by two signals "0" and "1", and each data are recorded at a cycle of 1/8-4 seconds.

Data such as altitude, speed and bearing are recorded every second, data suddenly changeable such as acceleration every 1/8-1/4 second, data such as time every 4 seconds, and all data are covered through in a 4 seconds cycle. In DFDR decoder, data check is done every second, and if there is an unreadable portion due to insufficient signal level or signal distortion, or when an error in the data format is discovered, an error mark is registered to indicate "unreadable ".

2. Error Correction by Decoder

As described earlier, on DFDR tape of the accident aircraft were found cuts or wrinkles, and at the time of read-out many error marks were registered on the portion involving the cuts, the wrinkles and others. It was found that the appearance of error marks relevant to low signal level or large signal distortion are dependent on conditions such as individuality of read-out equipment used, tension of the tape when being read out and others. For this reason the read-out was tried changing the equipment or tape tension for an optimum condition. By this method, error marks could be lessened.

However, the error mark still remained at three portions, i.e. about 1824:35, about 1840:34, and a Portion of more than one minute after 1855:12, which needed data recovery by the method in (3) below.

3. Error Correction by Computer

As to portions unreadable by the ordinary decoder due to low output level or distorted wave shape, decoding was done by taking out the signals from the intermediary stage in the play back process of DFDR, and converting them into an array of digital signals "0" or "1" through a computer after rectifying the wave shape using various devices. Normally the signals indicating "0" and "1" are arranged under a regular rule, but in some of portions involving errors the arrangement of signals was far out of the rule, for which such a computer processing was done as to try decoding by allowing variable bit-cells in the PCM signal.

As a result of the above, most of portions where the signal level exceeds a certain degree became readable, but other portions, specifically portions where the signal distortion is large, remained unreadable with the data processing by computer, where such human decipherment became necessary as finding out data based on signal patterns before and behind.

4. Outline of Results of Error Correction

By the afore-mentioned methods, most of portions where originally had an error mark became readable. In the portion of continuous errors after 1855:12, the error correction work was conducted only on factors related to dynamic analysis of flight course, attitude of aircraft, etc. (altitude, speed, acceleration, bearing, attitude angle, engine output level, etc.).

The DFDR record corrected for. errors by the methods above is shown in. Attachment 5. Portions corrected were indicated by the correction mark. Non-corrected data in the continuous error portion are also shown for reference in Attachment 5.

Flight Situation and Flight Course of Accident Aircraft based on DFDR Record (Reference Material - Addendum 6)

Situation before and after Occurrence of the Abnormal Situation (1) Sequence of Events (refer to Attachment 5)

From the analysis of DFDR, the following events are conceivable to have taken place before and after the occurrence of abnormal situation:

a. Longitudinal Acceleration (LNGG)

The longitudinal acceleration at 1824:35.70 shows a spike of about 0.047 G as compared to those before and after the abnormal situation occurred. When the aircraft weight at that time is taken into account, it is estimated that an external force of as much as about 11 tons acted forward, and that the rupture of the aft fuselage occurred at about this time.

Great changes in longitudinal acceleration recorded for a few seconds after 1824:36.20 are conceivable to have been due to the aircraft motion.

b. Lateral Acceleration (LATG)

Between 24:35.73 and 35.98, a first significant change is recorded in lateral acceleration. This change in the lateral acceleration occurred after the protrusion of the longitudinal acceleration and is considered to endorse the estimation that the rupture of the empennage occurred before 24:35.73 hours.

For a few seconds after 24:35.98 an oscillation having a maximum total amplitude exceeding 0.08 G is observed in the lateral acceleration. Judging from the fact that it completely decayed in a few seconds, it is considered that it was a free oscillation excited by an abnormal external forces.

c. Displacement of Horizontal Stabilizer Position (HSTB)

Up to 1824:35.13. the position was at the normal trim position of -1.2° . At the next recording time i.e., 36.13 seconds and thereafter, values exceeding the HSTB sensor limit are recorded. It is estimated that HSTB sensor or the signal wiring was broken between 35.13 and 36.13 seconds.

d. DFDR Error

DFDR records several errors in the neighborhood of 1824:35.64 and 35.73. It is considered that the errors occurred because DFDR was installed on the upper part of the fuselage portion to which the vertical fin is attached and was subjected to strong shocks due to the structural destruction.

e. Control Column Position (CCP) and Auto-pilot Channel A (CMD 1)

After the occurrence of the abnormal situation, CCP as a whole was in an extraordinarily forward position. Judging from the fact that no corresponding change in pitch attitude was recorded, it is estimated that the normal relationship was lost between the control column position and the power control package output position of the elevator within a comparatively short period after the occurrence of the abnormality.

Auto-pilot Channel A was in "command mode" up to 1824:37.92, and was "off" after 38.92 seconds.

f. Vertical Acceleration (VRTG)

Vertical acceleration that is indicative of normal flight conditions are recorded up to 1824:35.66. Thereafter to 31.16 seconds the vertical acceleration increased slightly, and at 36.28 seconds it jumped by about --0.24 G, causing a disturbance to begin.

It is estimated that the vertical fin ruptured nearly at this time.

g. Rudder Pedal Position

PED had been in the normal neutral position of 0° up to 1824:36.22, and changed radically to more than 25° to the right not later than 36.72 seconds. This time almost coincides with the time when the oscillation in lateral acceleration originated. PED varied abruptly thereafter from 20° right to 15° left, but the heading and roll angle did not respond as expected to such a large PED input. From this, it is estimated that the rudder had lost its effective control moment after 36.22 seconds.

2. Numerical Analysis of Aircraft Motion

a. Purpose

The purpose of the analysis is to confirm that there is no significant contradiction among DFDR data and to estimate external forces arising from jet streams or changes in the exterior shape after the abnormal condition had occurred and theory to confirm that the process of destruction is consistent with the descriptions in item (1) above.

b. Study on the Assumption that no Abnormal External Forces had existed

When the aircraft motion is calculated on the assumption that the elevator angle and the thrust are given by those which were recorded in DFDR as control column position and EPR (engine output), the responses well coincide with DFDR record for the period before the occurrence of the abnormal situation. However, significant differences between the calculated response and the record begin to exist after 1824:36, as to the altitude, speed, angle of attack and pitch angle. From this, it was found that the DFDR record could not be accounted for unless abnormal external forces had come into action after the occurrence of abnormality.

c. Estimation of External Forces resulting from Jet Streams and Changes in the Exterior Shape at the Occurrence of the Abnormal Situation

133

In order to reconstruct DFDR record, the response of the aircraft (change in speed, altitude, acceleration, attitude, etc) was analyzed numerically, assuming abnormal external forces. From the numerical calculation. it was found that an abnormal external force (not exceeding about 11 tons) directing forward coming into action from about 1824:35.60 and an abnormal external force directing downward having its peak at 36.60 seconds were necessary.

The lateral abnormal force, if any, could not be estimated from DFDR record

Change-in Stability and Control due to partial Loss of the Empennage and vertical Fin

Loss of the empennage/fin brought about decrease in stability due to- change in the aerodynamic shape and deterioration of the control due to loss of rudder surface, damage to control cables, loss of hydraulic pressure, etc. Therefore, the following study was made by a numerical analysis:

1.   Shapes of the Empennage/Fin after their Rupture

From wreckage investigation, and analysis of DFDR record and photographic image, it is estimated that the empennage portion aft of 13S2658 was separated immediately after the abnormal situation occurred. However, the shape of the vertical fin after it ruptured is not necessarily clear. The motions of the accident aircraft could best be accounted for if the shape of the vertical fin is assumed to have varied as shown in the figure below (lost portions are indicated by hatched lines).

Figure-15. Lost Portion

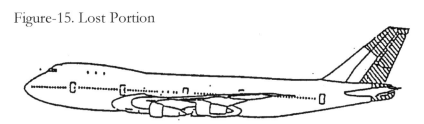

2. Longitudinal Stability

The direct effect of the partial loss of the empennage is to such an extent that the non-dimensional damping coefficient of the phugoid is somewhat increased with increase in aerodynamic drag. It is noted that both the gear down and the increase in stationary descent angle help the phugoid mode to subside.

3. Longitudinal Control

Throughout the flight after the occurrence or the abnormal situation, phugoid mode was excited, together with dutch roll mode. Regulating attitude by altitude control is the fundamental requirement for suppressing phugoid motion. From an early stage after the occurrence of the abnormal situation, it is considered that the elevator had been in a floating condition due to loss or hydraulic pressure. and HSTB had been kept fixed by the jack screw. Under such conditions, normal attitude control should have been impossible.

As alternative longitudinal control elements other than the elevator, there are controls either using engine thrust, or flap operation by alternate extension Although the period of phugoid is long, the driving speed of flaps by the alternate system is extremely slow and therefore it does not contribute to practically suppress the phugoid mode.

It is theoretically possible to stabilize the phugoid mode which is brought into existence due to loss of the longitudinal attitude control by operating the thrust lever. It does never mean that the task is easy for a pilot to accomplish.

4. Lateral-Directional Stability

Different from the case of longitudinal motion, the lateral stability is decisively affected by a partial loss of the vertical fin. After the loss, both the directional stability and the damping-in-yaw decrease due to reduced area of the vertical fin, with the results that the undamped natural frequency of the dutch roll mode decreases considerably (the period increases considerably), and the non-dimensional damping coefficient changes from positive to negative (stable to unstable within the assumption of linearization). The spiral mode is stabilized on the contrary, and the time constantin roll subsidence decreases to some extent.

When the abnormal situation occurred, it is estimated that the aircraft was flying at a height-speed combination such that the dutch roll mode would become unstable under the assumption of linearization if the empennage had really broken to the afore-mentioned configuration. It is also estimated that the ruptured aircraft entered a flight region of more unstable dutch roll mode as flight speed decreased thereafter. Actually, the aircraft is estimated to have been brought into a limit cycle as amplitude increases.

5. Lateral-Directional Control

Out of the rudder and the aileron-spoiler systems originally used for lateral-directional control, it is considered that the rudder had been separated almost at the same time when the abnormal situation occurred. As a result, function of Yaw dampers were also lost immediately thereafter, and it is estimated that the situatioin was such that an external disturbance, if any, would have excited the dutch roll mode.

Judging from the response of the aircraft as recorded on DFDR, it is considered that the aileron have functioned for more than one minute, but thereafter did not at all due to loss of hydraulic pressure in the same manner as the elevator.

Suppressing of dutch roll mode by use of the differential thrust between the right and left engines is estimated practically impossible for a pilot.

6. Effects of Flaps on Lateral-Directional Stability

When part of the vertical fin is missing, the contribution of the empennage to the total directional stability decreases and the contributions of the wings and fuselage relatively increases to give a dominant effect on the directional stability. The contribution of the wings on the directional stability depends to a large extent upon the trimmed angle of attack as well as setting angle of the flaps. Since the trimmed angle of attack also depends on the setting angle of the flaps, the directional stability with the partial loss of empennage varies with the flap setting angle in very sensitive and complicated manner.

Unless the flap angle is adjusted with fastidious precision to speed and altitude, the aircraft would easily be caught into the region of dutch roll instability at least within small amplitude.

Estimated Flight Course by DFDR

The estimation of flight course of the accident aircraft was made on the basis of radar records and decoded DFDR data. The status of propagation of radar wave began to remarkably worsen due to effects of mountains from approximately 1848 at which the aircraft initiated a flight towards the mountainous area, causing disorder in radar records. For this reason the estimation for the period approximately 1846 to the last of DFDR record (1856:27) was made mainly based on the decoded data from DFDR. The estimated flight course is shown in Attached Figure-1. The flight course is almost consistent with statements of eye witnesses.

According to the estimation above, the aircraft, after approached Mt. Senpei, initiated an abrupt right turn, and crashed turning clockwise and making an ellipse of about 3.4 km east to west, and about 2.5 km north to south on the north side of Mt. Mikuni.

Estimation by DFDR of Flight Situation immediately before Crash

About 1854:40 when the aircraft was south of Mt. Mikuni,

the flap angle became about 8 units, but a right bank abnormally increased due probably to unbalance between the right and the left flap effectiveness, and a right turn was initiated. The flap continued to go down, and sometime after 1855 the right roll angle reached 30° - 40 ° when the aircraft was west of Mt. Mikuni, gradually steepening the right turn. After 1855:40, engine power on the left wing became slightly higher than that on the right wing, which situation continued up to the crash.

At 1855:44 the flap angle became about 25 units. A flap-up action was immediately initiated, but the right bank further increased to 50° - 60° . It is estimated that a situation was sustained that is susceptible of unbalanced effectiveness between the right and the left flaps since the flaps were kept operated from about 1851:14 to the crash.

At approximately 1855:57 the pitch angle exceeded -15° and the nose continued to go down. For this reason the power would have been increased abruptly, by which the engine powers were rised from 1.15 to 1.50 level. The altitude at this time was about 10,000 feet.

Asymmetric right and left thrusts of considerable amount were applied to the aircraft of nose down pitch attitude and roll attitude of several ten degrees. The aircraft plunged into a dive increasing the right roll angle to more than about 80°, and supposedly entered a steep right turn due to increase in lift, resulting from quick velocity increment, onto the situation of large right bank angle. At 1856:07 the nose came down as much as about -36° , the rate of descent became 15,000 feet/minute on the average, temporarily more than 18,000 feet/minute. It is estimated that the aircraft lost altitude rapidly, because the increase in lift following the increase in airspeed did not help prevent the descent with the resultant large upward vertical acceleration, but only causing a steep turn due to the deep bank.

Approximately 1856:17, at an altitude of about 5,500, the

right roll angle recovered up to about 40° at which time the airspeed exceeded 340 knots. It is estimated that about this time engine power was brought near the maximum, because the GPWS had been activated (CVR record). Although the steep turn still continued, the descent of the aircraft stopped, for a reason, among others, that the right roll angle became less than before (to about 40°), with a result that an upward vertical acceleration of about 3G's continued for 5-6 seconds.

Sometime after approximately 1856:23 a shock of backward 0.14 G was recorded on the longitudinal accelerometer, and the right bank deepened suddenly, and at the same time the nose which was up was going down again abruptly, after which output of the 3rd and 4th engine on the right side decreased at an abnormal speed; especially power of the 4th engine dropped to EPR 0.50 which is indicative of zero output. However, EPR of the 1st and the 2nd engine on the left side were normal, and EPR of the 3rd engine remained at about 0.86. From this record together with a contact sound recorded on CVR taken into account, it is estimated that at this time a portion of the right wing involving the 4th engine cut off trees in the vicinity of the single larch tree, and the 4th engine was separated from the airframe.

About 3 seconds thereafter, the aircraft became subjected to a large rearward G's, and abnormal changes began to appear in heading and in longitudinal acceleration. From the abnormality and the flight distance from single larch tree. as well as the second contact sound recorded on CVR taken into account, it is estimated that this was the initial contact with the U-ditch. Almost at the same time output of the first and second engine on the left side began to indicate an abnormal drop in the same lanner as the fourth engine, being followed by drop in output of the third engine. It is conceivable that at this time the 1st, 2nd and 3rd engines were separated from the airframe and dispersed 500-700 meters ahead by locally concentrated force resulting from considerable aftward and lateral forces applied at the time of the contact and large engine thrusts corresponding thereto.

At about 1856:27 the aft acceleration reached 0.26G, and at the same time the lateral acceleration reversed from +0.5G to -0.5G. From this, it is conceivable that the airframe was subjected to a force more than 200 tons starboard to port, at which time the aircraft scooped deep the U-ditch with the right wing tip.

It is conceivable that the remaining vertical fin and horizontal tail were separated and dispersed of which strength had deteriorated due to the progress of destruction since the airframe had been subjected to very severe impacts in the course of events at the U-ditch.

The analysis by DFDR data was possible up to the point (1856:27.25 hours) the aircraft would have proceeded about 40-50 meters from the U-ditch toward the crash site. The attitude of the aircraft recorded last was pitch angle - 42.2° roll angle 131.5° heading 277.1° , and airspeed 263.7 knots, probably with deep nose-down and almost upside side down. The track(bearing)at this time is estimated as 304°.

Flight Simulation Test on Accident Aircraft
(Reference Material — Addendum 7)

1. Purpose

For the purpose of clarifying what would have been like, to the flight crew (hereinafter referred to as the "crew" in this para.), the flight of the accident aircraft of which stability and control have deteriorated extremely due to damage at the aft airframe, simulation tests were conducted with the objectives of determining the following:

a. Did the aircraft have the possibility to survive the accident?
   i.   in case the crew was ignorant of adequate control procedures to cope with this particular emergency condition, or
   ii. in case the crew was well trained with the optimum descent procedures

b. what control systems at least are required to remain normal, in order that the possible survivability is assured to the accident aircraft?

c. How could the pilot detect malfunctions of various control systems on the accident aircraft ?

In this accident the flight would have been conducted under severe conditions such as decompression and lack of oxygen associated therewith, and psychological pressure in an unexpected emergency situation, but such conditions cannot be simulated in the flight simulation test.

2. Test Equipment

The simulation was carried out on a training simulator for the aircraft of the same type as the accident aircraft owned by All Nippon Airways Co., Ltd. with some modification necessary for the test purpose. With regard to the objective (c) above, a flight experiment was conducted, using an in-flight-simulator of National Aerospace Laboratory (Variable Stability and Response Airplane, VSRA) to obtain the necessary motion cue.

3. Test Plan

a. Failure Configuration

Config. of Failure	①	②	③	④	④'	⑤
Auto Throttle	off					
Auto Pilot	off					
Yaw Damper	on	off				
Vert.Stab & Rudder	normal			lost		
Horiz.Stab.& Elev.	normal			inoper.	normal	inoper.
Aileron & Spoiler	normal					inoper.
Flap	normal hyd. source			alternate		
Landing Gear	normal hyd. source			alternate		

Failure configuration ② through ⑤ were assumed as specified in the above table. The basic configuration ① was set forth as a reference base for comparison with the other failure configurations, and is a normal configuration except that both autothrottle and autopilot were brought to "off". Config. ② in the same as Config. ① except for "yaw damper off".

It is estimated that the aircraft was brought into configuration ⑤ within 1 to 1.5 minutes after the abnormal situation occurred.

Failure configuration ③, ④ and ④' are set up for investigating relationship between the mode of failure and possible survivability of the accident. It is not intended to simulate with these configurations any situations where the aircraft was actually involved, except that the aircraft is considered to have been in configuration ④ for 1 to 1.5 minutes after the abnormal situation occurred.

Assuming that the functions of subject pilots are those of a pilot who is trained to the standard level, the focus of the test was placed on a piloting problem to let down the aircraft of with deteriorated stability and control on a runway or on the sea (without specifying the touchdown point) with as much safety as possible. No consideration was given at all to such factors as crew-coordination, pilots' concern to the passenger cabin, communications with the ground, and abrupt decompression and effects to the crew due to lack of oxygen resulting there from.

b. Test Sequence

Four crews A through D were organized for this test, each consisting of an experienced captain of the instructor class, a copilot and a flight engineer. Each crew underwent one round test (4 hours) a day for two days, a total of two rounds. Prior to starting the simulation test, each group was given the caution that the simulator had been modified to simulate some failure conditions for the purpose of investigation of this accident, and that the personal experience on the tests be not communicated to each other.

After termination of the tests on crew A through D, test data were fully reviewed from the viewpoint of stability and control and an optimum operating procedure was set up. Using the optimum descent procedures, crew E (the captain of crew E was selected from among crew A through D) carried out one round of the test on failure configuration 5 only. In other words, the test case (ii) i.e. *"the case where the crew was well trained with the optimum descent procedures"* was conducted exclusively by crew E. In the all testings, a light turbulence was input, and a cross wind (from 060°) 10 knots was added in the approach and landing to Runway 33R of Haneda.

4.   Test Results and Review

a.   Detection of Abnormality

The time required for crews A through D to detect abnormality in each control system is as follows:

Each captain first of all detected malfunction of the pitch control system through inability to correct pitch attitude excursion, or unusual feeling on response to his input to the elevator or the horizontal stabilizer, and then detected abnormality of the roll control system through inability to suppress dutch roll motion and poor response to the aileron control. Detection of malfunction of the directional control system came firstly in the form of noticing inoperation of the yaw damper because of apparent dutch roll oscillation, and it took a considerable time to recognize the abnormality in response itself to the pedal input. In average, the time required for the detection on the second day became shorter to some extent than that on the first day.

Since in the simulator test each crew had been cognizant of a summary of this accident and the information was given in advance stating that some abnormal situation should arise in this particular test run, the abnormalities were detected within 30 seconds for the pitch control system, within 1.5 minutes for the roll control system, and within 4 minutes at latest for the yaw control system, respectively, judging only from the response to each control system input.

In the flight experiment by the VSRA, the detection of the abnormality was earlier in most cases than in the simulator test. However, when disturbance simulating an input such as the gust or asymmetrical thrust was added without notice, there was found a trend to obstruct significantly the early detection.

b. *Survivability with Failure Configuration* ⑤

The test was suspended of an altitude of 30 feet of the radio altimeter in order to avoid possible adverse effect upon the simulator on the occasion of simulating hard water landing.

All captains of crews A through D gave up to land to the runway and decided to make an emergency water landing. They encountered severe dutch roll and phugoid motions in the same manner as the accident aircraft. In most cases, all of the captains judged that it was impossible to accomplish any of assignments, such as regulating attitude, changing heading, setting descent rate or making safe water landing, even if they made their best efforts.

However, from the simulation by the captain of crew E who had been advised beforehand the optimum descent procedure, a comparatively stable touchdown condition was obtained where the air speed is less than 200 knots, the rate of descent less than 500 feet per minute, the pitch angle near 0 ° , and the roll angel is less than 2° - 3° , with the gear down at an altitude of 30 feet by radio altimeter.

According to the test results of the simulation, on the assumption that the failure configurations was the same as for the accident aircraft, and the crew had never experienced such an emergency situation as the accident aircraft,

1. landing to a runway was tried by every test crew but never succeeded, and

2. even if the touchdown area was not specified, the airspeed required at water landing was unable to decrease below 200 knots, and furthermore, taking a wide variation in touchdown parameters such as descent rate, attitude into consideration, the possibility to survive is hardly expected.

c. *Possible Survivability with other Failure Configurations*

Failure Configuration ③

All trials were made on landing at Haneda Runway 33. Although it is natural that strength of cross wind and effect of gust component must be taken into account, but conclusion was that the landing on the Haneda runway was possible even if a portion of the vertical fin and the rudder were lost, provided control functions of the aileron system and the elevator system remained normal.

Failure Configuration ④

In all cases except for one example in which landing on Haneda Runway 33R was tried, landing on the runway was given up, and a water landing was selected. Water landings were possible with an airspeed slightly over 200 knots, if functions of the aileron and spoiler system had remained normal. However, the variation in pitch angle at touchdown is of considerable amount.

Failure Configuration ④'

In failure configuration ④' where only the elevator system remains effective, the captains gave up landing on the runway, and instead tried a water landing. The simulation test indicated that water landings were possible with an airspeed under 200 knots, a rate of descent under 300 feet per minute, and a pitch angle over 3°

Voice Analysis of CYR Record

(1) Stress estimated from CVR Record

Many studies have been reported on the correlation between stress and the voice fundamental frequency of pilots and other crew members. An analysis was conducted to estimate stress of the crew of the accident aircraft from their voice record based on a method developped by Aeromedical Laboratory of Air Self-Defense Force (* Note).

The voice fundamental frequency is the frequency per second of vibration of the vocal cords, and it is said there is a difference of about one octave between man and woman. In this analysis, 150 Hz for man and 240 Hz for woman, which are said to to be voice fundamental frequencies in normal conversations of the Japanese, were taken as standard frequencies.

Table-8 is a grade table by which to evaluate a stress, in case it was caused, into grades (1) to (9) with reference to increase of the voice fundamental frequency over the standard frequencies.

Although a great number of the crew's voices are recorded in CVR and ATC communication record, the analysis was carried out on 67 cases of voice communication in the following six flight segments set up in the light of change in flight situation of the accident aircraft, and others:

A. departure
B. immediately before the abnormal situation occurred
C. immediately after the abnormal situation occurred
D. about 15 minutes after the abnormal situation occurred (altitude about 22,000 feet)
E. about 25 minutes after the abnormal situation occurred (altitude about 9,000 feet)
F. immediately before crash

146

Results of the analysis are shown on Table-9.

(*) Note   Kuroda.l., 0.Fujiwara, N.Okamura, andN.Utsuki. Method for determining pilot stress through analysis of voice communication. Aviation Space and Environmental Medicine. 1976

a.   Stress until the Sound like "bang" occurred after Take-off (see Table-9)

Stress of the captain, as estimated from voice in ATC communication record during a climb from take-off at Haneda till 1818:38 hours, varies within grade (1) to (3) of the 9 grade system. Such degrees of stress are considered normal in a take-off to climb step, and there would be less possibility that at this time the captain was cognizant of occurrence of some abnormality.

The CVR record of the accident aircraft starts with a intercom. call from a cabin attendant to the cockpit at 1824:12 *"Someone want to do. May I permit it?"*. The stress estimated from this female voice is grade 3 as shown in Table-9, and judging from her collected way of talk, there would be less possibility that at this time the cabin attendant was cognizant of some abnormality.

Stresses of (5) to (7) of the 9 grade system were estimated from voices of the flight engineer and the copilot answering to the ordinary request of the cabin attendant. These figures indicate high stress considered somewhat abnormal under the normal flight condition. Therefore, it is conceivable that the flight crew had perceived at this time some trend of such an abnormality as to raise their stress.

b.   Stress after the Sound like "bang" occurred

The stress, as estimated from voices of the captain, copilot and flight engineer immediately after the sound like "bang" occurred, varied within grade (6) to (8), and thereafter gradually increased its extent repeating some variation up to grade (9) immediately before the crash. Such change in stress would be considered natural in view of the fact that the accident aircraft fell into, so to speak, the most unfavorable emergency condition.

(2) Hypoxic Hypoxia as reviewed from CVR Record

According to CVR record, the altitude alert of the passenger cabin rung for about one second from 1824:37 immediately after the sound like "bang" was heard, and after an interruption of 26 seconds resumed to ring until 1847:28 at which time the altitude became less than 10,000 feet. It is, however, estimated that the flight crew did not wear the oxygen mask, judging from the fact that voices of the crew were recorded on CVR through the microphone for picking up sounds within the cockpit (hereinafter referred to as "area mike"), which should have been impossible if they had perceived the depressurization within the airframe by the alert sound and had put on the mask.

An investigation was made on any possible symptom of hypoxic hypoxia to the flight crew who are estimated from CVR record to have flown for about 18 minutes without wearing oxygen mask under no pressurization at altitudes more than 20,000 feet. The results were as follows:

As seen in Table-9, there are many entries of the remark *"unclear"* in column *"maximum of voice fundamental frequency"* of Section D of the table. The entry means that in this portion high harmonics of the voice fundamental frequency are unclear, which is said to be symptomatic of hypoxic hypoxia. The unclear harmonics may have been caused by hypoxic hypoxia they suffered from. The following are a list-up of portions regarded as hypoxia-related in CVR voice record. (see Attachment-6).

a. The volume of conversation between the captain and the copilot from the latter half of 18 hours 29 minutes through 36 minutes was remarkably little, and the conversation among the flight crew was also extremely little from 18 hours 40 minutes to the first half of 43 minutes. (It is noted that after about 1845 when the flight altitude became less than 20,000 feet the conversation within the cockpit started to increases, and their answer was made to calls from the ground)

b. Although it was suggested by the flight engineer twice about 1833:50 to wear the oxygen mask, the captain disregarded it, just replying "yes" in either case.

c. They did not respond to call made by Japan Air Tokyo 4 times during 1833 to 1843. In this connection, about one minute was necessary for the crew to decide to which of Tokyo and Osaka they were to answer.

d. For about one minute after about 1835 the tone of voice of the captain had been extremely raised.

Table-8. Stress (Grade) Conversion Table

Stress	Voice Fundamental Frequency (Hz)			
(Grade)	Male		Female	
(1)	—	150	—	240
(2)	151	— 164	241	— 262
(3)	165	— 182	263	— 290
(4)	183	— 201	291	— 322
(5)	202	— 228	323	— 365
(6)	229	— 261	366	— 418
(7)	262	— 308	419	— 492
(8)	309	— 374	493	— 598
(9)	375	—	599	—

Grade (1)-(3) represent degrees of stress caused generally under normal conditions.

(4)-(6) represent degrees of stress caused generally under conditions somewhat abnormal but not yet reaching an emergency.

(7)-(9) represent degrees of stress caused generally under an emergency. From past examples, it has been accepted that cool-headed disposition or judgement would become difficult to do under stress(9).

149

Table-9 Stress Analysis Table (Reference Material – Addendum 6)

Time Zone	No.	Time	Utter-er	Content of Utterance	Maximum Voice Fundamental Frequency and Stress Grade
A	1	17:53:17	CAP	Ah TOKYO clearance JAPAN AIR 123	136Hz(1)
	2	:59:38	CAP	Clearance delivery JAPAN AIR 123 – –	154 (2)
	3	18:03:43	CAP	Roger JAPAN AIR 123, 15 left	165 (3)
	4	:07:43	CAP	Alfa 4 A runway to charlie 7 – – –	150 (1)
	5	:09:45	CAP	Into position and hold 15 – – – – –	150 (1)
	6	:12:24	CAP	Roger JAPAN AIR 123	138 (1)
B	7	:16:35	CAP	Roger own navigation direct ah– – –	162 (2)
	8	:16:55	CAP	TOKYO CONTOROL JAPAN AIR 123 passing – –	168 (3)
	9	:18:38	CAP	Present position direct SEAPERCH– –	170 (3)
	10	:24:12	STW	Someone want to do. May I permit it.	267 (3)
	11	:〃:15	COP	Be careful.	250 (6)
	12	:〃:16	F/E	Ok, be careful please.	290 (7)
	13	:〃:17	COP	Quick.	220 (5)
	14	:〃:18	STW	Yes, thank you. ⎤ simultaneously	300 (4)
	15	:〃:18	F/E	Be careful please. ⎦ recorded	210 (5)

C	16	:24:35		"Bang"		
	17	:″:39	CAP	Something exploded?	250	(6)
	18	:″:42	CAP	Squawk 77	290	(7)
	19	:″:43	COP	Gear door	260	(6)
	20	:″:43	CAP	Check gear, gear.	240	(6)
	21	:″:44	F/E	What	300	(7)
	22	:″:44	CAP	Check gear, gear.	270	(7)
	23	:″:46	CAP	Engine?	270	(7)
	24	:″:47	COP	Squawk 77	260	(6)
	25	:″:48	F/E	All engine ···	320	(8)
	26	:″:51	COP	Look at this.	275	(6)
D	27	:38:29	CAP	Use both hand, both hand.	unclear	
	28	:″:30	COP	Yes.	″	
	29	:″:32	F/E	How about gear down? Gear down.	340	(8)
	30	:″:34	COP	Shall we gear down?	unclear	
	31	:″:45	CAP	Doesn't work. Gear does't go down.	″	
	32	:″:54	CAP	Lower the nose.	″	
	33	:″:55	COP	Yes.	″	
	34	:39:13	F/E	Shall I lower it slowly by alternate?	″	
	35	:″:18	CAP	Yes, wait a moment.	″	
	36	:40:00	CAP	Ah, lower the nose.	350	(8)
	37	:″:01	COP	Yes.	240	(6)
	38	:″:22	F/E	I have lowered the gear.	300	(7)
	39	:″:23	COP	Yes.	240	(6)
	40	:″:41	CAP	Lower the nose.	280	(7)
	41	:″:42	COP	Yes.	210	(5)
	42	:41:00	CAP	Lower the nose.	332	(8)
	43	:″:01	CAP	Never mind that.	320	(8)
	44	:43:23	CAP	Lower the nose.	unclear	
	45	:44:22	CAP	Is the wheel pushed all the way?	″	
	46	:″:23	COP	All the way, it's all the way.	″	
E	47	18:47:53	CAP	We'll hit a mountain!	330	(8)
	48	:″:″	COP	Yes.	250	(6)
	49	:47:59	CAP	Max. power.	300	(7)
	50	:48:00	COP	Max. power.	280	(7)
	51	:″:02	F/E	Keep trying.	354	(8)
	52	:″:10	CAP	Left turn, this time.	362	(8)
	53	:″:19	CAP	Ah, right right, lower the nose.	368	(8)
	54	:″:23	CAP	Lower the nose.	400	(9)
	55	:″:25	COP	Wheel is pushed all the way.	325	(8)
	56	:″:51	COP	Shall I increase power?	280	(7)
F	57	:55:44	CAP	Hey, halt the flap.	326	(8)
	58	:″:47	CAP	Flap, stop crowding together.	400	(9)
	59	:″:56	CAP	Power.	370	(8)
	60	:″:58	CAP	Flap.	410	(9)
	61	:″:59	F/E	It is up.	318	(8)
	62	:56:04	CAP	Raise the nose.	360	(8)
	63	:″:07	CAP	Raise the nose.	400	(9)
	64	:″:10	CAP	Power.	380	(9)

3. *Alert Sound in CVR Record (refer to Addendum 8)*
   In CVR were recorded the sounds of the cabin altitude alert, take-off alert, altitude alert, fire alert, stall alert and ground proximity alert.

   The times at which the alert sounds were made and classifications of the sounds are shown in Attachment-6 "CVR Record".

4. *Pre-recorded Announcement (hereinafter referred to as "PRA") (refer to Addendum 8)*

   According to CVR record in Attachment--6, at 1824:37 the cabin altitude alert rung indicating that the pressure altitude of the cabin (including the cockpit, the same applies hereinafter) became about 10,000 feet.

   Soon thereafter, pressure altitude of the cabin increased to about 14,000 feet, at which time oxygen masks would have dropped, and at the same time PRA would have started. However, since PRA at this time was not recorded in CVR, an investigation was made on whether PRA was started without delay.

   From the investigation, it is estimated that the automatic playback equipment was activated at about 1824:38, and 6-7 seconds thereafter started the announcement. The reason an initial portion of the announcement was not recorded is that the recording priority was given to a live announcement being in progress by a purser.

5. *Alert Sound for Release of Autopilot*

   DFDR record indicates that the autopilot switched from command mode to off position immediately after the sound like "bang" occurred, but it was unable to confirm the alert sound to be emitted at release of autopilot in CVR voice record. Although an investigation was made on the alert system for the reason, but it could not be determined.

It is noted that a voice of the captain *"don't bank so much. It's manual"* was recorded at 1826:03, which may be construed as the autopilot having been released already at this time.

Acoustic Analysis of CVR Record (Reference Material Addendum 9)

Investigation on Acoustic Propagation Characteristics of Airframe as well as Playback Characteristics of CVR

In CVR were recorded voices, sounds, radio communications, etc within the cockpit for about 1824:12 hours to about 1856:28. The CVR has 4 record tracks: one for voices from the mike; the other three for voices of radio communication or intercom. selected by the captain, the copilot, and the flight engineer, respectively.

Since the acoustic signal analysis requires to measure in advance the acoustic propagation characteristics in the airframe as well as the recording and playback characteristics of CVR, the following investigations were conducted:

1. *Investigation on Acoustic Propagation Characteristics of the Airframe*

   An area mike is installed near the center of the cockpit ceiling. As propagation paths through which a sound originating in an aft fuselage area distant from the cockpit reaches the area mike, the paths through the solid airframe as well as paths through outside of the airframe must be taken into consideration, in addition to the paths through inside of the airframe.

   The acoustic propagation characteristics are considered considerably complicated, because, propagation of sound is affected by pressures in and out of the airframe, air temperature, and airspeed. Therefore, the investigation was made during flight as well as on the ground for items which require measurement in flight, using the same type of aircraft as the accident aircraft.

As a result of the investigation, it was found that the propagation of sound from aft fuselage is mainly through inside of the airframe, because the sound insulation effect of the airframe is great and the attenuation of propagation of sound through solid is also considerably great.

2. Investigation on Recording and Playback Characteristics of CVR

An investigation was made on the recording and playback characteristics of the CVR, using CVR of the same type as used in the accident aircraft.

From the investigation were obtained the frequency characteristics and extent of leakage of frequency components of the power supply which are necessary for analysis of played-back signals of CVR.

Acoustic Analysis of CVR Record

1. *A Sound like "bang"*

A sound like "bang" was heard from 1824:35.5--35.6 to 1824:37.0. The frequency analysis made on playback signals of CVR around this period indicated that the sound was composed of several groups. The playbacked wave of CVR and its sound spectrogram are shown in Figure-16

Since a wide distribution of frequencies involving extremely low frequencies is seen in the initial portion of this sound, the sound is estimated to have been an impulsive sound accompanied by a voluminous air flow. It is further estimated that the series of sound subsequent thereto was a complicated combination of sounds from several different sources and sounds generated by resonance or reflection from parts of the airframe.

Although the Initial sound began at 1824:35.5--35.6 as far as it heard auditorily, a further precise frequency analysis showed there was a symptom that this sound had already started in a frequency band earlier at about 1824:35.3 — 35.4.

Then, the frequency variation of leak components of the CVR power supply frequency (400 Hz) was investigated, for the purpose of analyzing the vibration to which the CVR proper was subjected. The investigation revealed that a large frequency variation attributable to a vibration had been recorded in the neighborhood of 1824:35.2 which Is 0.1--0.2 second earlier than the time the above symptom was recognized.

The reason such a large frequency variation was recorded is estimated to be that an airframe vibration of such a large extent as not to be absorbed by the damping device as well as violent air flows occurred in the neighborhood of' the place the CYR proper is installed.

If it is presumed that the remarkable frequency variation recorded In CVR and the initial sound were of the same source, from above results, It is estimated that the source should be located several tens of meter distant from the area mike when the time difference between them and the velocity of sound are taken into account, and this is not inconsistent to the distance of about 54 meters between CVR proper and the installed location of the area mike.

2. *Whistling Sound*

From about 1829:30 up to the crash are intermittently recorded whistling sounds which continued for 1 to 6 seconds and might be considered as wind sough. The major frequencies of these sounds are 1,350 Hz, 1.140 Ilz, or 680 Hz. The duration and strength of each sound are irregularly variable as a whole, but In some portion they are repeated with a certain cycle.

Check by a comparison of sounds recorded on CVR with flight conditions recorded on DFDR indicated that all these sounds were caused when lateral acceleration was minus (leftward acceleration) and that their occurrence was related also to pitch toward nose-down as well as comparatively high engine output.

From the above, the possibility would be high that the whistling sounds are wind soughs caused when air currents which strike the cockpit and its vicinity meet a certain condition, but the origin of the sounds and others could not be clarified

3. *Noises*

On the track for the area mike of C|VR were recorded noises attributable to engines, or frictions of air currents around the airframe throughout from the beginning to the end of record. These noises vary from time to time depending on the flight conditions (altitude, velocity. attitude, engine power, etc) of the accident aircraft.

156

Figure-16. CYR Playback Wave and its Sound Spectrogram CYR Playback Wave O and its Sound Spectrogram.

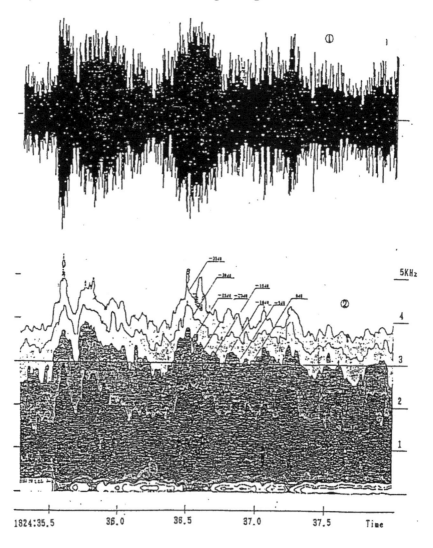

Tests and Investigation on Variation in Behavior related toHypoxic Hypoxia (Reference Material — Addendum 10)

When the air at a very high altitude is breathed, hypoxic hypoxia is suffered from because the organism cannot take in a sufficient amount of oxygen due to low oxygen tension in inspired air in the air.

Under hypoxic hypoxia, supply of oxygen to the brain tissue decreases, capability to perform intelligent work and activity deteriorate, although different for each individual, with the risk of causing unconsciousness, depending on the altitude and duration of exposure.

It is conceivable that the flight crew of the accident aircraft suffered from hypoxic hypoxia because they might have been in flight for about 18 minutes without pressurization nor oxygen mask at an altitude more than 20,000 feet. In order to study whether they suffered from hypoxic hypoxia or not, the following tests and investigation were conducted, using a low pressure chamber of Aeromedical Laboratory of Air Self-Defense Force.

Test Method

1.   Test 1

To investigate deterioration of ability to perform intelligent work due to hypoxic hypoxia at an altitude of 24,000 feet, two subjects (male A, age 26; male B, age 28) were taken on board the low pressure chamber with oxygen masks put on, and the chamber was depressurized to a pressure equivalent to an altitude of about 24,000 feet in about 8 minutes.

The subjects took off the mask at the altitude and worked on an assignment for about 12 minutes.

The assigned work consisted of a subtraction of two-digit figures involving borrow and reading aloud of a short sentence issued alternatively at a 15 second interval. Each assignment was periodically displayed on a CRT by a a desktop computer. The answer to the subtraction was input by the subject through keyboard and pushing return key.

When the input answer was correct, the display to that effect was made. When it was erroneous, the display to that effect was made together with a beep, and re-try was requested. However, if 15 seconds has elapsed from the onset of an assignment, it was erased from the screen regardless of the subject's response, and a next assigned sentence to be read aloud came into display on CRT.

The sentence to be read aloud was displayed in "hiragana" and "katakane (Japanese systems of alphabets), and the subjects were requested to read it aloud.

2. Test 2

One subject (male, age 48) and three fellow riders (male, age 31; male, age 29 also acting as attendant doctor); female, age 24), were taken on board the low pressure chamber with oxygen masks put on except for the subject. In order to simulate roughly the pressure change in the cockpit and passenger cabin of the accident aircraft, depressurization was carried out in such a manner that the Pressure was first decreased to that equivalent to the passenger cabin altitude of 650 feet, then decreased to the pressure equivalent to the altitude of 24,000 feet in almost five seconds, and thereafter was maintained at the pressure equivalent to an altitude of more than 20,000 feet for about 20 minutes.

The subject worked on the same assigned task as in Test 1 above without the oxygen mask from start to end of the Lest. The two fellow riders other than the attendant doctor were engaged in a selective response task with oxygen masks for the first 10 minutes. and without masks for the succeeding 10 minutes, in the period of 20 minutes after the abrupt depressurization. The remaining fellow rider, acting as attendant doctor, was subjected to the selective response task with the mask on for the 20 minutes period.

In the selective response task, a fellow rider was requested to push the switch at hand when the lamp of pre-assigned color for him was lit among three lamps of red, blue, and yellow which was irregularly lit. If the switch was pushed correctly, the lit lamp went off.

The reaction time from the lamp was turned on till the switch was brought on was measured by a desktop computer and recorded.

Through Test 1 to Test 2, a medical doctor was on board the chamber, to ensure the safety of personnel on board and chamber operators.

3. *Supplementary Test*

In the tests above, the amount of oxygen exhausted from persons with the oxygen mask put on may not be negligible, because a number of persons were on board the low pressure chamber of a relatively small scale.

The tension of oxygen In the chamber was, therefore, measured in a flight conducted under the same conditions as in Test 2 with the same number of persons on board as in Test 2.

Although the partial pressure of oxygen at a pressure altitude of 24,000 feet used in Test 2 should be theoretically about 62 mm llg, the oxygen tension measured 64.4 mm 11g. which was equivalent to the partial pressure of oxygen at an altitude of about 23,000 feet.

4. *Test Environment*

In the tests above, subjects and fellow riders got on board the low pressure chamber with the previous knowledge that they would be placed under a hypoxic condition while working there. Temperature, humidity and noise were not regulated in the low pressure chamber.

Test Results

1. *Test 1*

A to the task of subtraction, correctness and response time of the answer were analyzed; while as for the task of reading aloud of a short sentence, measurement was made of the average voice fundamental frequency, utterance time (time from start to end in reading the sentence), and the maximum value of sound level.

Results of the assignment tests were reviewed in comparison with those obtained in advance using the same method on the ground (under the standard atmosphere).

In the test on the ground under the standard atmosphere, a reduction in response time to the subtraction was seen. False answers were found in a comparatively early stage, but they disappeared in the latter half of the period, due probably to familiarization to the assigned task.

As to the voice index, the reading-aloud in the first time showed a somewhat high average voice fundamental frequency, but remained constant thereafter.

In the test at the 24,000 feet altitude, the subject "A" showed, after the elapse of about 5 minutes. significant increase in response time, frequent false answers, decrease in the average voice fundamental frequency, increase in utterance time, and decline in maximum sound level. Furthermore, the abnormality was also found that he tried to read aloud the same sentence several times.

With regard to harmonics of the fundamental voice frequency, the sound level started to decrease 5 minutes after the onset of the task mainly in frequencies over 500 Hz, and the trend was maintained until the end of the work.

On the other hand, the subject "B" made frequent false answer after the elapse of about 4 minutes. and showed a slight increase in response time after the elapse of about 9 minutes. No distinct change in the average voice fundamental frequency was observed. The utterance time seemed to indicate a somewhat increasing trend. There was no change in maximum sound level. Abnormality in utterance behavior was observed only one time at the elapse of 11 minutes.

As to harmonics components, a decrease in the acoustic pressure of the order of 2 KHz--3 KHz was seen at the elapse of 3-4 minutes after the task was started, but it recovered thereafter.

There was found no individual difference between the two subjects in the assigned work on the ground, but the difference was observed under the hypoxic conditions at the altitude of 24.000 feet.

2. *Test 2*

(i).No subjects and fellow riders showed symptoms of decompression sickness when the rapid decompression was induced to the pressure of equivalent to the altitude of 24.000 feet.

(ii) Response time of the subject was inclined to increase

with the elapse of time in the same manner as Test 1. The average voice fundamental frequency showed a significant increase after the elapse of about 8 minutes. followed by rather reduction in utterance time.

After the elapse of about 3 minutes, many utterances in which high harmonic components decreased were seen, but no constant trend was observed.

The selective response times of the fellow riders were as follows:

(a).No change was found of the base line of the response time of the fellow rider (doctor, male age 29) with the oxygen mask put on always during the test.

(b).As to another fellow rider (male, age 31) who took the oxygen mask off in the test, response time increased obviously after about 4 minutes since he took off the mask, but it resumed to a normal level after he wore the mask again.

(c). As to the other fellow rider (female age 24), there was some period after she removed the mask, in which response time increased, but it resumed a former level thereafter.

3. *Comparing results Test 1 and 2*

When results of Test 1 and Test 2 are compared with those of the test on the ground, it could be concluded that in either case of Test 1 and Test 2, hypoxic hypoxia manifested on the behavior level of one subject in the Test 1 and the subject in Test 2, although there was some difference in the time it occurred.

The change In the behavior level of a subject of Test 1 was not significant as compared with other subjects of Test 1 and 2.

As to reactions of the fellow riders of Test 2, obvious change in the behavior level, deemed to be due to hypoxic hypoxia, was observed on a male rider. but none of evident changes was on a female rider.

As to the average voice fundamental frequency, none of the changes in common to the subjects was observed. The reason is estimated to be that emotional change due to hypoxic hypoxia was different with each subject.

To summarize, in either Test 1 and Test 2, both the subjects and fellow riders showed decrease in their capability to deal with intelligent work 4 to 8 minutes after they were brought under hypoxic conditions, but no loss of consciousness was observed.

In the light of the fact that there were persons who did not show obvious decrease in capability to perform the intelligent work, it is estimated that with regard to manifestation of the symptom of hypoxic hypoxia, there is a considerable individual difference in the latency before manifestation and the extent they suffer.

OTHERS

Analysis of Photographic Images of Vertical Pin (Reference Material - Addendum II)

An analysis was made on the status of damage to the vertical fin of the accident aircraft, based on a photograph taken from the ground of the aircraft flying over Okutama City, Nishitama County, Tokyo at about 1850 hours. August 12. Data used were the photograph of the aircraft (see Attached Photo--124), a model of Boeing,and the damge chart of the vertical fin (see Attached Figure-27 and - 28).

For the image processing was used the TIAS (Tokai Image Analysis System)2000, developed by Tokai Research and Information Center, Tokai University.

The residual area rate of the vertical fin was 41.7% in the orthographic projection, and, when supplemented with data of damage chart, was 41.6196, both results being almost the same. In actuality a possibility is conceivable that part of a hidden portion added up to this, in which case still the increase would remain within 2--3 % for the reason that the upper part of the lower rudder is lacking in the damage chart and that the possibility of the lower rudder remaining in such a shape is almost unconceivable from the structural view point.

From the above, it is estimated that more than at least 55% of the vertical fin of the aircraft had been lost at the time the photograph was taken.

Estimation of Crash Time by Seismic Shock Wave

A seismic shock wave regarded as related to the crash of the aircraft was recorded on a short-period seismometer installed in Shin-etsu Earthquake Observatory of Seismological Laboratory of Tokyo University, located at the point (elevation 1,430 meters, 35° 56' 25" N, 138° 40' 28" E) about 7 km (horizontal direct distance) SSE of the crash site of the aircraft. (see Figure-17)

Figure-17. Recorded Seismic Shock Wave

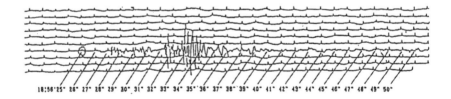

18:56'25" 26" 27" 28" 29" 30" 31" 32" 33" 34" 35" 36" 37" 38" 39" 40" 41" 42" 43" 44" 45" 46" 47" 48" 49" 50"

The time recorded on the seismometer is accurate because it is automatically collated with the Japan Standard Time.

Since the propagation speed of seismic shock waves varies with the geological features of their course, its accurate value is not determined, but generally accepted as about 3.0--3.5 km in shallow layers. According to this, the time required for the seismic shock wave to reach the observation point from the crash point would be estimated as 2.0--2.3 seconds.

On the seismometer of the observatory the vibration was recorded from about 1856:27.2 hours. At the outset a bit-by-bit wave continued for about 3 seconds, and thereafter about 56' 31.2" a wave of high frequency was acknowledged, and from about 1.5" thereafter, which is about 56' 32.7" a big wave was recorded, followed by vibrations which were repeated for more than 10 seconds but gradually subsided.

A big wave recorded at approximately 1856:32.7 is regarded as caused by the crash on the ground of the accident aircraft, and the time the aircraft crashed is estimated to have been 2.0--2.3 seconds earlier, i.e., approximately 1856:30.5. The time above is almost consistent with the crash time estimated from DFDR record.

The bit-by-bit wave and the high frequency wave recorded before approximately 1856:32.7 are estimated to be ones originated at the time engines and part of the airframe dropped down, and the waves thereafter are estimated to be reflexed or scattered waves of the shock caused at the time of crash of the accident aircraft.

Detectability of Cracks by Visual Inspection
(Reference Material — Addendum 12)

At rivet hole edges of L18 splice of the aft pressure bulkhead of the accident aircraft, a number of cracks were initiated and propagated. A study was made on the possibility of detecting these fatigue cracks by visual inspection at the time of inspection and maintenance.

The crack length detectable by the visual inspection depends on crack length, crack shape, location where the crack exists, accessibility to the crack for inspection, existence of coating/stains, experience and ability of the inspector, and other factors.

As to the relationship between the crack length and the crack detectability, documents relating to the study on the damage tolerant design, records prepared by aircraft operators on the basis of their inspection and maintenance results and others, are so far available, but their data of detectable crack length are considerably different from each other due to involvement of the various factors mentioned above. However, it would be possible to say that cracks of 1--2 inches are detectable in the average case where there would be less related factors to impede the detection.

(1) Fatigue cracks in L18 splice of the aft pressure bulkhead of the accident aircraft

Based on the fatigue crack data of L18 splice an estimation was made on the length of fatigue cracks at the time No.11C maintenance was conducted on. December 1984 before this accident. The estimation indicated that large ones would have been of the order of average of both side 10 mm long (visible crack length: 8 mm *1) at this time.

> *1 The visible crack length is the length of the crack to be visible when the aft pressure bulkhead is inspected from the back, subtracting hidden portion by the manufactured rivet head and the strap from estimated crack length.

(2) Probability of detecting fatigue cracks in L18 splice of the aft pressure bulkhead of the accident aircraft

A study was conducted on the probability of detecting the fatigue cracks which were propagating at a number of rivet hole edges of L18 splice by a visual inspection at the time of No.11C maintenance corresponding to G2 level where locations to be inspected are not directed (refer to Attachment 2).

(a) Major assumptions used in the study were as follows:

The probability of detecting a crack by a visual inspection

corresponding to G2 level is a function of crack length and is represented by a three-parameter Weibull distribution function.

0.08 inch (2 mm) and 0.12 inch (3 mm) are used for the minimum detectable crack length, and the probability of detecting a crack of one inch (25.4 mm) long is 50 96.

(b). The study revealed the following results:

The probability of detecting a fatigue crack of the order of 10 mm in visible crack length was calculated to be roughly 10 96.

The probability of detecting at least one out of a number of fatigue cracks propagating at L18 splice was calculated to be of the order of 14--60 96.

In case the possibility of detecting fatigue cracks is discussed using this result, consideration should be given to the assumptions mentioned in (a) and to the influences of other factors relating to the detection of cracks.

ANALYSIS

CHAPTER 5

ANALYSIS

General Matters

1. The flight crew were properly qualified and had passed the established medical examination.

2. The accident aircraft flew a detour south of the usual route, for the reason that the echo from cumulonimbus in the vicinity of Kowa has not vanished completely on the meteorological radar screen and almost no echo was recognized on the sea to the south.

    It is not conceivable that meteorological conditions in areas related to the flight course of the aircraft from the occurrence of the abnormal situation up to the crash directly affected the flight of the aircraft, judging from meteorological data and statements of eye witnesses, although the areas were scattered with low, middle and high layer clouds.

3. Functions and operational conditions of aids to navigation related to the flight of the aircraft are acknowledged to have been normal.

4. The aircraft had a valid, airworthiness certificate, and had undergone the established maintenances and inspections.

Repair of damage following the accident at Osaka International Airport in 1978 as well as operations and maintenances/inspections of the aircraft thereafter.

A study was made on the relationship to this accident of the repairs of damage by the accident at Osaka International Airport in June 1978 (refer to Attachment 1) and the situation of operations, maintenance and occurrence of discrepancies thereafter (refer to Attachment 2).

1. Repairs of damage by the accident at Osaka International Airport

a. It is acknowledged to have been proper that the repair work related to structures of the aircraft was accomplished by the Boeing Company for JAL by the contract, because the aircraft was manufactured by the company and that the company had much experience in the repairs with satisfactory achievements in the past

b. The repair plan of the aircraft agreed on between JAL and the Boeing Company is considered to have been virtually proper.

c. When the lower half of the aft pressure bulkhead deformed by the accident was removed and was being replaced by the new one in accordance with the repair plan,. it was found by an inspector of the Boeing Company that there were locations where the edge margin around the rivet holes on the splice surface (L18 splice) between webs of the upper half and the lower half of the bulkhead was less than value specified in the structural repair manual.

The reduced edge margin is estimated to have been caused by, one or a combination of the following:

a. disorder in alignment of rivet hole rows existent on the upper half of the aft pressure bulkhead

b. deformation of the upper and the lower half of the bulkhead which is of a thin plate structure,

c. deformation of an aft portion of the fuselage due to shock at the time of the accident,

d. deformation caused by removal of part of an aft portion of the fuselage for the repair work, and

e. short dimensions of the cut end of the upper edge of the web of the lower half of the bulkhead.

To prevent the airframe from deforming, the aft fuselage was supported by additional jacks; nevertheless, some deformation might have remained in the aft fuselage. In this connection, it might have been possible to use special tools in order to prevent the fuselage from deforming and to facilitate the installation of the lower half of the aft pressure bulkhead, but no such work was carried out.

From this, it is considered that concern against deformation of the aft fuselage, etc. was somewhat insufficient in the repair work of the aft pressure bulkhead.

d. As a corrective measure of the shortage of edge margin mentioned above, an instruction to make a splice joint by inserting a splice plate was issued by an engineer of the repair team of the Boeing Company. The instruction is considered to have been virtually pertinent.

e. During the repair, work was carried out in which one splice plate narrower than described in rework instructions, and one filler were applied, instead of one splice plate. No written record, however, was found to the effect that such work was done.

It is estimated that during this rework, part of L18 splice which should have been spliced by two-row rivets became spliced by one-row rivets, with the result that the strength of this part decreased to about 70% of the original strength. From this, it is estimated that these portions was brought under a condition susceptible of occurrence of fatigue cracks.

This work was inspected by an inspector of the Boeing Company, but he could not find that it was different from the instruction.

f. On the webs of the aft pressure bulkhead repaired in such a way were found six oil cans. It is conceivable that they were caused by the effect of deformation which might have been remaining on the aft fuselage as stated in (c) above, or by the difficulty in splicing with rivets the bulkhead having not enough rigidity in a workshop.

g. Inspection on the repairs accomplished by the Boeing Company was made by their inspector in accordance with the regulations of the Boeing Company as approved by FAA. JAL made confirmation by their inspectors and other personnel on whether each work item had been accomplished as stipulated in the contract, and at the same time conducted an acceptance inspection including attendance at inspection on items established in advance.

Civil Aviation Bureau, on application from JAL of inspection on repair or modification in accordance with the Civil Aviation Law, made inspection on the repair plan, the process of repair and the condition after completion of the work.

It is considered that such inspection methods were in conformance with what was accepted as the general inspection method on repair and modifications. This involves checks by the airworthiness engineers of CAB on the repair planthrough reviewing the drawings submitted from the applicant, checks on the repair process based on work records, as well as inspection on the condition after completion of the work such as general external inspection, functional tests on the ground and flight test (refer to 11 of Attachment 1).

h. It is conceivable that the confirmation by a visual inspection of the work results inconsistent with the afore-mentioned instruction was impossible after the repair work of the bulkhead had been completed, because the edge of the said splice portion was covered by fillet seal.

i. It is considered that the method of management for the work including the inspection of working process was in part insufficient in pertinence.

(2) Operation, Maintenance and Malfunctions after 1978

a. The accident aircraft underwent an incident at the time of landing at Chitose Airport August 1982, in which No.4 engine pod struck the runway. But, repaired were only the engine and the engine cowling, and none of these are considered as relevant to this accident.

b. In operations of the accident aircraft, after July 1978, a considerable number of discrepancies were reported. Out of these, the discrepancies related to the aft fuselage and the vertical fin were investigated. The investigation showed that they were not related to this accident except for malfunctions of lavatory doors as referred to in (c) below, because their occurrence is common to other aircraft of the same type.

c. During the period February-August 1985, 33 cases of malfunction of lavatory doors were reported, out of which 28 cases were with the lavatory located aft most of the passenger cabin, and 22 cases were on the Guam flight (Osaka—Guam, Guam—Osaka), Investigation made of the malfunctions on the Guam flight (refer to 1.6.2 of Attachment 2) revealed that they would be attributable to loading a large amount of supply materials in the coat room aft of the passenger cabin, which had been specific to the Guam flights.

However, the possibility could not be denied completely that deformations caused in aft portions of the airframe by the accident of June 1978 had been connected to malfunctions of the lavatory doors.

d. It is considered that the intensity of cabin pressurization affected the propagation speed of fatigue cracks found in L18 splice of the aft pressure bulkhead (refer 1.7 of Attachment 2).

e. The maintenance procedure which had been applied to the accident aircraft is as shown in Attachment 2 and it is the procedure JAL is applying ordinarily their fleet of Boeing 747SR-100.

f. Detailed maintenance of the airframe is mainly carried out by C maintenance (every about 3,000 hours). Maintenance work is conducted in accordance with each work card. With regard to the aft pressure bulkhead there are 10 work cards, mainly concerning inspection of corrosion on the lower part of the bulkhead and inspection on the Y chord etc. The juncture of webs such as L18 splice of the bulkhead was not designated as special inspection locations, and its inspection was not designated as specified inspection locations, and its inspection was made within the overall visual inspection (equivalent to G2 level) of the rear surface of the aft pressure bulkhead.

The reasons such maintenance procedures were adopted would be the judgement that a general visual inspection mainly for corrosion would be sufficient because enough margin of strength is provided at the web splice joint in the design of structural strength of Boeing 747, and there were no precedents in which defects such as dangerous cracks were found on this portion in the operations of other aircraft of the same type.

g. Up to the occurrence of this accident, C maintenance was conducted 7 times including C maintenance made together with the repairs of July 1978 (No.5C). None of the discrepancies matters found in these maintenance nor in A maintenance (everyabout 250 hours) subsequent thereto were recognized as relevant to this accident. Several cases are recorded of defects (such as leak of air) on L-5 and R-5 door (aftmost doors of the passenger cabin), but they could not be considered as relevant to this accident, because these were caused by deterioration of door seal, etc.

h. Tabacco nicotine found adherent between webs of L18 splice of the aft Pressure bulkhead was concentrated at rivets No.21--78. Blow-out of nicotine to the non-pressurized side was found at two places between the lower web and the splice plate in the neighborhood of No.41 and No.50.From these, it is conceivable that the repair work made to L18 splice contributed to the adhesion and blow-out of nicotine. However, the nicotine adhesion to the splice surfaces between webs could not have been discovered by the visual check on the surface. It was impossible to determine whether the blow-out of nicotine to the non-pressurized side already existed or not at the time of the previous C maintenance (No.11C).

i. A number of fatigue cracks were under progress on rivet hole edges of L18 splice of the aft pressure bulkhead of the accident aircraft as shown in Table-4 and Figure-7. It is estimated that some of these fatigue cracks had reached as much as 10 mm in length at the time of No.11 C maintenance in December 1984.Inspection on this portion at the time of C maintenance is a visual inspection equivalent to G2 level as referred to in (f) above. The probability to discover a fatigue crack by such a visual inspection is dependent upon length, shape, and location of the fatigue crack, and technique and experience of the person in charge of the inspection, and other conditions.

Result of a study made on the probability of discovery indicated that no definite decision could be made on whether it could have been possible or not to' discover the fatigue cracks in L--18 splice by the inspection method applied in the C maintenance.

j.　The inspection method of the aft pressure bulkhead in the time of C maintenance might have been an appropriate method, because it was unconceivable at the time of the said C maintenance was conducted that a number of fatigue cracks came into existence in this portion, provided the bulkhead was manufactured normally and repair work was done properly.

However, it is considered that the inspection was not complete in part, in view of the fact that such fatigue cracks as in this case which caused the aft pressure bulkhead to rupture were overlooked, although they were results of the original repair work.

Analysis of Damage to Airframe in Initial Stage after Occurrence of the Abnormal Situation

A study was made on the process of destruction of the constructural parts and major materials whose damage would have progressed in the early stage of flight after the abnormal situation occurred, based on status of wreckage of the airframe, the test and research for analysis of destruction, and analytical calculations, and also reference being made to analytical results of DFDR record and CYR record.

Rupture of Aft Pressure Bulkhead

The rupture of the aft pressure bulkhead located at B.2360 is estimated to have progressed as follows:

1. *Propagation of fatigue crack at L18 splice*

   A number of fatigue cracks regarded as caused by the repetitive load of fuselage inner pressure were found on rivet hole edges of L18 splice. From an observation by the electron microscope, the number of repetition of the inner pressure load required for the propagation of these fatigue cracks was estimated as the order of 10,000 times, which almost coincide with the number of flights 12,319 after the repair of the aft pressure bulkhead in 1978.From this, it is estimated that fatigue cracks at L18 splice began to generate immediately after the repair of the bulkhead, and propagated on hole edges of a half of the rivets with repetition of flight, reaching as much as about 280 mm in total length immediately before the accident.

2. *Rupture of L18 Splice*

   It is estimated that at the time the accident aircraft climbed to about 24,000 feet, the differential pressure between the pressurized passenger cabin and outside atmosphere became 8.66 psi, and L18 splice having the afore-mentioned fatigue cracks was brought into a total fracture, initiated by fracture of bay 2 as has been described earlier.

3. *Progress of Subsequent Rupture*

   It would be difficult to make a detailed analysis of the

progress of ruptures after the fracture of L18 splice, because the ruptures were impulsive and followed by considerable deformations. However, the following would be a destruction process considered highly probable in which status of ruptures, structural dimensions, etc are taken into account:

The fracture which progressed rightward (as viewed from aft of the aft pressure bulkhead) of L18 splice detoured clockwise along the collector ring located in the center of bulkhead and advanced upward along R6 and L2 stiffener. On the other hand, the fracture which progressed leftward of L18 splice advanced upward along Y chord on the outboard side.

Subsequent to these ruptures, the portion of the bulkhead involving part 1 and part 2 (see Attached Figure-32) was blown up and rearward by pressure, and collided with the fuselage frame located at BS2412. The bent as shown by dotted lines in Attached Figure-32 is considered to have been caused at this time.

The area of the opening caused in such a way is estimated to have been of the order of 2-3 square meters.

The part 2A portion is considered to have been separated from part 2 which was blown up, being restrained by cables running through therein. The part 1 portion would also have been subjected to a restraint due to several cables passing through it.

Rupture of Empennage including APU Firewall

The pressurized air of the passenger cabin would have discharged from part 1 and part 2 of the aft pressure bulkhead accompanied by a shock wave. However, it would be unconceivable that the APU firewall was damaged by the shock wave, in the light of the fact that the cross section of the fuselage aft of the aft pressure bulkhead is by far larger than the area of the opening in the aft pressure bulkhead and that there are many obstacles within the empennage such as the pass-through portion of the horizontal stabilizer and fuselage frames. It is therefore estimated that the rupture of structures due to discharge air was caused by a static increase of pressure.

1. Pressure Relief Door

    This door was discovered in the vicinity of the crash site. A breakup investigation and tests were conducted on whether this door was opened in the early stage of this accident, but it was impossible to clarify it.

    However, the possibility is considered high that the door opened because of the design to open at a pressure differential of 1.0--1.5 psi, and the condition of damage of the door. Even if the door opened, the pressure inside the empennage would have increased abruptly because the opening area was not large enough to discharge the air which flowed in from the opening of the aft pressure bulkhead out of the aircraft.

2. *Rupture of Structures in the Vicinity of the APU Firewall*

    It is estimated that the APU firewall buckled first at lateral beams except 2 and 4 due to-abrupt rise of pressure in the empennage and then the entire firewall was separated together with structures including the APU proper located aft thereof by a differential pressure of the order of 3--4 psi.

3. *Other Ruptures*

    Almost simultaneously with the ruptures above, the position sensor of the horizontal stabilizer installed aft of the pass-through portion of the horizontal fin would have ruptured.

Rupture of the Vertical Fin

It is estimated that the inner pressure of the fore portion of the empennage and the inside of the vertical fin leading thereto increased, although the Pressure relief door opened, the APU firewall Was broken, and the air was discharged outside of the aircraft; and that when the pressure reached about 4 psi, rupture of the vertical fin started at the fixture between the aft torque box's stringer and the rib chord.

Subsequent to the above, rupture of main structural materials of the aft torque box, collapse of the rear spar, and separation of the rudder would have been caused. However, it was impossible to determine in detail the destruction process

The striped black marks found on a part of the vertical fin-skin could be considered aluminum alloy powder which was caused by friction in flight of the skin with rivets loosened when the vertical fin fractured by the inner pressure and developed into a striped form up to the time the aircraft crashed, being mingled with a part of the hydraulic liquid gushed out due to fracture of the hydraulic line.

Rupture of Hydraulic Line for Control System

As to the hydraulic line for the control system, it was impossible to locate parts due to severe damage caused by crash.

However, since the hydraulic line to the rudder PCP is laid down from the fuselage near BS2540, along the rear surface of the vertical fin's aft torque box, to the upper portion of the vertical stabilizer, it is conceivable that subsequent to the collapse of the aft torque box and the separation of the upper and the lower rudder after the abnormal situation occurred, the four systems of hydraulic lines to the rudder PCP's were fractured at the bent between the fuselage near BS2540 and the stabilizer, or near the lower half portion of the vertical stabilizer's aft torque box, with the result that the hydraulic liquid was lost.

From the result of investigation it is also estimated that a portion of the lost hydraulic liquid gushed out to the inside of the fuselage aft of the aft pressure bulkhead.

Rupture of the Aft Passenger Cabin

It is acknowledged that the aft most lavatory of the passenger cabin and part of cabin interior materials in the vicinity were damaged by air current which flowed out of the broken aft pressure bulkhead, and dispersed aft of the pressurized cabin, judging from the fact that a considerable amount of thermoinsuling materials installed on the inside of the pressurized cabin was found aft of the pressurized cabin and inside of the pressurized fin, and that apart of panels of the aft most lavatory in the cabin and fragments of cabin interior materials were discovered from the ground where the operating gymbal of the horizontal fin fell down.

The possibility is conceivable that other parts were also damaged, but it was impossible to clarify it.

Time Required for the Airframe to rupture in the Initial Stage after the Occurrence of the Abnormal Situation

The time required from rupture of aft pressure bulkhead to rupture of the empennage including the APU firewall and rupture of most of the vertical fin is estimated to have been as short as several seconds.

Analysis of the Situation at the Time of Crash and Fracture of the Airframe thereafter

Status of the Accident Aircraft at the Time of Crash

1. Status of the Accident Aircraft immediately before Crash.

The last data readable from the DFDR record of the aircraft are as follows:
- Airspeed   (CAS) : 263.7 knots
- Heading   (HIM) : 277.1
- Pitch angle (PCH)   : —42.2°
- Roll angle   (RLL) : 131.5°

The track at this time is estimated 304° . The aircraft was devoid of 4 engines, the vertical fin, the horizontal fin and aft empennage aft of BS2484, and the right wing tip structure including the skin and part of the leading edge and the trailing edge flap would have been separated from the airframe.

2. Status of the Accident Aircraft at the Time of Crash

The time the aircraft crashed is estimated to be approximately 1856:30 hours based on the time of contact with the U-ditch, etc. From the last data recorded on DFDR and the status of scattered wreckage at the crash site, the status of the aircraft at the time of crash is estimated as follows:

Heading (IIDO   : 220±40°
Pitch angle (PCB)   :-70±20°
Roll angle (RLL)   : 60± 30°
Flight course : 310±10°

From the data, the possibility is considered high that the aircraft, taking an almost upside-down attitude with the nose down and heading to the south-west and with the tail turned up and toward the north-east, crashed with the righthand wing turned down and the lefthand wing up.

Progress of Destruction of the Airframe by Crash

(1) Status at the crash point (see Attached Figure-14 and -15)

The possibility would be high that the collision and rupture of the aircraft at the crash point progressed as follows:

a. First, the right wing tip smashed into a point slightly below the provisional heliport on the slope. And almost at the same time, the upper part of the leading end of the fuselage smashed into a point about west of the smash point of the right wing tip.

b. Thereafter, the rupture due to the smash progressed from the right wing tip and the upper part of the leading end of the fuselage.

c. The rupture of the right wing advanced up to its base portion, during which structural parts of the wing were broken into small fragments and most of them were dispersed on a north slope on the side of the 3rd branch of Sugeno Dale.

d. In the same manner, the rupture of the fore fuselage advanced up to B1480-1694 (mid fuselage). Since the fuselage smashed into the ground from its upper portion, the upper structural parts were compressed and broken into small fragments, while the lower structural parts broken into comparatively large fragments, and both were dispersed near and along the ridge line. The cockpit and internal structures of the passenger cabin fore of the vicinity of BS1480— 1693 were also destroyed during this period.

e. The fuel which would have dispersed from the fuel tank due to shock at the time of crash catched fire, and burnt down the wreckage scattered in the vicinity of the provisional heliport as well as trees.

f. While the rupture of the fuselage reached BS1480--1694, the left wing was separated from the fuselage and came to a stop on a slope about 30 meters SI of the provisional heliport.

g. It is difficult to estimate the strength of the shock caused by the aforementioned smash of the right wing and the fore fuselage into a spot near the Provisional heliport, but figures analogized from the referential materials (K) are: the strength of shock reaches as much as hundreds of G in the vicinity of the smashed portion, decreasing with distance from the portion to Lens of G at the end of the aft fuselage. The duration of the shock is considered as 0.05-0.2 second.

(* 1) ①NASA Tech. Paper 1210, Light Airplane Crash Tests at Three-Path Angle. 1978

②AIAA Paper 79--0780. NASA/FAA General Aviation Crash Dynamics Program. 1979

(2) Status of the Aft Fuselage The possibility is high that the rupture of the aft fuselage progressed as follows:

a. The aft fuselage aft of BS1480—1693 would have been subjected to hundreds of G at the forward end and tens of G at the end at the time of smash into the crash point. By the shock a total destruction would have been caused of structures in the vicinity of the forward end, and at the same time rupture would have been caused of the majority of the flooring, seating, galley, etc within the fuselage. The more severe would have been the rupture of the flooring, seating and gallery, the nearer they to the forward end, and the damage was comparatively slight at the aft end portion.

Most of the broken flooring, seating, gallery, etc would have been dispersed aft within the fuselage by the shock.

(*2) The flooring, seating, gallery, etc and their fixture are designed to bear an ultimate load of the order of 10 G's.

b. The aft fuselage aft of BS1480--1694 did not directly contact with the hillside. It dropped on the north slope with the right hand aft portion of the fuselage ahead after the fore fuselage was destroyed by hitting the hillside, and collided with the ground and trees and proceeded about 240 meters, separating part of structure, flooring, seating. galley. etc, but keeping itself in a body to the last. The left hand aft fuselage aft of the vicinity of BS2000 is considered to have come to a stop on the 3rd branch of Sugeno Dale.

c. The shock the aft fuselage was subjected to when it fell down on a north slope would have been less than 10 G's.

An Analysis on Fail-safe Capability of the Accident Aircraft

All principal structural components of Boeing 747 aircraft except for the nose landing gear are designed on a fail-safe concept. The fail-safe concept was based on the provisions for airworthiness of the FAA at the time the aircraft was developed.

In the case of the accident aircraft, during the repairs in 1978 (refer to 3.2.2 and Attachment 1). the repair different from the rework disposition was carried out in which a portion of L18 splice of the aft pressure bulkhead was connected by one-row riveting. A study on the fail-safe capability of the accident aircraft under such condition was made asfollows.

A Study on Fail-safe Capability of the Aft Pressure Bulkhead

(1) The aft pressure bulkhead is designed on the concept of the so-called one-bay fail-safe. This is a design based on the premise that even if a crack is initiated and propagated, it can be detected and is repaired while its propagation remains within one bay (one area surrounded by stiffeners and tear straps). In the concept of one-bay fail-safe, there is no presumption of cases where cracks are initiated and propagated simultaneously in several bays.

In the design of the bulkhead of the aircraft, the residual strength is verified analytically with the condition that the bulkhead with one-bay crack shown in Figure-18 can withstand the expected maximum cabin pressure differential (the maximum operating pressure of the over pressure relief valve: 9.4 psi) considered as the fail-safe load. Furthermore, as to detection of crack, the principle is adopted that if the crack is propagated to a certain length, it can be detected by a visual inspection, or from indication such as leak of pressurized air from the crack and abnormality of the web.

(2) In the case of the accident aircraft, a number of cracks were initiated and were propagated mainly on bay 2 and bay 3 of L18 joint connected with one-row riveting during operations of the aircraft after the repairs of damage by the accident at Osaka International Airport in 1978. Such situation was not presumed in the one-bay fail-safe design concept, as mentioned previously.

It is conceivable that the premise of the one-bay fail-safe, that is, a crack was detected and repaired while it was staying within one bay, collapsed for the reasons that it was difficult to detect the fatigue cracks of the accident aircraft by visual inspection or by air leakage because the cracks were small and propagated along rivet holes at web overlaps.

Figure-18. Failsafe Analysis of the All Pressure Bulkhead.

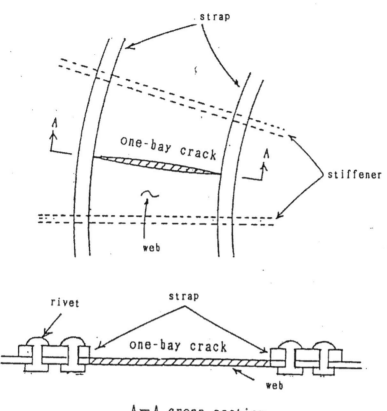

A—A cross section

A Study on Fail-safe Capability of Structures of the Fuselage Tail and the Vertical Fin

1. In case Part. of the aft pressure bulkhead is fractured and the press air flows out, the internal pressure of the fore part of the fuselage tail (BS2360 - 2658) and the vertical fin rises, and these portions may be fractured. To prevent this possibility, such design to ensure fail safe is adopted that the pressure relief door automatically opens to release the air so that the pressure difference at these portions does not rise to more than 1.0--1.5 Psi. The area of the relief door's opening

(approximately 0.49 square meters) satisfies the target that the differential pressure does not rise to more than 1.5psi even if one hay area of the aft pressure bulkhead (the maximum area about 0.14square meters) should be failed and the pressurized air flows out from the area.

2. However, in the case of the accident aircraft it is estimated that the aft bulkhead was fractured as much as 2--3 square meters at the time the abnormal situation occurred in flight, and therefore, it is conceivable that even if the afore-mentioned relief door might open, the internal pressure of the fore part of the fuselage tail and the vertical fin exceeded the pressure presumed in the fail-safe design, resulting in the rupture of the APU firewall and the vertical fin.

Study on Redundancy of Control System

1. Such redundancy is incorporated in the design of the control system that control surfaces are divided, and 10 hydraulic pumps are provided, and 4 systems of piping are laid for the hydraulic system for the control.

2. In this accident, functions of all the four hydraulic systems were lost and the control systems became all inoperative soon after the abnormal situation occurred in flight.

   The reason would be that the piping of all the four hydraulic systems was fractured and hydraulic fluid leaked out due to rupture and separation of more than half of the vertical fin including rudders, but it is considered that such ruptures or separation were situations out of scope of considerations in the fail-safe design.

Fail-safe Capability of Boeing 747 aircraft

As afore-mentioned, the fail-safe design was in accordance with FAR25.571, a provision concerning fatigue in FAR 25 on airworthiness of transport aircraft of the FAA(*), which was in effect at that time.

Provisions on airworthiness set forth the minimum requirements for capability which aircraft should provide, but they would not guarantee the airworthiness under conditions possible only in a very rare case, nor caused by inappropriate repair work. In order to maintain and improve the fail-safe capability of the aircraft structures, it is required to conduct appropriate modification, inspection and maintenance, incorporating improvement based on service and experience.

In the case of the accident aircraft, several fractures successively occurred, reducing the airworthiness seriously. That is, fracture of the aft pressure bulkhead, fracture of the aft part of the fuselage tail and the vertical fin, fracture of all the four hydraulic lines systems for the control system, and loss of all primary control functions occurred successively.

It is conceivable that the reason ruptures propagated as a chain reaction in this accident is that prior concern had not reached as far as to the prevention of such situation from occurring, although the fail-safe design of the aircraft in the development stage, and inspection and maintenance methods which incorporated service experience were proper to meet the provisions concerned.

(*1) The provision on the fatigue was revised thereafter in 1978 for incorporation of the damage tolerant design technology, but the basis of the concept on fail-safe capability as referred to herein remains unchanged.

Analysis of Flight Capability of the Accident Aircraft after Occurrence of the Abnormal Situation

An analysis was made of the flight capability of the aircraft after the occurrence of the abnormal situation, based on the DFDR records, CVR records and results of the test and research and analysis described in earlier paras.

The Status of the Control System after the Occurrence of the Abnormal Situation

Itis estimated that most of control functions were lost. The status of the control system of the aircraft was as follow:

1. It is estimated that with the rupture of the vertical fin, the rudder was separated, and control functions of the rudder were lost immediately after the abnormal situation occurred.

2. Since the hydraulic fluid was run out of hydraulic pressure lines for the control system which was cut off due to rupture of the vertical fin, it is estimated that the control function of the rudder was lost immediately after, and the control function of the aileron and the spoiler were lost 1.0--1.5 minutes after, the occurrence of the abnormal situation.

3. It is estimated that at the same time as above, the operational function of the flap and the landing gear, and the trimming function of the horizontal stabilizer driven by the hydraulic pressure were lost. As to the flap, the electromotive operation was possible by an alternative system, while as to the gear, both gear-up and -down become impossible due to loss of the system hydraulic pressure but gear-down only was possible electrically.

Stability and Control of the Accident Aircraft after the Occurrence of the Abnormal Situation

It is estimated that the stability and control worsened to an extreme degree as follows:

1. *Longitudinal stability and control*

    It is estimated that ruptures caused to the aircraft did not bring about change in the longitudinal stability of the aircraft for a reason that the horizontal stabilizer had been fixed in a virtually balanced position. However, because both of the attitude control capability of the elevator and the attitude trim capability of the horizontal stabilizer were lost, the aircraft is estimated to have been in such a situation that operations necessary to perform missions such as maintenance of attitude, set-up of climb rate/descent rate, and pull-up were impossible by ordinary methods. Due to the inability to control the attitude, it became difficult to control phugoid motion excited by variation in engine thrust and external disturbance of air turbulence, etc, and sometimes the phugoid motion reached as much as about 15° in pitch angle, about 0.3G in vertical acceleration, about 100 knots in speed variation, and about 4,000 feet in altitude change.

2. *Lateral-directional stability and control*

It is estimated that by the ruptures caused to the aircraft, the lateral stability of the aircraft slightly increased in the spiral mode, but in the dutch roll mode became more unstable.

Since the direction and attitude control capabilities of the rudder, aileron, spoiler were lost, the dutch roll motion became uncontrollable, with result that the dutch roll motion was excited during most of the flight except for a descent made at about 1845 hours, and the flight continued under the condition of a constant vibration of a large amplitude (a limit cycle condition), and the motion was sometimes as severe as about 40° in roll angel and about 0.5G in lateral acceleration.

It is considered virtually impossible to make a directional control of the aircraft by setting differential thrust between the right and the left engines, because it would be accompanied by undesirable trends such as excitement of dutch roll motion.

3. It is considered that the aircraft was not able to continue a stable flight and any flight as intended by the captain was difficult and that a safe landing or landing on the water by the captain having no such experience was next to impossible, due to the afore-mentioned deterioration in stability and controllability both longitudinal and lateral.

Reaction of the Flight Crew in the Abnormal Situation

About 12 minutes after takeoff, an abnormal situation occurred to the aircraft, being followed by a sequence of abnormal phenomena adverse to the operation of the aircraft, and such flight conditions continued for about 30 minutes thereafter. The following analysis was conducted on reactions of the flight crew during this period, based on DFDR record, CVR record and results of the relevant tests and research.

Recognition of Status of Damage to Structures of the Aircraft

It is estimated that the flight crew become cognizant of the occurrence of the abnormal situation without delay, judging from the fact that following the voice of the captain that something exploded, a voice of squawk 77 indicative of occurrence of an emergency as well as utterances relating to their search for its cause were recorded in CVR.

It is, however, estimated that they were not able to know at this time where and how the abnormality occurred.

Judging from the fact that on CVR was recorded at about 1831 hours conversation between the flight engineer and a cabin attendant concerning an irregular status of structures in the vicinity of the cargo room in the aft passenger cabin, it is estimated that the flight crew become cognizant at this time of the damage to part of structures of the aft cabin, but was and continued to be ignorant of the occurrence of critical defects such as separation of part of the vertical fin as well as the rudder.

Reaction to Depressurization and Emergency Descent

1. The flight crew would have become cognizant of the depressurization in the aircraft soon after the occurrence of the abnormal situation by the cabin altitude alert and the indication of the cabin altimeter. However, since no call-out for an emergency of depressurization was recorded in CVR immediately after the occurrence of the abnormal situation, it is conceivable that none of measures to be taken in case of depressurization was performed.

2. As to the emergency descent of the aircraft, according to CVR record, the aircraft requested at 1825:21 a descent to 22,000 feet to Tokyo Control and after 1826:36 were repeatedly recorded utterances indicative of the intention to make an emergency descent and transmissions that the aircraft was in an emergency descent. However, according to DFDR record, it was after 1840 that the aircraft actually started descent.

   The flight crew continued flight for about 18 minutes without pressurization at an altitude over 20,000 feet, not making an emergency descent to the safety altitude 13,000 feet and only requesting the descent to 22,000 feet, although they were aware of the depressurized condition within the aircraft. In this regard, it was unable to clarify the reason therefore.

   It is, however, conceivable that the emergency descent action was not taken because the flight crew devoted themselves to the quest of causes of the occurrence of the abnormal situation in an early stage after it occurred, and afterwards to the control of the aircraft to stabilize the flight attitude.

3. As to wear by the flight crew of the oxygen mask, talks

between them were recorded several times in CVR after 1826:30. It is estimated that none of these 3 crewmembers wore the oxygen mask during this period, because their voices which should not have been recorded if they had worn the mask were recorded on the area mike channel.

It was impossible to determine the reason the flight crew who had had education and training on the wear of the mask did not wear it, being confronted with such depressurization.

However, it is conceivable that the flight crew gave priority to the control operation for continuation of flight although minding the need to wear the mask, because a depressurization to such an extent as might have been in the aircraft would not have caused instantly aversion nor pains to man, although there are individual variations as can be seen from the test results.

It is conceivable also that the judgement and operation ability of the -flight crew deteriorated to some extent by hypoxic hypoxia, because they neither made an emergency descent nor did wear the oxygen mask.

4. It is estimated from CVR record and witness of survivors that the actions to be taken by cabin attendants under the depressurized condition for wear by passengers of the oxygen mask were initiated without delay after the occurrence of abnormal situation.

With regard to the use of the portable oxygen bottle (hereinafter referred to as P02 bottle) in the vicinity of R--5 (141) where there was a trouble in supply of oxygen, the P02 used at that time might have been a bottle distributed to the vicinity of R-5 temporarily in accordance of the instruction of the flight engineer to a cabin attendant at 1830:38 hours, judging from the statement of a survivor that the cabin attendant at that time were making confirmation of passengers wearing of the oxygen mask, taking oxygen from the oxygen mask of an empty seat, not using the P02 bottle on whose usage they should have been educated and trained.

It is conceivable that the trouble of oxygen supply regarded as having occurred in the vicinity of R-5 was caused by damage to part of equipment of the system located in the ceiling due to shock at the time of occurrence of the abnormal situation, but it was impossible to clarify the cause.

(*1) The aircraft is equipped with 24 P02 bottles for cabin attendants or for first-aid purpose in an emergency, being installed in the vicinity of each cabin attendant seat.

Stress to Flight Crew in the Cockpit

The stress to the flight crew after the occurrence of the abnormal situation was considerably high in grades of stress. It increased gradually, repeating some variation, and showed the highest figure immediately before the crash. This is considered natural in the light of the fact that the aircraft ran into, so to speak, the most unfavorable emergency condition.

Meanwhile, in conversations between a cabin attendant and the flight crew starting 1824:12 which was before the occurrence of the abnormal situation, whose contents were not clear, the utterance "be careful" was repeatedly used by the flight engineer and the copilot, and from these voices high stress figures considered rather irregular as those in a normal takeoff and climb were measured.

From the above, it is conceivable that the flight crew might have noticed some abnormality at this time, and that the cause for the high stress of the flight crew might have been only within the knowledge of the crew in the cockpit, from the fact that the voice of the cabin attendant on the other hand remained in a normal strength of stress.

However, it was impossible to clarify the cause for the high stress of the flight crew prior to the occurrence of the abnormal situation, because no records relevant to the high stress to the flight crew were found in DFDR record, and portions prior to the said conversations did not remain on CVR.

Reactions to Abnormality in the Control System

1. Judging from the fact that an instruction of the captain to correct for an excessive bank angle was recorded in CVR at 1825:53, it is estimated that the flight crew had no cognizance at all at this time of the abnormality in the control system due to drop in hydraulic pressure.

2. Judging from the fact that utterances on the drop of hydraulic pressure were repeatedly recorded in CVR from about 1826 which was about one and one half minutes after the occurrence of the abnormal situation, it is estimated that the flight crew was cognizant of the abnormality in the control system due to drop in hydraulic pressure, and thereafter at 1828:35 the captain reported for the first time to Tokyo Control that the aircraft was uncontrollable.

3. In CVR were recorded conversations on gear-down operation after 1838, and subsequently conversations on flap-up operation were also recorded in the DFDR. It is estimated that these operations were made electromotively, the alternate means in case the hydraulic system becomes inoperative.

4. Although the hydraulic pressure dropped to zero and the rudder, the aileron, spoiler, and elevator became inoperative, the crew continued control operation as evidenced by CVR and DFDR records. It is estimated that the steering conducted corresponding to attitude variation without giving up control even under the condition the control system was inoperative was for the purpose of restraining the dutch roll and phugoid movements.

5. From 1842:53 to 1844:43 the voice of the flight crew "heavy" was recorded four times in CVR. At that time the movement of the control cable would have been in restraint due to destruction of the bulkhead , etc. The utterance would be related to the considerable steering force which would have been required because of the restraint, but it was impossible to clarify the reason.

Other actions

1. The flight crew selected Tokyo International Airport as return airport after the occurrence of the abnormal situation, as recorded in CVR, but not Osaka International Airport which was the destination airport nor Nagoya Airport which was comparatively near the flight course. The selection is considered to have been proper in the light of the scale, runway length, other facilities and environment of the airport.

2. Judging from the voice of the captain recorded in CVR that *"You'll have to control pitch with power."*, it is estimated that the flight crew attempted pitch control by control of engine thrusts after the occurrence of the abnormal situation. However, it is estimated that the aircraft was not brought into a stable condition by this operation, for the reason that by this operation phugoid motion would have been controlled, but the operation should have also excited the dutch roll arising from differential thrust between the right and the left engines. Furthermore, it is possible to change the bearing by setting a thrust difference between the right and the left engines, but no evidence was found that such was attempted

3. The copilot was performing the captain's duties seated in the left-hand seat, while the captain performing the copilot duties seated in the right-hand seat. After the occurrence of the abnormal situation, as seen from CVR record, it is

acknowledged that the coordinated operation was made of the copilot and the flight engineer by the instruction of the captain; the captain issued all instructions concerning the operation and was engaged in communications in the early stage; and the copilot was concentrated mainly on the control operation. It is also acknowledged that the flight engineer took charge of communications on behalf of the captain, and cooperated in gear-down and flap operations by the alternate system, and power control.

4. It is estimated that severe dutch roll motion and phugoid motion, which are impossible to aircraft in normal conditions, occurred and deteriorated the judgement, together with the depressurization, and control ability of the flight crew.

5. Flight crews have been educated and trained so that in case of an emergency reactions to the emergency to be taken after the stability of flight attitude has been secured by the control operation.

    However, such a situation where part of the vertical fin is separated and the hydraulic pressure of all four systems decrease to zero and most of control functions are lost would be out of the scope of the education and training or knowledge the crew have received or acquired as to reactions to emergency or abnormality. For this reason, it is conceivable that the crew was not able to control the aircraft.

6. After the occurrence of the abnormal situation, the flight crew not only fell into an abnormal situation which was out of the scope of the education and training they received or the knowledge and experience they had, but also was unable to comprehend fully the substance of the abnormal situation, and furthermore they were brought into a severe environment of being subjected to severe motion and

depressurization of the aircraft. For these reasons, it is conceivable that they were concentrated on the operation to stabilize the flight while not able to make a pertinent judgement on how to cope with the situation.

Analysis of Support from Ground to the Flight of the Accident Aircraft

The accident aircraft, after the occurrence of the abnormal situation, continued flight receiving support by communication from the ground. An analysis was made of the support including the related matters (refer to Attachment 3,4 and 6)

Support by ATC/Communications Services

1. The aircraft, some time after 1817 hours while climbing after take-off, established communication with Tokyo Control. Communication with Tokyo Control was made by the captain seated at the copilot seat. Radio frequencies selected by the flight crew in flight were 123.7 MHz (Tokyo Control), 121.5 MHz (emergency frequency), and 131.9 MHz (company frequency, Flight Operation Dep., JAL Tokyo Branch Office).

2. In response to the report from the captain on the occurrence of the abnormal situation and the request to return to Haneda, Tokyo Control immediately acknowledged them and instructed the aircraft to make a right turn pursuant to the intention of the captain, and initiated radar vectoring. Then, immediately after the emergency was confirmed, Tokyo Control informed the Rescue Coordination Center of occurrence of the emergency, and at the time began to provide radar vectoring to other aircraft approaching the aircraft for the collision avoidance purpose.

3. At 1831, in response to the inquiry of Tokyo Control whether the aircraft could land at Nagoya, the accident aircraft replied that they request to return to Tokyo. Then Tokyo Control approved the aircraft to use Japanese in communication and the aircraft acknowledged it.

4. At 1840, in response to the inquiry of Tokyo Control whether the frequency could be changed to 134.0 MHz, there was no reply from the aircraft. Therefore, Tokyo Control requested other traffic to change their ATC communication frequency to 134.0 MHz. and not to transmit until further noticed. However, some of the traffic still remained in 123.7 MHz for communication.

5. Yokota Approach requested the aircraft to contact the Approach several times after 1845 using the emergency frequency (121.5 MHz), but there was no reply from the aircraft.

6. At 1853, in response to the request of Tokyo Control to change the frequency to 119.7 MHz (for exclusive use of Tokyo Approach), there was a reply from the aircraft that they had completed selection of the station, after which there was acknowledgement of the aircraft for each transmission from Tokyo Approach of position information and others.

7. After 1855, there were no responses from the aircraft to transmissions from Tokyo Control and Tokyo Approach.

Other Supports

1. The accident aircraft established communication at 1820 during climb after take-off with JAL on the company frequency (131.9 MHz).

2. In response to repeated calls from JAL after 1833. a reply was made by the aircraft that R--5 door was broken, together with the request to monitor all subsequent transmissions, which was acknowledged by JAL.

3. Against calls from JAL thereafter, there were made no responses.

Study on the Status of Supports

1. The action taken by Tokyo Control immediately after the occurrence of the abnormal situation to vector the accident aircraft proved fruitless, because the aircraft was brought into an uncontrollable condition. The instruction which was given to other essential traffic to evade the aircraft is regarded as pertinent.

2. It would have been from a consideration to help reduce the burden of the flight crew that Tokyo Control kept use of the frequency 123.7 MHz for communication with the accident aircraft. Meanwhile, since other aircraft were also using 123.7 MHz, there were cases where the aircraft received transmissions of other aircraft. However, it would not have caused such situation as to obstruct communication between Tokyo Control and the aircraft.

3. To avoid jamming, it is desirable to have the frequency between Tokyo Control and the aircraft separated from the frequency of other aircraft well in advance. The action for frequency separation was taken at 1840.

The aircraft, other than the accident aircraft, which were requested to change the frequency from 123.7 MHz to 134.0 MHz should have complied with the instruction without delay.

4. The reason the support to the aircraft remained within the scope as referred to in para.3.2.8.1 and 3.2.8.2 would be that the situation of the aircraft was unknown except that the aircraft was uncontrollable, and that no request of support except for ATC was made by the flight crew.

5. Supports to the accident aircraft, beside the above, such as provision of advice from personnel in charge of operation, engineering or maintenance, and assistance by dispatch of a follower aircraft are conceivable, but even if such support had been provided, no effects would have been expectable.

Analysis of Search and Rescue Activities for the Accident Aircraft

Collection of Flight Information of the Accident Aircraft

Rescue Coordination Center, upon receipt of the notification that the abnormal situation occurred to the aircraft, began to collect information immediately. It is regarded as actions pertinent to the state of affairs that the information collection was made in close coordination with Tokyo Control and JAL, in the light of the fact that the flight information of the aircraft was made known by ATC radar and communications.

The center was not able to grasp the substance of the abnormal situation caused to the aircraft, but it would be considered natural, as would be seen from contents of communications recorded in CYR.

Actions taken after the Target on Radar Scope disappeared

The actions which were taken by Tokyo Control and Rescue Coordination Center after the target on the radar scope disappeared as well as the actions taken by Police Agency, Defence Agency, etc upon receipt of this notification are considered as virtually pertinent.

Confirmation of the Crash Site and the Aircraft

Upon confirmation by a Defense Agency aircraft at 1921 of flames at a place supposed to be the crash site, the search was initiated to confirm the crash site and the aircraft. Early morning of August 13, the crash point and the aircraft were confirmed by aircraft of Defense Agency and Nagano Prefectural Police.

Considerable time was necessary for confirmation of the point, but it could not be helped in the light of the fact that the crash point was located in a mountainous area thickly covered with trees and furthermore that the search was conducted in the. night time.

Rescue Activities

The crash point is located about 12 kilometers SW of the hall of Ueno Village, where the Countermeasure Headquarters of the Accident was set up, and was accessible via Hontani Woodland Path along Kanna River upstream to the end of the road, and from there by climbing about 4 km, an elevation difference of about 600 meters. Since there was no climbing path in the vicinity of the crash site, and the mountainous area searched was dangerous because of the risk of falling rocks, the rescue activities were an extreme difficulty. It is acknowledged that efforts to the maximum extent were made by every organization who participated in the activities.

Analysis of Injuries to Passengers and Crew

A study was made on the status of injuries to passengers and crew caused by shock at the time of crash of the accident aircraft as well as by shock due to breakage of the airframe.

Injuries to Passengers and Crew in the fore Fuselage

It is estimated that the passengers and crew in the fore fuselage fore of the vicinity of BS1480--1694 were instantly killed by a strong shock as much as hundreds of G at the time of collision against the crash point as well as total destruction of the fore fuselage structures at that time (* 1).

*1. Man's anti-G capability depends on direction of G (shock acceleration), method of supporting him such as by a band, and duration of G load. Man's anti-G capability (the limit of G within which no fatal injuries are caused) studied by NTSB in reference to aircraft accidents is shown, as an example, as follows:

Source material: NTSB--AAS--81--2, Cabin Safety in Large Transport Aircraft, 1981

Duration of G	: 0.1 — 0,2 second
Rate of G	:50 G/second

(with belt)

Direction of G	Strength of G
Forward	20 — 25
Downward	15 — 20
Sideways	10 — 15
Upward	20

Passengers and Crew in the Aft Fuselage

Out of passengers and cabin attendants who were in the aft fuselage aft of the vicinity of BS1480-1694, those seated on forward seating are estimated to have been killed almost instantly due to a possible strong shock in excess of 100 G's at the time of collision against the crash point. The shock persons seated on aft seating were subjected to was also of the order of tens of G, and by this shock most of them are estimated to have undergone fatal injuries. Moreover, a considerable portion of flooring, seating, galley, etc in the aft fuselage were dispersed up to the aft end of the fuselage together with passengers and cabin attendants. Therefore, the possibility is conceivable that the injuries were deepened by the secondary disaster of collision with these substances in which severe bruises and oppressions were caused. Furthermore, it is conceivable that the degree of injuries was enlarged by the shock during drop along the slope on the side of the third branch of Sugeno Dale.

Four persons survived this accident

They were all seriously injured. All of them were seated at the aft portion of the aft fuselage and are estimated to have subjected to tens of G, but they were able to escape death miraculously. The conceivable reason would be that their seating attitude, status of belting, status of damage to the seat, surroundings of the body, and others at the time of collision chanced to help soften the impact and that they were less subjected to collision with dispersed internal substances of the fuselage such as flooring, seating and galleies.

The status of injuries

The status of injuries to the bodies and recovered places of the bodies were such as to back up virtually the estimations above.

CONCLUSION

CHAPTER 6

CONCLUSION

Summary of Analysis

General Matters

- The flight crew were properly qualified and had passed the established medical   examination.

- It is acknowledged that the then existent meteorological conditions were not directly relevant to the occurrence of the abnormal situation.

- Functions and operational conditions of aids to navigation and ATC unit are acknowledged to have been normal.

- The aircraft was certificated and maintained according to approved procedures.

Flight of the Accident Aircraft up to the Occurrence of the Abnormal Situation

- On August 12, 1985, the accident aircraft took off Tokyo International Airport 1812 hours as Flight 123, subsequent to preceding four scheduled flights on the day. There were neither reports of abnormality nor flight discrepancies regarded as relevant to this accident in the preceding four flights as well as in the inspection and maintenance conducted between them (including the pre-flight check as flight 123).

- At 1824:35 hours, about 12 minutes after take-off, an abnormal situation occurred so as to exert serious influence on continuation of the flight, up to which time the flight is considered to have been normal.

Repairs for Damage caused by the Accident at Osaka International Airport

- It is acknowledged to have been proper that the repair work related to structures of the aircraft was accomplished by the Boeing Company for JAL by the contract, because the aircraft was manufactured by the company, etc.

- The repair plan of the aircraft agreed on between JAL and the Boeing Company is considered to have been proper in general.

- When the lower half of the aft pressure bulkhead deformed by the accident was removed and was being replaced by the new one in accordance with the repair plan, it was found that there were locations where the edge margin around the rivet holes at the splice (L18 splice) of the upper and the lower webs of the aft pressure bulkhead was less than drawing requirements. This is considered to have been caused by somewhat insufficient concern against deformation of the aft fuselage in the repair work of the aft pressure bulkhead.

- For the above, the corrective measure to make a splice joint by inserting a splice plate between webs of the upper half and the lower half of the aft pressure bulkhead, which is considered as proper, was planned. But, during the repair, improper work was conducted in which different from the intended corrective measure, one splice plate narrower than drawing requirements, and one filler were applied instead of one splice plate.

- In inspections during and after the repair work, the afore-mentioned improper part of the work could not be found.

- It is considered that the method of management for the work including the inspection of working process was in part insufficient in pertinence.

- It is estimated that during this rework, part of L18 splice which should have been spliced by two-row rivets became spliced by one-row rivets, with the result that the strength of this part decreased to about 70% of the strength to be obtained by the original splice method. From this, it is estimated that these portions was brought under a condition susceptible of occurrence of fatigue cracks.

From the above, it is conceivable that the aft pressure bulkhead of the accident aircraft was lacking at this time in fail-safe capability.

Fail-safe Capability of Boeing 747 Aircraft

The fail-safe design of Boeing 747 is in accordance with standards on airworthiness of transport aircraft of the FAA, which was in effect at that time.

Provisions on airworthiness set forth minimum requirements for capability which aircraft should provide, but they would not guarantee the airworthiness under conditions caused in a very rare case, nor caused by improper repair work.

It is conceivable that the reason why ruptures propagated as a chain reaction in this accident is that prior concern had not reached as far as to the prevention of such situation from occurring, although the fail-safe design of the aircraft in the development stage, and inspection and maintenance methods which incorporated service experience were proper to meet the provisions concerned.

Operation and Maintenance of the Accident Aircraft after the Osaka Accident

- The flight hours and the number of flights (number of landings) of the aircraft after the repairs for the accident at Osaka International Airport in June, 1978 up to this accident were 16,196 hours and 12,319, respectively.

- During this period, in L18 splice of the aft pressure bulkhead, a number of fatigue cracks were caused and propagating mainly at one-row rivet connection portions.

- It is considered that there were neither abnormalities nor flight discrepancies deemed to be related to this accident in flights during this period.

- During this period C maintenance (a maintenance every 3,000 hours) was conducted 6 times, at which time visual inspection was made, but fatigue cracks which had been existent at the rivet connected portions of L18 splice were not found.

  The inspection method of the aft pressure bulkhead in the time of C maintenance might have been a proper method, because it was unconceivable at the time the said C maintenance was conducted that a number of fatigue cracks came into existence in this portion, provided the bulkhead was manufactured normally and repair work was done properly.

  It is considered that the inspection method was not proper

in part, in view of the fact that such fatigue cracks as to cause the aft pressure bulkhead to rupture were not found, although they resulted from the improper repair work.

Outlines of the Abnormal Situation

The conditions of the abnormal situation in which the accident aircraft was brought are considered as follows:

- At about 1824:35, when the aircraft climbed to an altitude of about 24,000 feet, the pressure differential between the pressurized passenger cabin and outside atmosphere became about 8.66 psi, it is estimated that bay 2 whose residue strength had reduced remarkably by propagating fatigue cracks was fractured, being unable to bear the pressure differential, and taking this opportunity, L18 splice went into a total fracture at a stroke.

- It is considered that the fracture propagated thereafter upward in the central portion of the bulkhead along the collector ring, and furthermore progressed upward along R6 and L2 stiffeners, and meanwhile in the outer edge portion of the bulkhead, the fracture propagated upward along Y chord.

- As a result of such progress of the fracture, part of the web of the upper half of the aft pressure bulkhead was blown up aft by the air pressure of the passenger cabin to make an opening. The area of the opening is estimated as of an order of 2-3 square meters.

- It is estimated that the inner pressure of the empennage increased by the pressurized air of the cabin flowed in through the opening of the aft pressure bulkhead, thereby the APU firewall was broken, and part of the empennage structure including the APU proper located aft of the wall was destroyed and separated.

- It is estimated that part of the pressurized air of the passenger cabin which flowed into the empennage rushed into the vertical fin through the opening in the lower portion of the aft torque box of the vertical fin, thereby increasing the inner pressure of the vertical fin, and the fixture between the stringer and the rib chord in the upper half of the aft torque box was destroyed at first. It is estimated that thereafter destruction of the internal structures of the aft torque box and peel-off of the skin were caused, followed by separation of the upper half of the forward torque box, most of the aft torque box, the wing tip cover, etc.

- It is estimated that the damage to the aft torque box of the vertical fin caused separation of the rudder, and four systems of hydraulic pressure line for the rudder control system were all fractured.

- It is estimated that such destruction of the aircraft progressed within a period as short as a few seconds.

- It is estimated that the pressure in the cabin including the cockpit reduced to the atmospheric pressure within a few seconds due to the opening of the aft pressure bulkhead.

- It is estimated that by the afore-mentioned destruction of the airframe, control functions of the rudder and elevator and the trim function of the horizontal stabilizer were lost immediately after the abnormal situation occurred. It is also estimated that control functions of the aileron and the spoiler, and operational functions of the flaps and the gear by hydraulic pressure were lost within 1.0--1.5 minutes after the abnormal situation occurred.

- It is estimated that due to loss of most of control functions and extreme deterioration of the lateral and directional

- stability, the maintenance of attitude and heading, and control of climb, descent, turn, and so forth became extremely difficult.

- It is estimated that severe phugoid motion and dutch roll motion, of which control were difficult, were caused to the aircraft.

- It is considered that the aircraft was not able to continue a stable flight and any flight as intended by the captain was difficult, and that a safe landing or landing on the water was next to impossible.

Flight of the Accident Aircraft after the Occurrence of the Abnormal Situation and Responsive Actions Taken by the Flight Crew

- It is estimated that the flight crew immediately became aware of occurrence of some kind of abnormality, but they remained ever since unaware of details of the damage such as rupture of the vertical fin and separation of the rudder.

- It is estimated that soon after the occurrence of the abnormal situation, the flightcrew became cognizant of depressurization of the airframe, and nonetheless the flight crew did not put the oxygen mask up to the last. The reason, however, could not be clarified.

- After the occurrence of the abnormal situation, the aircraft, without making an emergency descent, continued flight for about 18 minutes at an altitude of more than 20,000 feet, making phugoid motion and dutch roll motion. It is conceivable that the reason the emergency descent was not made during this period regardless of the intention expressed by the flight crew to make an emergency descent was that they were devoted to the control action to stabilize the flight.

attitude. However, the definite reason could not be determined:

It is conceivable also that the flight crew suffered from hypoxic hypoxia during this period, whereby their capability of dealing with intelligent work as well as their behavior were deteriorated to some extent.

- Thereafter, a gear-down operation was conducted, the aircraft entered into a descent and the phugoid motion subsided. When the aircraft descended to an altitude of about 7,000 feet, the flight crew noticed the aircraft was approaching mountains. As soon as they raised engine power immediately, the aircraft would have been brought into an unstable flight condition again, being accompanied by phugoid motion and dutch roll motion.

- After the occurrence of the abnormal situation, the flight crew not only fell into an abnormal situation which was out of the scope of the education and training they received or the knowledge and experience they had, but also was unable to comprehend fully the substance of the abnormal situation, and furthermore they were brought into a severe environment of being subjected to severe motion and depressurization of the aircraft. For these reasons, it is conceivable that they were concentrated on the operation to stabilize the flight while not able to make a pertinent judgement on how to cope with the situation.

Crash of the Accident Aircraft

- It is estimated that the aircraft which was in the unstable flight condition hit the single larch tree and the U-shaped ditch both short of the crash point, with the result that the remaining portion of the vertical fin and the horizontal fin as well as the engines, etc., were separated from the airframe at this time.

- It is estimated that thereafter the aircraft collided against the crash point with an attitude of the nose and the right wing both down. The time of crash is estimated as approximately 1856:30 hours based on records of the DFDR and seismometer, etc.

- BY the severe shock at the time of crash the fore fuselage and the right wing were broken into small fragments and dispersed. The aft fuselage is estimated to have been separated by the shock at the time of crash, and fallen into the 3rd branch of Sugeno Dale passing over the ridge line. The other parts were dispersed in a wide area involving the crash point.

- Fuel supposed to have been dispersed from the fuel tank flamed up, and the wreckage. dispersed in the vicinity of the heliport which had been constructed after the accident for rescue purpose was burnt down.

Injuries to Passengers and Crew

- It is considered that passengers and crewmembers in the fore and mid fuselage were all instantaneously killed by the shock estimated as much as hundreds of G as well as the total destruction of structures of the fore and mid fuselage at the time of crash.

- Out of passengers and cabin attendants who were in the aft fuselage, those seated on forward seating are considered to have been killed almost instantaneously due to a possible strong shock in excess of 100 G's at the time of crash.

  The shock persons on the aft seating were subjected to was also of an order of tens of G, and by this shock most of them are considered to have undergone fatal injuries. Moreover, the possibility would be considered high that since the flooring, seating, galley, etc were all destroyed and dispersed by the shock at the time of crash, they were killed enlarging the extent of injuries by bruise and oppression resulting from collision with such broken pieces.

- Four persons survived this accident, but they were all seriously injured. All of them were seated at the aft portion of the aft fuselage and are considered to have been subjected to tens of G, but they were able to escape death miraculously. The conceivable reason would be that their seating attitude, way to fasten the belt, status of damage to the seat, status of substances surrounding their body, etc., at the time of collision chanced to help buffer the impact, and that they were less subjected to collision with dispersed internal substances of the fuselage.

Support to Flight of the Accident Aircraft from the Ground

It is considered that provision of information to the accident aircraft and actions respondent to requests of the aircraft by ATC/Communications were conducted adequately on the whole.

Search and Rescue Activities

- Since the crash point was located in a remote area among a rolled mountainous district and the search was conducted in the night, considerable time was required to discover the aircraft and to confirm the crash point, which could, however, be justifiable under such conditions.

- It is acknowledged that rescue activities were carried out to the best with close coordination of organizations concerned which participated in the activities, although they were confronted with extreme difficulties.

Cause

It is estimated that this accident was caused by

deterioration of flying quality and loss of primary flight control functions due to rupture of the aft pressure bulkhead of the aircraft, and the subsequent ruptures of a part of the fuselage tail, vertical fin and hydraulic flight control systems.

The reason why the aft pressure bulkhead was ruptured in flight is estimated to be that the strength of the said bulkhead was reduced due to fatigue cracks propagating at the spliced portion of the bulkhead's webs to the extent that it became unable to endure the cabin pressure in flight at that time.

The initiation and propagation of the fatigue cracks are attributable to the improper repairs of the said bulkhead conducted in 1978, and it is estimated that the fatigue cracks having not be found in the later maintenance inspection is contributive to their propagation leading to the rupture of the said bulkhead.

CHAPTER 7

REFERENTIAL MATTERS

Actions and counter-measures taken up to May 31, 1987 by governmental organizations, aircraft manufacturers, and aircraft operators concerned, in reference to this accident are as follows:

The NTSB made the following safety recommendations to the FAA:

a. Design change on the empennage (Safety Recommendation A-85-133. Dec.5,1985)

Measures should be taken so that the empennage section of Boeing 747 and 767 will be protected against catastrophic failure in the event that a significant pressure buildup occurs in the normally unpressurized empennage.

b. Modification of the design of the hydraulic systems (Safety Recommendation A-85-134, Dec.5, 1985)

Design modification should be made so that the integrity of all four hydraulic systems will not be impaired in the event that a significant pressure buildup occurs in the normally unpressurized empennage.

c. Reevaluation of the fail-safe validity of the doomed aft pressure bulkhead (Safety Recommendation A--85--135, Dec.5, 1985)

Reevaluation should be made of the design of the aft pressure bulkhead of Boeing 747 and 767, and test be made to confirm their fail-safe validity.

d. Evaluation of procedures to repair the aft pressure bulkhead (Safety Recommendation A-85-136, Dec.5, 1985)

The current repair procedures of Boeing 747 and 767 aft pressure bulkheads should be evaluated to ensure that the repairs do not affect the fail-safe concept.

e. Revision of the inspection program for the aft pressure bulkhead (Safety Recommendation A--85--137, Dec.5, 1985)

In reference to the aft pressure bulkhead, an inspection program beyond the usual visual inspection should be established to detect the extent of possible multiple   site fatigue cracking.

f. Evaluation of the fail-safe Criteria of the domed aft pressure bulkhead (Safety Recommendation A-85-138, Dec.13, 1985)

Confirmation should be made on whether the fail-safe criteria have been satisfactorily evaluated for all domed aft pressure bulkheads of transport category airplanes.

g. Evaluation of repair procedures of the domed aft pressure bulkhead (Safety Recommendation A-85-139, Dec.13,1985.)

Procedures to repair the domed aft pressure bulkhead of all airplanes which incorporate the domed aft pressure bulkhead should be evaluated to assure that the affected repairs do not derogate the fail-safe concept of the bulkhead.

h. Issuance of a maintenance alert bulletin to persons responsible for the engineering approval of repairs (Safety Recommendation A--85--140, Dec.13, 1985)

A maintenance alert bulletin should be issued to persons responsible for the engineering approval of repairs to emphasize that the approval adequately consider the possibility of influence on ultimate failure modes or other fail-safe design criteria.

The FAA directed US operators of the Boeing 747 and the Boeing Company to make the following modifications, inspections, etc.:

a. Vertical fin access cover installation (Airworthiness Directive AD86-08-02, April 4, 1986)T

To install, within 6 months, a structural cover for the opening within the empennage which provides access to the vertical fin, to prevent destruction of the empennage structure due to a significant pressure buildup in the empennage. (A-85-133 related)

b. Reevaluation of the fail-safe validity of the domed aft pressure bulkhead

To request the Boeing Company to conduct a reevaluation of the design and tests concerning the fail-safe validity of the aft pressure bulkheads of Boeing 747 and 767. (A-85-135 related)

c. Evaluation of the repair procedures for the domed aft pressure bulkhead (Airworthiness Directive AD-85-22-12, Oct.25, 1985)

To request the operators to check on whether repairs of the aft pressure bulkhead of Boeing 747 have been carried out and to report the results to the Boeing Company.

No problems were found from the FAA's review on the results of reevaluation of the repair manuals of the aft pressure bulkhead of Boeing 707, 737, 747 and 767 issued by the Boeing Company.(A-85-136 related)

d. Review of the fail-safe criteria of the doomed aft pressure bulkhead

FAA's TACD (Transport Airplane Certification Directorate) formed a team with the major aircraft manufacturers to study on NTSB's safety recommendations, and they are making a review of large aircraft exceeding 75,000 pounds taxi weight. Through the review, modifications of and additions to inspection procedures were brought into.

Reevaluation of the damage tolerance design is also under way. (A-85-138 related)

e. Evaluation of the repair procedures of the domed aft pressure bulkhead

FAA requested the large transport airplane manufacturers to review the repair criteria for the domed aft pressure bulkhead by a letter dated Dec.12, 1985. (A-85-139 related)

f. Issuance of a memorandum to the engineering staff

A memorandum concerning repairs of important major structures of the aircraft was issued to the engineering staff belonging to each ACO (Aircraft Certification Office) (A-85-140 related)

g. Modification of the hydraulic systems

FAA initiated, with the Boeing Company in September 1985, a study on modifications necessary to prevent loss of functions of the hydraulic systems following major structural failure of Boeing 747. This work is still under progress, but indications are that functions of the elevator, ailerons, and spoilers could be secured by installing a fuse before No.4 hydraulic system where the hydraulic lines enter the vertical stabilizer. The Boeing Company has issued a service bulletin which provides for installation of the fuse on No.4 hydraulic system, and the SB is planned to become an FAA directive. (A-85-134 related)

The Boeing Company issued the following SB's and at the same time conducted design modifications, tests, etc. on new production airplanes:

a. Vertical fin access cover installation (SB747-53A-2264, Nov.25, 1985)

    The Boeing requested installation on airplanes in current use of the cover for the opening which provides access to the vertical fin. The installation on new airplanes was made from line number 626 (delivered Dec. 11, 1985).(A-85-133 related)

b. Modification of the hydraulic systems (SB747-29-2063, Dec.23, 1986) The Boeing requested installation on airplanes in current use of the fuse in No.4 hydraulic systems upstream of the vertical stabilizer. The installation of the fuse on No.4 hydraulic system of new production airplanes was initiated at line number 663 (delivered Dec.23,1986).The rerouting of the hydraulic line between BS1480 and 2460 will be incorporated in production starting with line. number 696, which will roll out of the factory in January, 1988. A SB which provides for rerouting of the hydraulic line will not be issued due to technical complexity unless requested by an operator through the Master Change process. (A-85-134 related)

c. Reevaluation of fail-safe validity of the aft pressure bulkhead of Boeing 747 and 767

The fatigue test and damage tolerance test of the aft pressure bulkhead on the current design model as well as on the improved model were completed in March 1986 and in July 1986, respectively. (A-85-135 and —138 related)

d. Evaluation of repair procedures of the aft pressure bulkhead

Boeing sent a telegram to the operators requesting them to check whether repairs have been carried out, and to report details of the repairs conducted. (A-85-136 and AD85-22-12 related)

e. Development of the reinforced aft pressure bulkhead

The reinforced aft pressure bulkhead was installed from line number 672 delivered in February, 1987. The modification added two tear straps, a cover plate to the center of the bulkhead, and doublers to the both sides of the bulkhead around the APU cutout. (A-85-135 related)

f. Revision on the inspection program of the aft pressure bulkhead (S8747-53-2275, March 26, 1987)

Boeing requested the visual inspection from the aft side at 1,000 flight-cycle intervals (freighters) or at 2,000 flight-cycle intervals (passenger airplanes); and after 20,000 flight-cycles, the detailed inspection by high-precision eddy current, ultrasonic wave and X rays at 2,000 flight-cycle intervals (freighters) or at 4,000 flight-cycle intervals (passenger airplanes).

As to 747SR, Boeing requested the visual inspection at 2,400 flight-cycle intervals; and after 24,000 flight-cycles, the detailed inspection by eddy current, etc. at 4,800 flight-cycle intervals. (A-85-137 related)

The Civil Aviation Bureau of the Ministry of Transport in Japan took the following actions for the safety operation of Boeing 747 and for the improvement of the search and rescue system for aircraft:

a. Instructions to conduct overall inspection of the vertical stabilizer and the rudder (Airworthiness Directive TCD--2483--85, August 15, 1985)

b. Instructions to conduct overall inspection of the aft part structure of the pressurized cabin (Airworthiness Directive TCD--2483--1--85, August 17, 1985)

c. Request was made to the airlines operating Boeing 747 in Japan to report results of repair of the aft pressure bulkhead to both the Boeing Company and Japanese Civil Aviation Bureau to reevaluate the repair procedure. (JCAB Document Ku—Ken 747, September 4, 1985)

d. Enforcement of an entry for inspection into JAL's Maintenance Department, and recommendation of service improvements based thereon for safety operation (September 5, 1985)

- to conduct overall inspection on Boeing 747s whose number of pressurized-flight times has reached the order of 18,000.
- to review the inspection items of C maintenance and others, and at the same time to improve work cards used in the inspection of airframe structures, for the reinforcement of airframe structure inspection of Boeing 747.
- to set up a long-range monitor program of airframe structures damaged by an accident or others.
- to review the sampling inspection procedures of airframe structures of Boeing 747, and at the same time to improve the technical evaluation procedures of the sampling inspection results.

Furthermore, to promote to development of preventive measures against the reoccurrence of major failures.

- to ensure the thorough implementation of instructions from the maintenance department to the engineering planning department.

- to reinforce the inspection and maintenance system of airframe structures as well as the all-round safety promotion system.

e. Notification to FAA of the inspection results of the pressurized cabin structures of JAL's Boeing 747SR's conducted pursuant to the service improvement recommendation, for FAA's further improvement actions to ensure the operation safety of the aircraft. (November 5/December 10, 1985)

f. Instructions to install a structural cover for the opening within the empennage which provides access to the vertical fin for the purpose of preventing the rupture of the fin structures due to flow-in of the pressurized air to the empennage aft of the pressure bulkhead. (Airworthiness Directive TCD--2611--86, May 7, 1986, A-85-133 related)

g. Instructions to incorporate SID items into the maintenance regulations as a measure to cope with the aging change of Boeing 747SR (Airworthiness Directive TCD--2636--86, October 13, 1986)

h. Up to Summer of 1986, the improvement of facilities of the Tokyo Airport Office where the Search and Rescue Center is located and the communications network among organizations concerned was completed, and the necessary staff was increased. Furthermore, on August 7, 1986, a joint training was carried out by the Civil Aviation Bureau and organizations concerned.

JAL has effected or is planning the following improvement actions, counter-measures, etc:

a. Design modification of the vertical fin (Airworthiness Directive TCD2611--86, AD86-08-02 and A-85-133 related)

On all Boeing 747's in current use the cover was installed to the opening which provides access to the vertical fin up to December 31, 1985. On JA8169 and the aircraft thereafter the cover is installed in their production.

b. Modification of the Hydraulic Systems

The installation of the fuse to the hydraulic systems on 4 aircraft incurrent use was completed by the end of May, 1987, and on the other aircraft in current use will be completed by the end of March, 1988. On JA8178 and the aircraft thereafter its installation is made at the production time. (A-85-134 related)

c. Evaluation of repair procedures of the doomed aft pressure bulkhead

Inspection on all aircraft in current use was made as to whether repairs were conducted and to what extent the work was carried out, and their results were reported to both the Boeing Company and the Japanese Civil Aviation Bureau. (A-85-136 and 139, AD85--22--12, the Boeing's Telegram, and JCAB Document Ku—Ken 747 related)

d. Revision of the inspection program of the aft pressure bulkhead

The eddy current inspections were implemented on six aircraft in the overall inspection of Boeing 747SR. (No cracks have been found) (A-85-137 Rescue related)

Comments

1. A further improvement is desirable of the DFDR's anti-impact capability, in view of the fact that the magnetic tape of the DFDR on board the accident aircraft was broken, and near the broken spot was found damage such as many small folds and wrinkles.

2. In the CYR of the accident aircraft, voices were recorded for approximately 32 minutes and 16 seconds, but information helpful to the accident investigation may have been recorded at a portion which had been erased. There were also found portions difficult to read, although the equipment was a product meeting the specifications MO C-84).

   It is, therefore desirable to develop a CYK covering more recording period, and to promote a study to improve the recording in terms of clarity through improvement of the total system involving the CYR.

3. Further enhancement is desirable of search and rescue capabilities through periodical enhancement of trainings etc., pursuant to agreements which have been concluded among organizations concerned to ensure prompt and effective search and rescue activities in an emergency.

By Aircraft Accident Investigation Commission:

/S/ Shun Takeda
Chairman

/S/ Yoshiomi Enomoto
Member

/S/ Kiyoshi Nishimura
Member

233

/S/ <u>Jiro Koo</u>
    Member

/S/ <u>Akira Azuma</u>
    Member

June 15, 1987

ATTACHED FIGURES

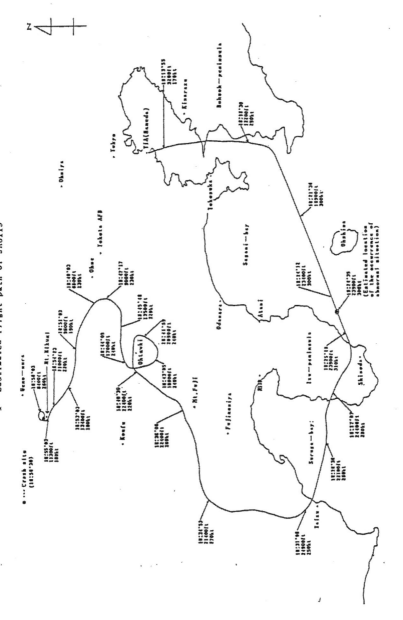

1 estimated flight path of JA8119

238

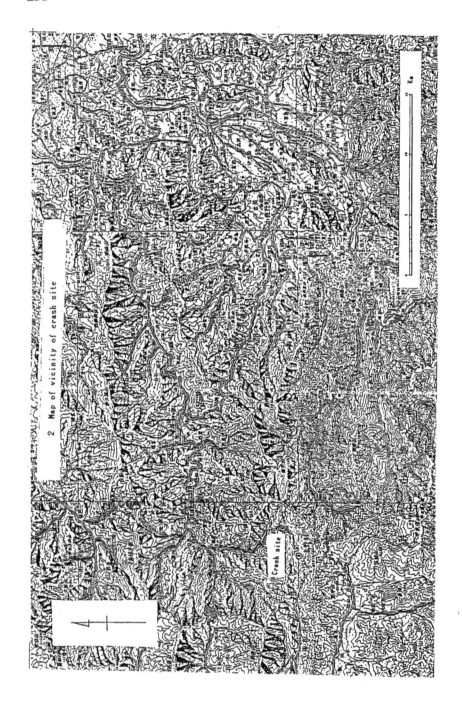

2 Map of vicinity of crash site

Crash site

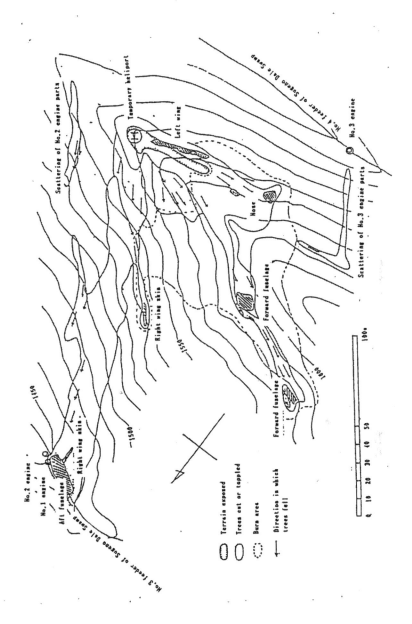

239

3 Situation of crash site

Temporary heliport

Left wing

Nose

Forward fuselage

Forward fuselage

Right wing skin

Right wing skin

Scattering of No.2 engine parts

Scattering of No.3 engine parts

No.3 engine

No.4 feeder of Sugeno Dale Swamp

No.2 engine

No.1 engine

Aft fuselage

No.3 feeder of Sugeno Dale Swamp

Terrain exposed

Trees cut or toppled

Burn area

Direction in which trees fell

100m

0 10 20 30 40 50

240

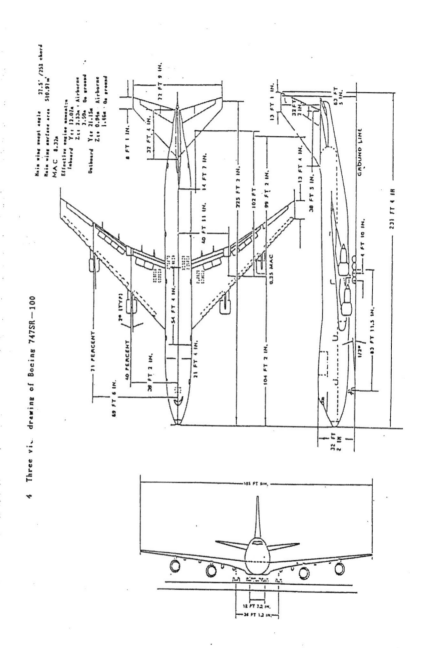

4 Three view drawing of Boeing 747SR-100

5 Fuselage station diagram and seat configuration

Seat configuration-R10
Maximum passengers 528

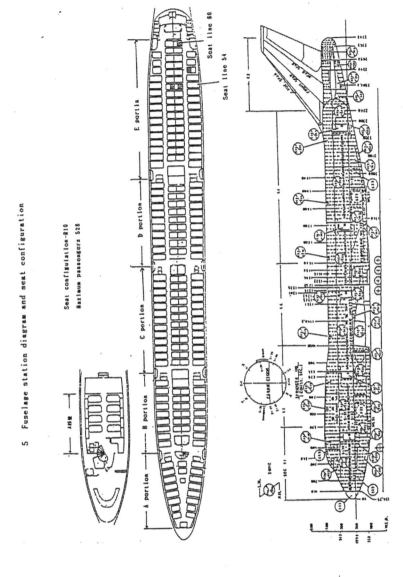

242

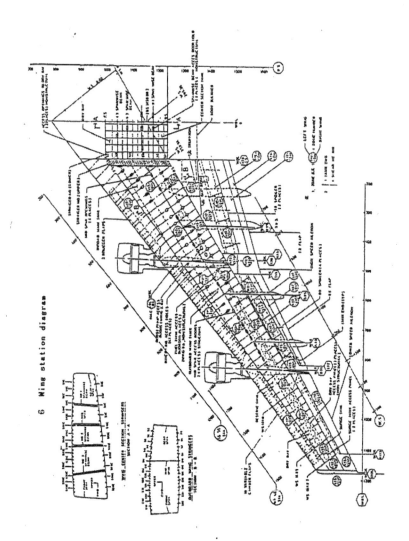

6 Wing station diagram

243

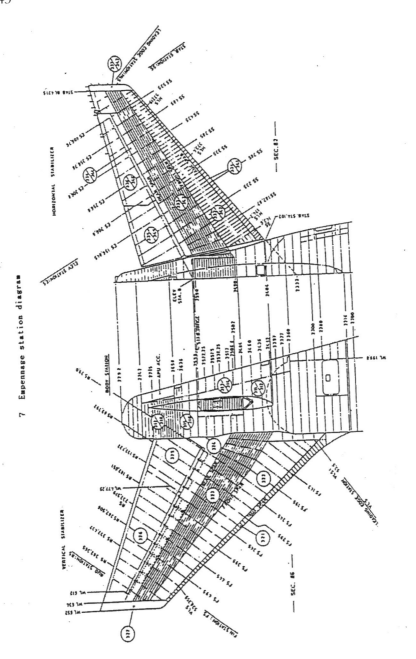

7 Empennage station diagram

244

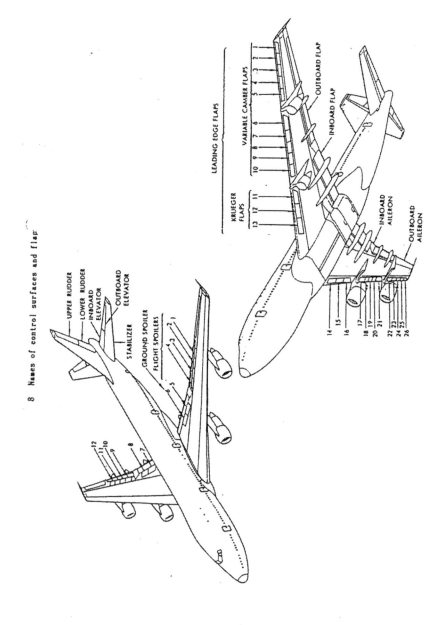

8　Names of control surfaces and flaps

LEADING EDGE FLAPS

VARIABLE CAMBER FLAPS

KRUEGER FLAPS

OUTBOARD FLAP

INBOARD FLAP

INBOARD AILERON

OUTBOARD AILERON

UPPER RUDDER

LOWER RUDDER

INBOARD ELEVATOR

OUTBOARD ELEVATOR

STABILIZER

GROUND SPOILER

FLIGHT SPOILERS

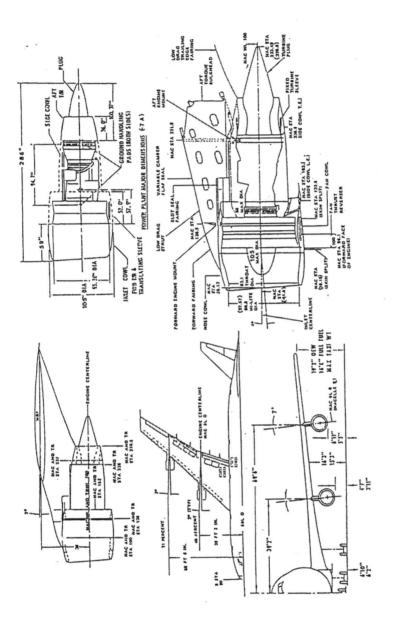

9 Engine installation

246

10 Engine cowling

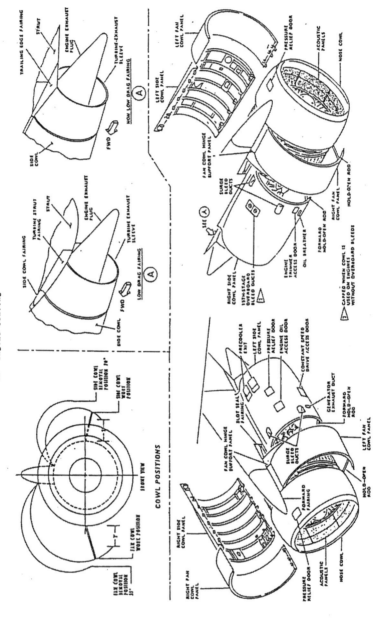

247

11 Engine cross section

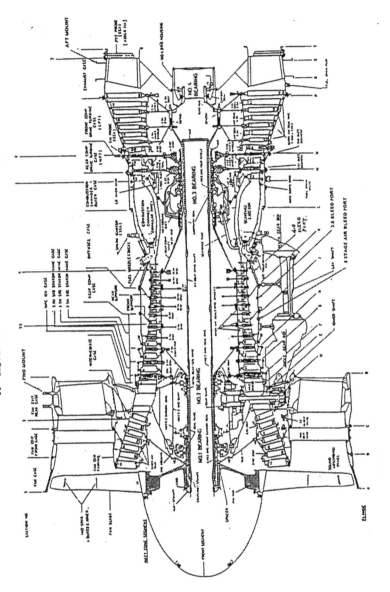

248

12 Flight compartment panels

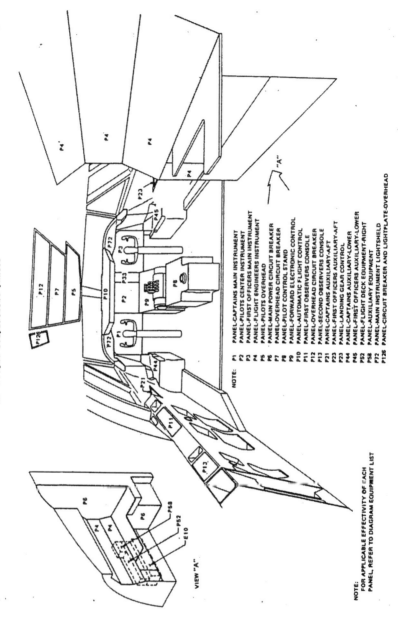

NOTE:

P1   PANEL-CAPTAINS MAIN INSTRUMENT
P2   PANEL-PILOTS CENTER INSTRUMENT
P3   PANEL-FIRST OFFICERS MAIN INSTRUMENT
P4   PANEL-FLIGHT ENGINEERS INSTRUMENT
P5   PANEL-PILOTS OVERHEAD
P6   PANEL-MAIN POWER CIRCUIT BREAKER
P7   PANEL-OVERHEAD CIRCUIT BREAKER
P8   PANEL-PILOT CONTROL STAND
P9   PANEL-FORWARD ELECTRONIC CONTROL
P10   PANEL-AUTOMATIC FLIGHT CONTROL
P11   PANEL-FIRST OBSERVERS CONSOLE
P12   PANEL-OVERHEAD CIRCUIT BREAKER
P13   PANEL-SECOND OBSERVERS CONSOLE
P21   PANEL-CAPTAINS AUXILIARY-AFT
P23   PANEL-FIRST OFFICERS AUXILIARY-AFT
P44   PANEL-LANDING GEAR CONTROL
P44   PANEL-CAPTAINS AUXILIARY-LOWER
P45   PANEL-FIRST OFFICERS AUXILIARY-LOWER
P52   PANEL-FLIGHT DECK EQUIPMENT-RIGHT
P58   PANEL-AUXILIARY EQUIPMENT
P72   PANEL-MAIN INSTRUMENT LIGHTSHIELD
P126 PANEL-CIRCUIT BREAKER AND LIGHTPLATE-OVERHEAD

VIEW "A"

NOTE:
FOR APPLICABLE EFFECTIVITY OF EACH
PANEL, REFER TO DIAGRAM EQUIPMENT LIST

249

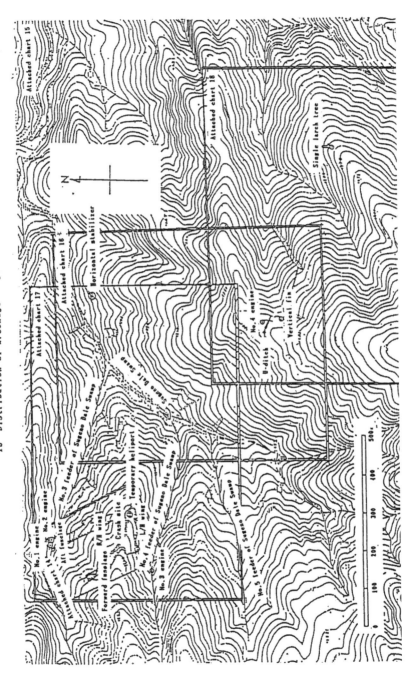

13 Distribution of wreckage — general

250

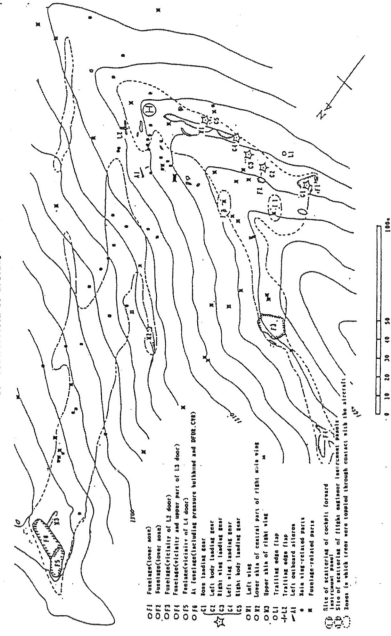

14 Distribution of wreckage — crash site

○F1 Fuselage(lower nose)
○F2 Fuselage(lower nose)
○F3 Fuselage(vicinity of L3 door)
○F4 Fuselage(vicinity and upper part of L3 door)
○F5 Fuselage(vicinity of L4 door)
○F6 At fuselage(including pressure bulkhead and DFDR,CVR)

C1 Nose landing gear
C2 Left body landing gear
C3 Right body landing gear
C4 Left wing landing gear
C5 Right body landing gear

○W1 Left wing
○W2 Lower skin of central part of right main wing
○W3 Upper skin of right wing
○L1 Trailing edge flap
+L2 Trailing edge flap
∠A1 Left outboard aileron

● Main wing-related parts
✕ Fuselage-related parts

Site of scattering of cockpit forward
instrument panel
Site of scattering of flight engineer instrument panels
Zones in which trees were toppled through contact with the aircraft

0 10 20 30 40 50   100m

15 Distribution of wreckage — right wing

252

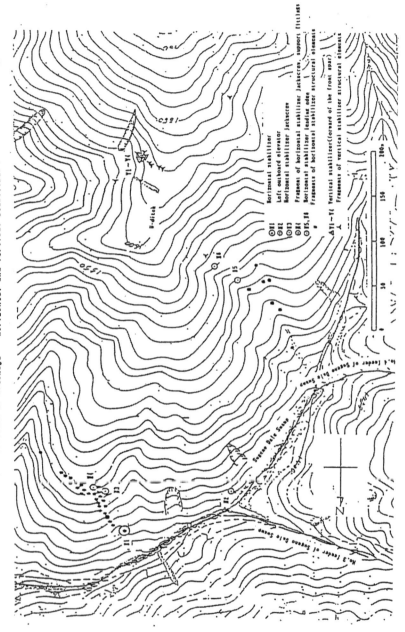

· 18 Distribution of wreckage — horizontal and vertical stabilizer ·

253

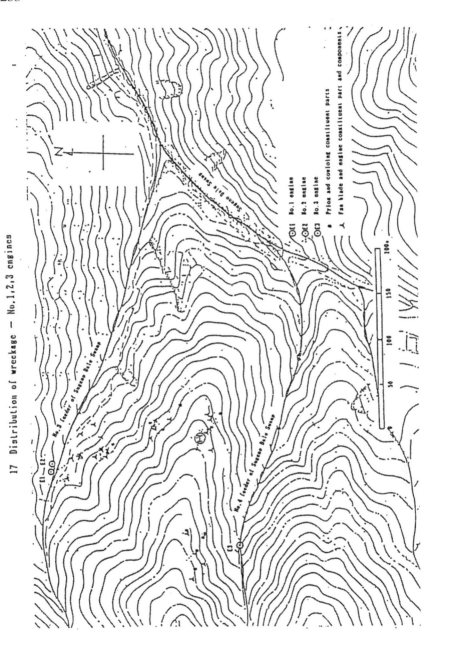

17 Distribution of wreckage — No.1,2,3 engines

254

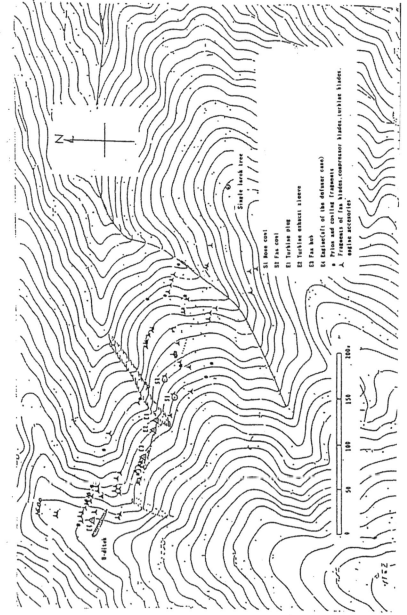

18 Distribution of wreckage — No. 4 engine

255

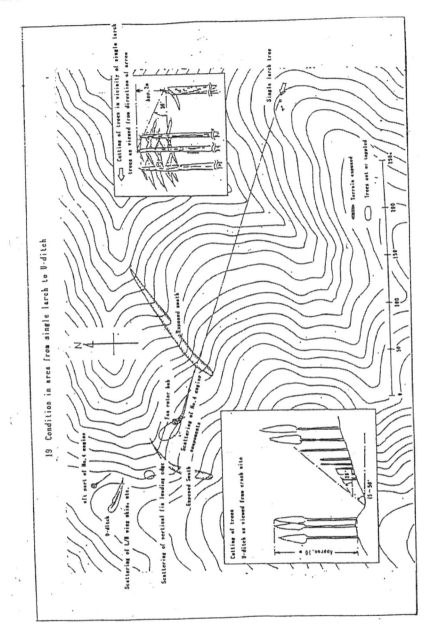

19 Condition in area from single larch to U-ditch

20 Locations of debris recovery from Sagami Bay, etc.

* Indicates "position on the airframe verified"

NO	DEG	MIN	SEC
①	34	43	49N
	139	01	54E
②	34	44	15N
	139	02	07E
③	34	44	35N
	139	03	10E
④	34	44	44N
	139	03	14E
⑤	34	44	43N
	139	02	37E
⑥	34	45	11N
	139	02	56E
⑦	34	45	19N
	139	02	51E
⑧	34	47	30N
	139	04	30E
⑨	34	46	35N
	139	04	30E
⑩	34	45	39N
	139	05	24E
⑪	34	45	54N
	139	04	23E
⑫	34	44	21N
	139	03	44E
⑬	34	44	27N
	139	02	53E
⑭	34	44	11N
	139	03	13E
⑮	34	44	09N
	139	03	31E
⑯	34	44	09N
	139	08	41E
⑰	34	45	58N
	139	04	2?E

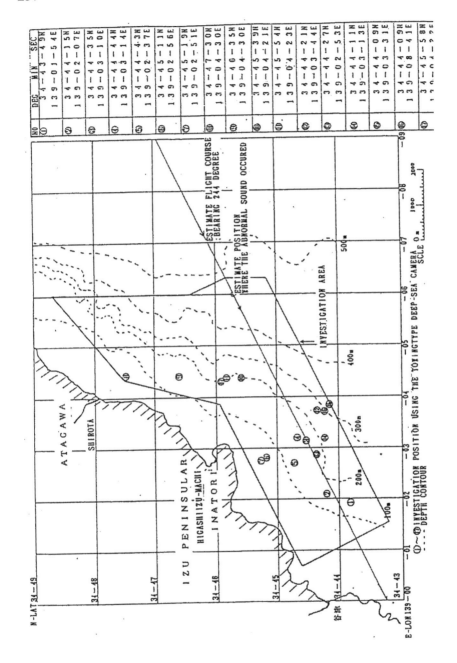

ATAGAWA

SHIROTA

IZU PENINSULAR

HIGASHIIZU-MACHI

INATORI

ESTIMATE FLIGHT COURSE : BEARING 244 DEGREE

ESTIMATE POSITION WHERE THE ABNORMAL SOUND OCCURED

INVESTIGATION AREA

500m 400m 300m 200m 100m

①~⑰INVESTIGATION POSITION USING THE TOYINGTYPE DEEP-SEA CAMERA
--- DEPTH CONTOUR

SCALE 0m   1000   2000

N-LAT 31-49   31-48   31-47   31-46   31-45   31-44   34-43

E-LON 139-00

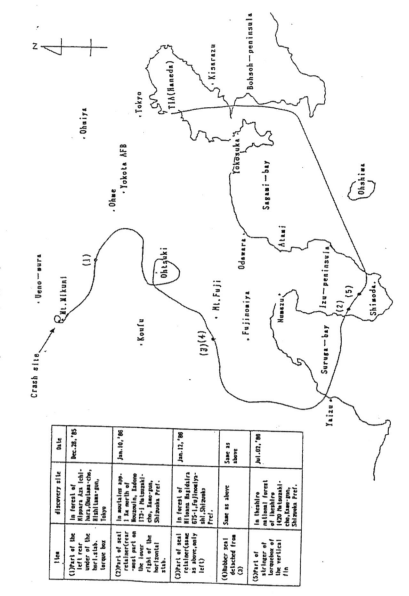

22 Wreckage discovered on flight course

259

23 Tokyo Radar sketch chart (1800)

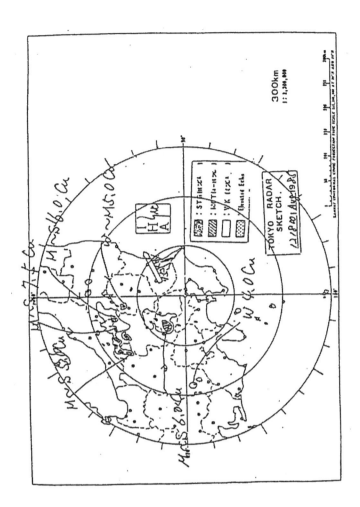

24 Tokyo Radar sketch chart (1900)

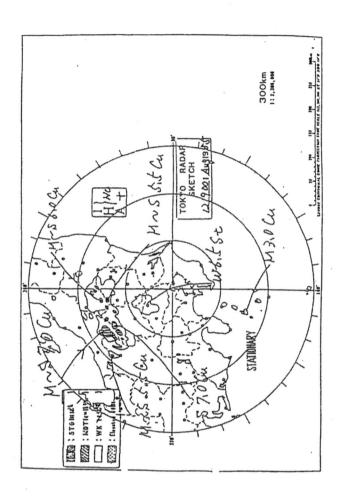

261

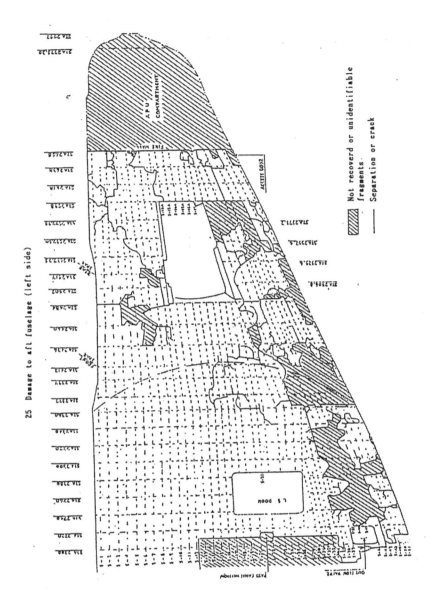

25 Damage to aft fuselage (left side)

262

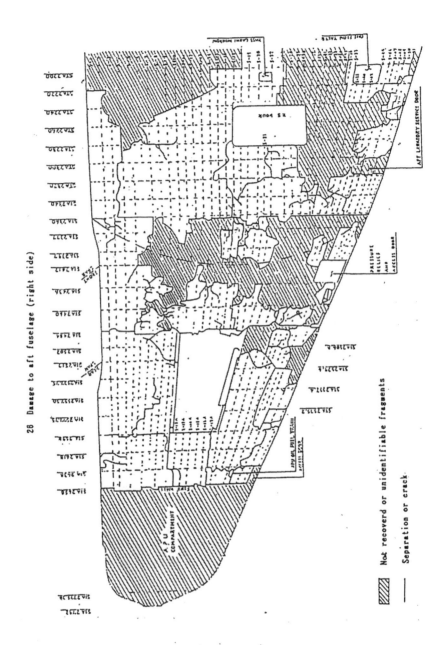

28 Damage to aft fuselage (right side)

Not recoverd or unidentifiable fragments

Separation or crack

263

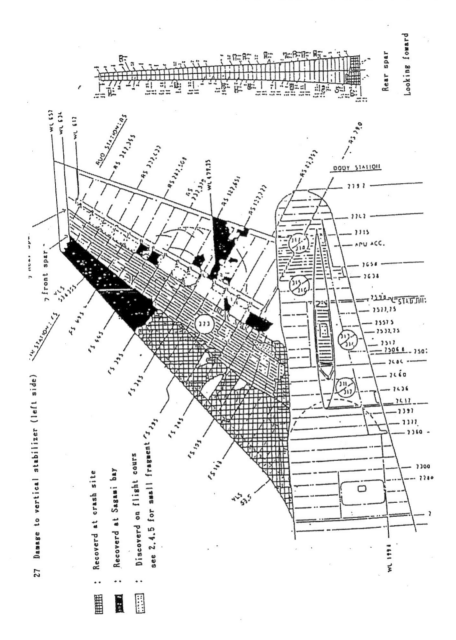

27 Damage to vertical stabilizer (left side)

: Recoverd at crash site

: Recoverd at Sagami bay

: Discoverd on flight cours
see 2,4,5 for small fragment

Looking foward

Rear spar

264

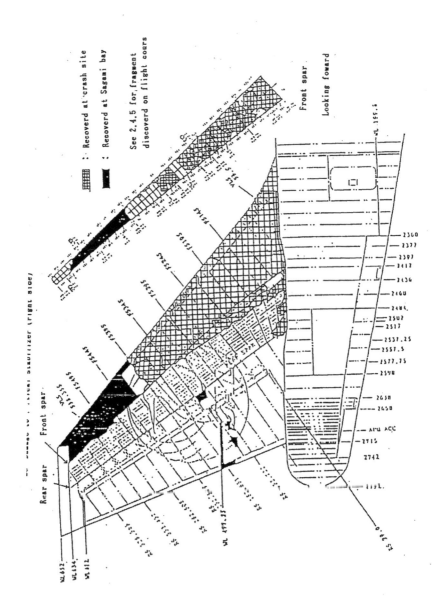

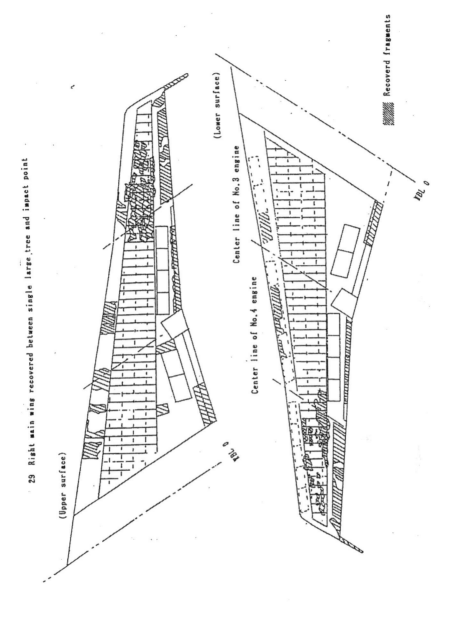

29 Right main wing recovered between single large tree and impact point

266

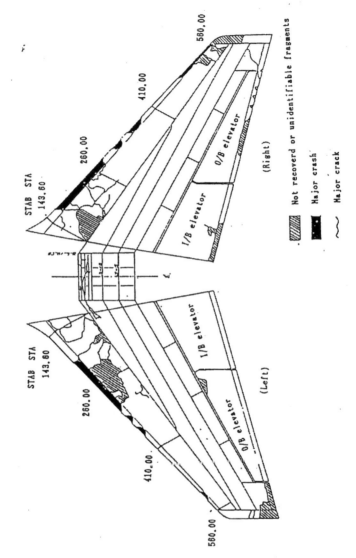

30 Damage to horizontal stabilizer (upper surface)

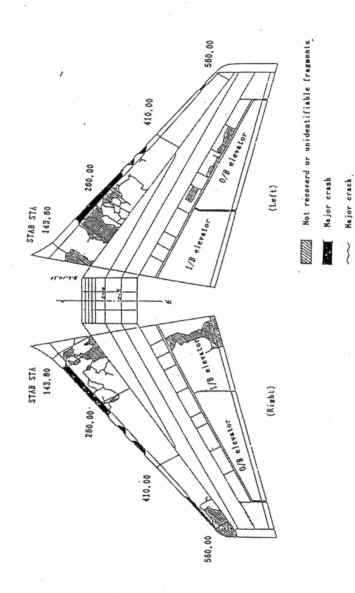

31 Damage to horizontal stabilizer (under surface)

268

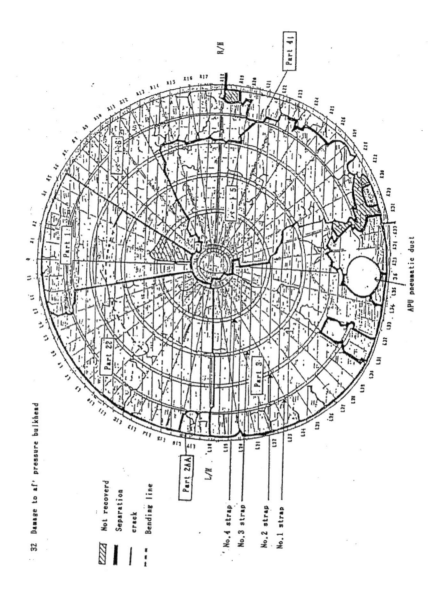

32 Damage to aft pressure bulkhead

Not recoverd
Separation
crack
Bending line

No.4 strap
No.3 strap
No.2 strap
No.1 strap

Part 1
Part 22
Part 2AA
Part 3
Part 4
APU pneumatic duct

R/H
L/H

33 Latch mechanism of pressure relief door

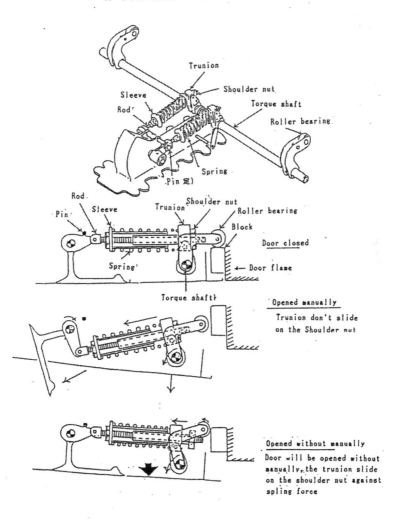

Trunion

Shoulder nut

Sleeve

Torque shaft

Rod

Roller bearing

Spring

Pin 図)

Rod

Shoulder nut

Pin

Sleeve

Trunion

Roller bearing

Block

Spring

Door closed

← Door flame

Torque shaft

Opened manually

Trunion don't slide
on the Shoulder nut

Opened without manually

Door will be opened without
manually, the trunion slide
on the shoulder nut against
spling force

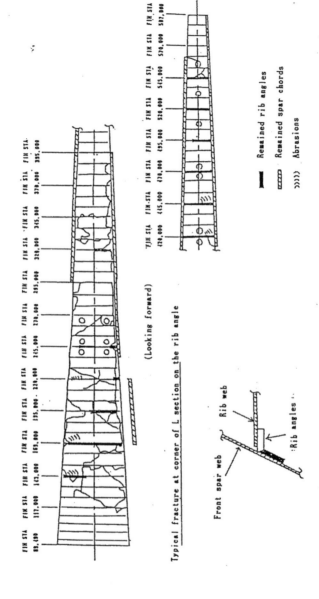

34 Damage to vertical fin front spar

FIN STA 90.000, FIN STA 117.000, FIN STA 143.000, FIN STA 169.000, FIN STA 195.000, FIN STA 220.000, FIN STA 246.000, FIN STA 272.000, FIN STA 295.000, FIN STA 320.000, FIN STA 345.000, FIN STA 370.000, FIN STA 395.000

FIN STA 420.000, FIN STA 445.000, FIN STA 470.000, FIN STA 495.000, FIN STA 520.000, FIN STA 545.000, FIN STA 570.000, FIN STA 597.000

(Looking forward)

Typical fracture at corner of L section on the rib angle

Front spar web

Rib web

Rib angles

Remained rib angles

Remained spar chords

Abrasions

Black colored section was remained Remained rib angles

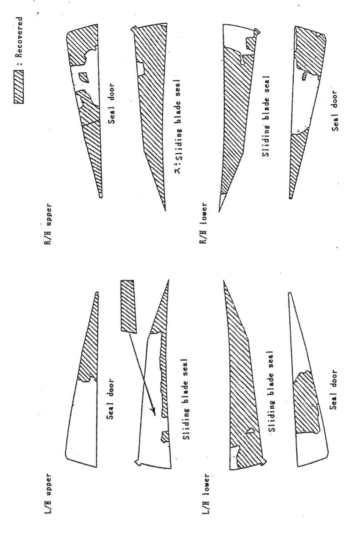

35 Damage to body seal

272

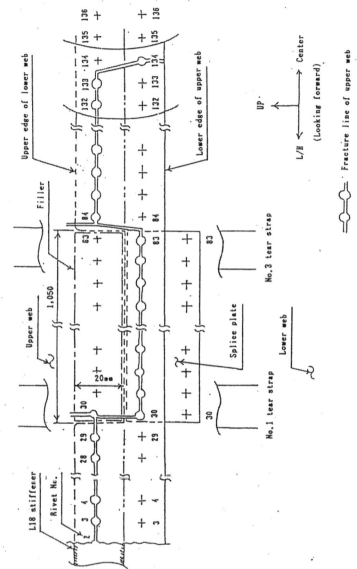

36 L18 splice of aft pressure bulkhead (simplified)

273

Figure-37 Fracture of webs along stiffener L18

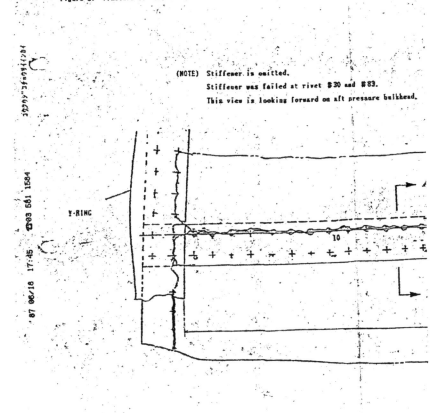

(NOTE) Stiffener is omitted.
Stiffener was failed at rivet #30 and #83.
This view is looking forward on aft pressure bulkhead.

Y-RING

10

274

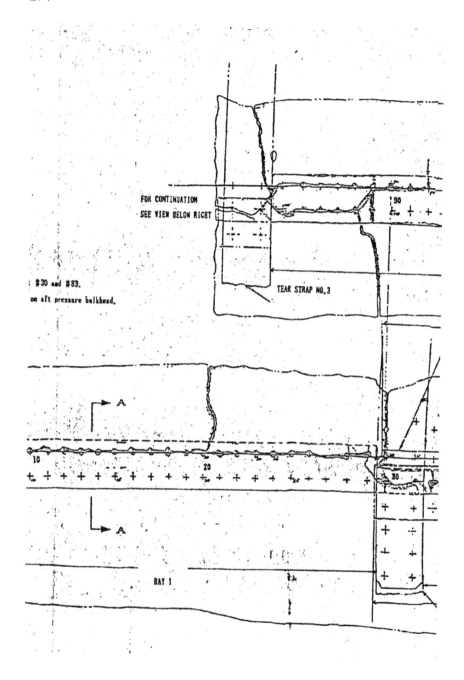

FOR CONTINUATION
SEE VIEW BELOW RIGHT

#30 and #83.
on aft pressure bulkhead.

TEAR STRAP NO.3

A

A

BAY 1

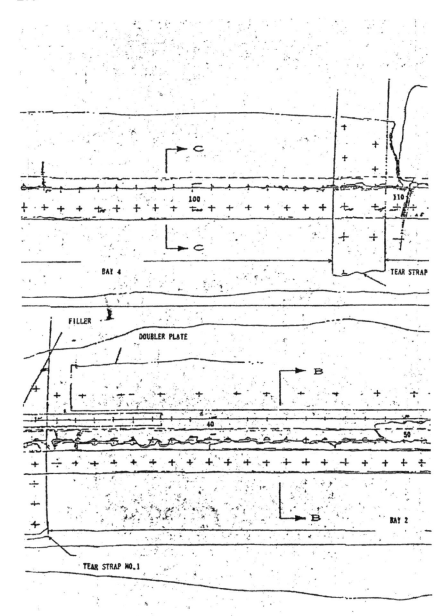

C

C

100

110

BAY 4

TEAR STRAP

FILLER

DOUBLER PLATE

B

40

50

B

BAY 2

TEAR STRAP NO. 1

276

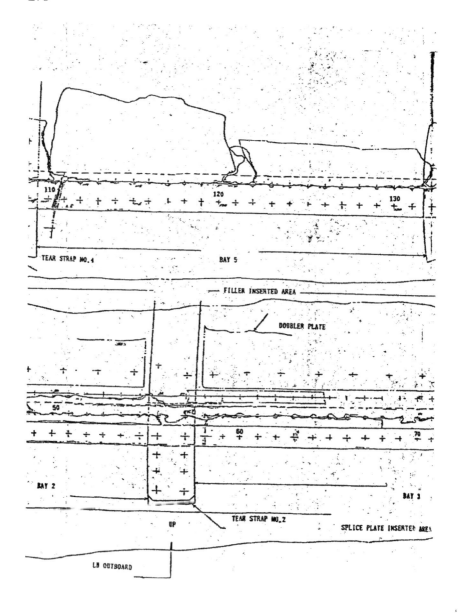

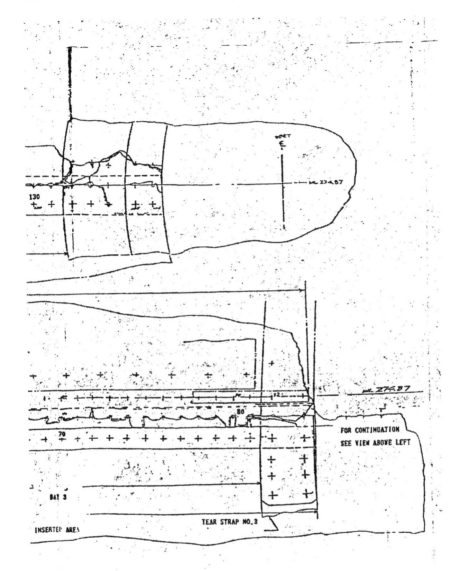

278

Figure-38 Details of fracture c

(a)

SECTION A-A AND C-C

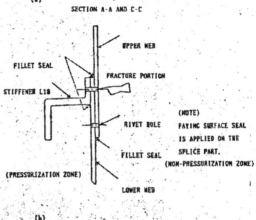

(NOTE)
FAYING SURFACE SEAL
IS APPLIED ON THE
SPLICE PART.
(NON-PRESSURIZATION ZONE)

(b)

SECTION B-B

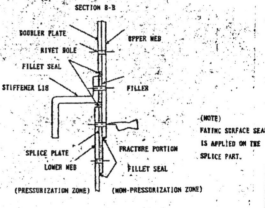

(NOTE)
FAYING SURFACE SEAL
IS APPLIED ON THE
SPLICE PART.

...ils of fracture of webs along stiffener L18

(c)

TYPICAL FRACTURE ASPECT

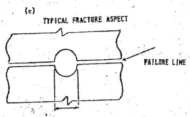

FAILURE LINE

HOLE WIDTH ON FRACTURE SURFACE

CE SEAL
IN THE

(ION ZONE)

(d)

ASPECT OF FRACTURE NEAR EDGE OF PLATE

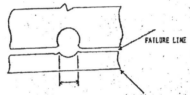

FAILURE LINE

HOLE WIDTH ON   HOLE   EDGE OF PLATE
FRACTURE SURFACE   DIAMETER

(e)

ASPECT OF SHEARING FRACTURE OF HOLE EDGE

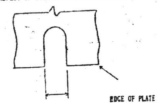

SURFACE SEAL
IED ON THE
PART.

EDGE OF PLATE

HOLE WIDTH

ATTACHED PHOTOS

283

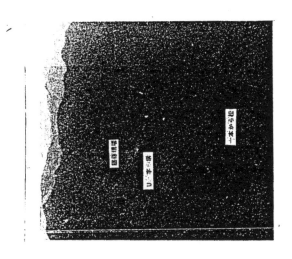

1   Distant view of crash site (1)

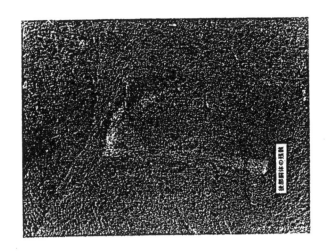

2   Distant view of crash site (2)

284

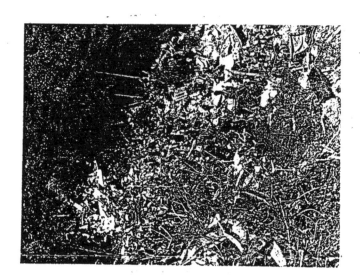

4　Debris of aft fuselage (1)

3　U-ditch

5　　Debris of aft fuselage (2)

6　　Horizontal stabilizer

286

7   No.1 engine

8   No.2 engine

9   No.3 engine

10   Part of No.4 engine

11　Fractured part of tierod link

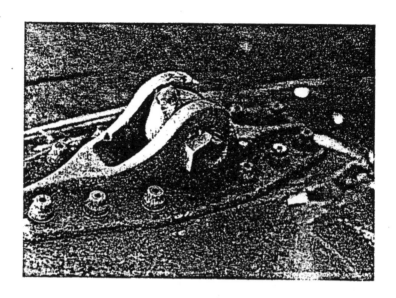

12　Recovered aft pressure bulkhead (1)

13   Recovered aft pressure bulkhead (2)

14   APU air intake recovered from sea

15   Part of vertical fin recovered from sea (1)

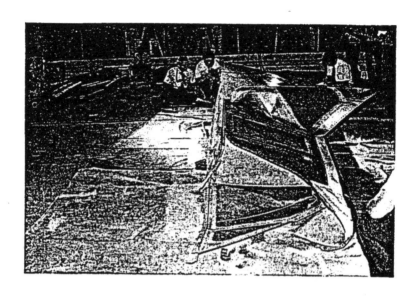

16   Part of vertical fin recovered from sea (2)

17   Wreckage discovered on flight path (1)

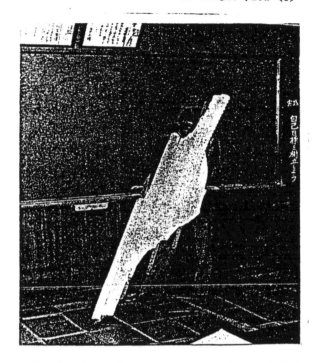

18   Wreckage discovered on flight path (2)

19   Wreckage discovered on flight path (3)

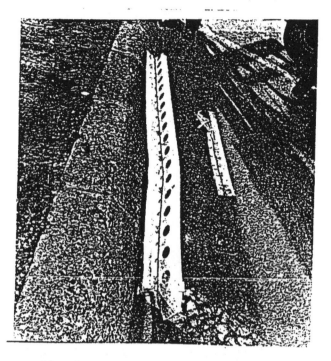

20   Wreckage discovered on flight path (4)

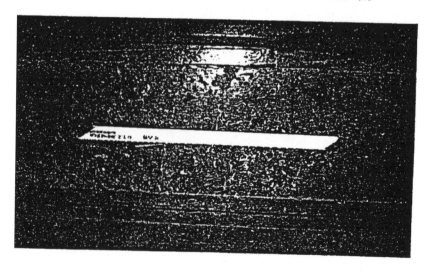

21   Reconstruction of aft fuselage (left side)

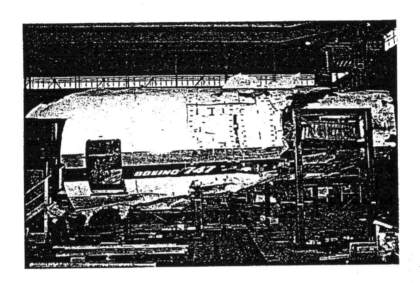

22   Reconstruction of aft fuselage (right side)

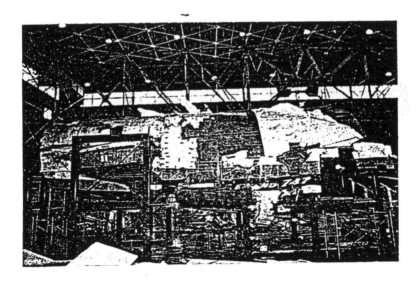

23   Vertical fin spread view

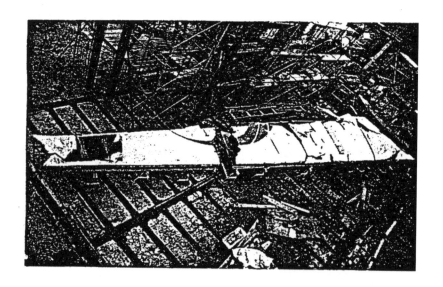

24   Reconstruction of aft pressure bulkhead

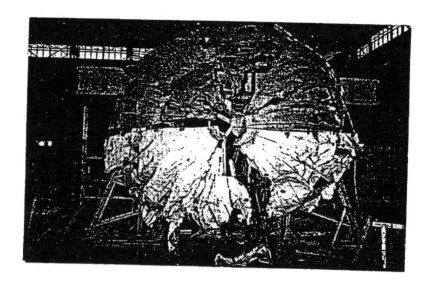

25 Pressure relief door

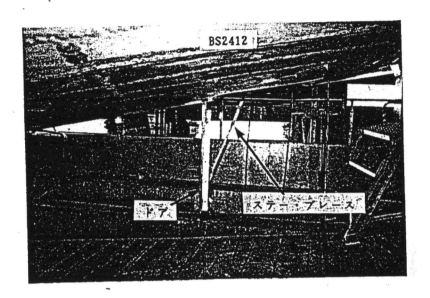

26 Pressure relief door (outside)

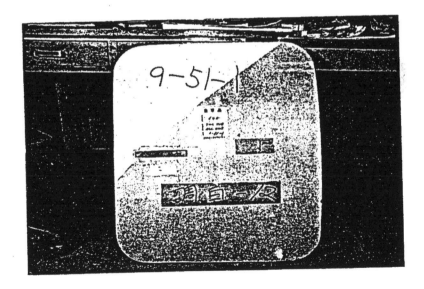

27   Pressure relief door (inside)

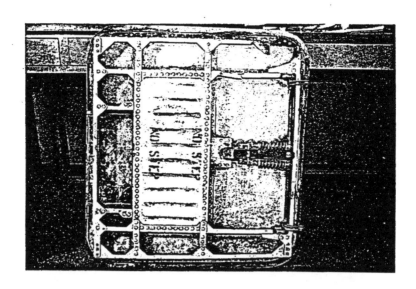

28   Deformation of skin at left door hinge
of pressure relief door

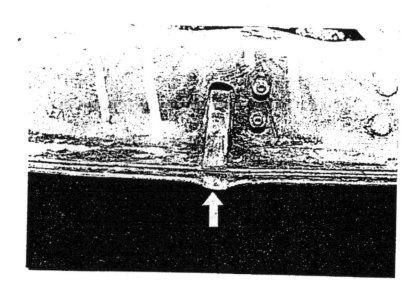

29   Deformation of skin at right door hinge·
of pressure relief door

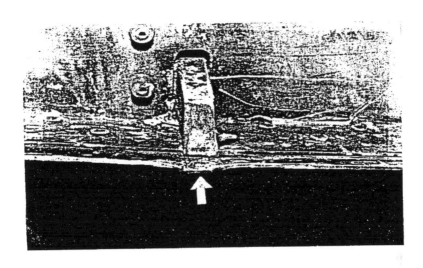

30   Abrasion on the shoulder nut of
the pressure relief door (left side)

これらの傷は、分解作業のため発生したものである。

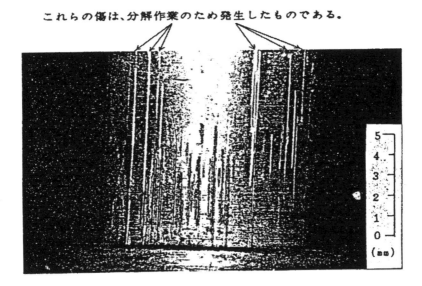

31   Abrasion on the shoulder nut of
      the pressure relief door (right side)

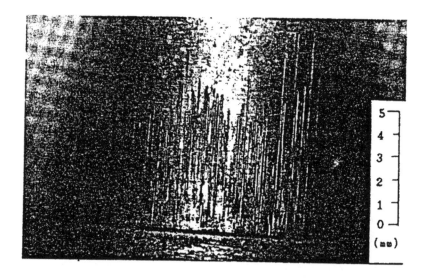

32   Pressure relief door latch mechanism

33   Rupture of BS2658 APU firewall
      installation parts between S1L and S1R

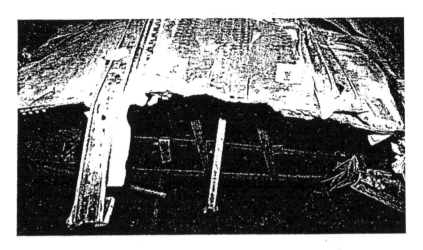

34   Hinge support channel of APU air intake duct

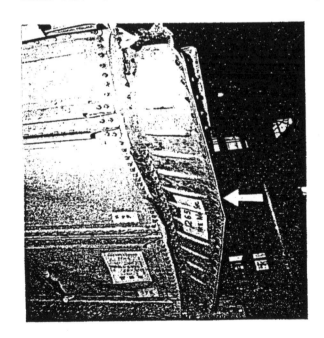

36   Damage of APU firewall installation section at
     BS2658 near S23R

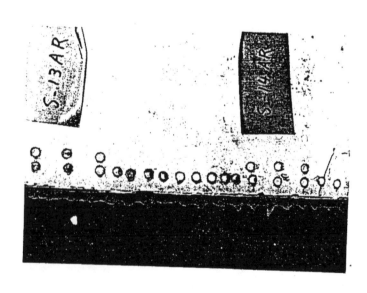

35   Damage of APU firewall installation section at
     BS2658 near S14AR

301

38 Warped doubler in APU firewall installation section at BS2658 near S25R

37 Damage of APU firewall installation section at BS2658 near S25R

40   Damage of APU firewall installation section at
      BS2658 near S14AL

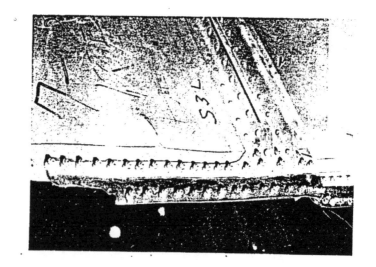

39 · Damage of APU firewall installation section at
     BS2658 near S3L

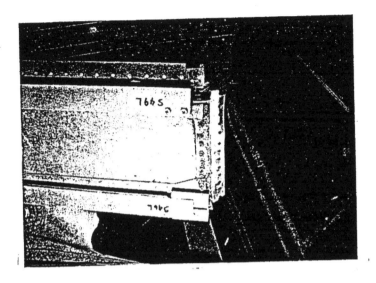

42   Damage of APU firewall installation section at
     BS2658 between S46L and S49L

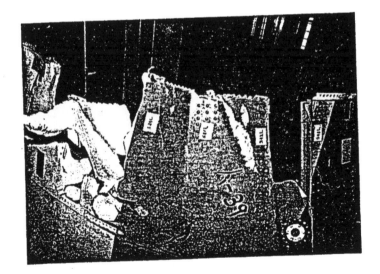

41   Damage of APU firewall installation section at
     BS2658 near S26L

43 Insulation materials that appear to have blown
through fastener holes in fuselage skin at BS2638

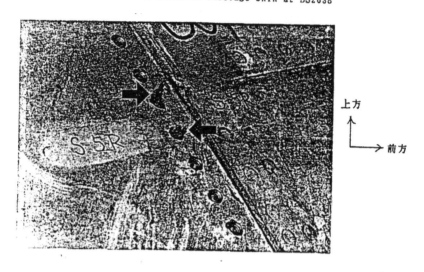

44 Fractured skin at vertical stabilizer forward
torque box front spar left chord

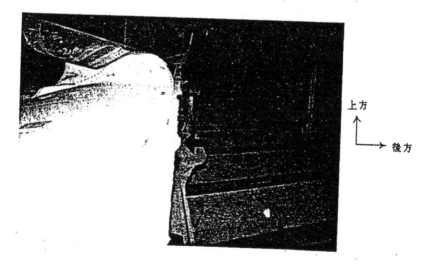

305

45   Fractured rivets at vertical stabilizer
      forward torque box front spar left chord

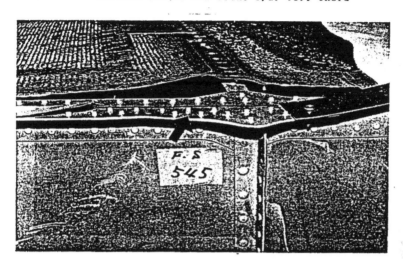

46   Fractured skin at vertical stabilizer forward
      torque box front spar right chord

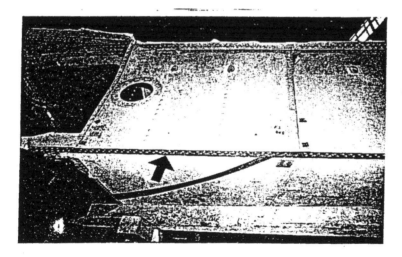

47   Fractured rivets at vertical stabilizer forward
      torque box spar right chord near FS545

48   Fractured skin at vertical stabilizer forward
      torque box front spar right chord near FS495

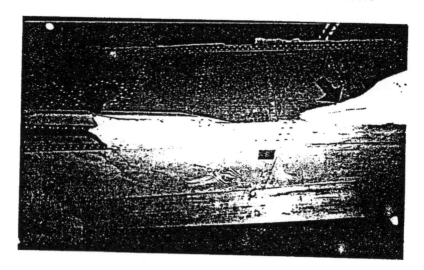

49   Vertical stabilizer front spar rib angle at FS545

50   Vertical stabilizer front spar rib angle at FS520

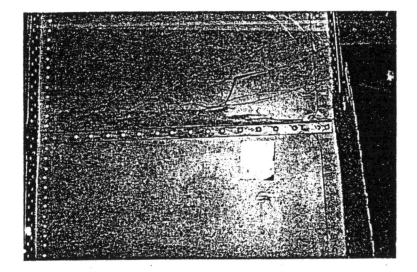

51　Vertical stabilizer front spar rib angle at FS195

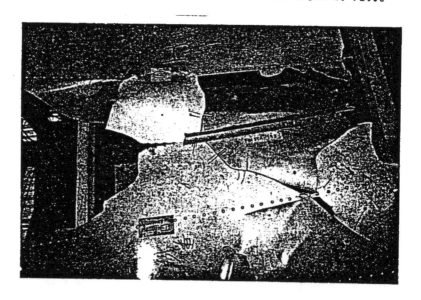

52　Vertical stabilizer front spar rib angle at FS169

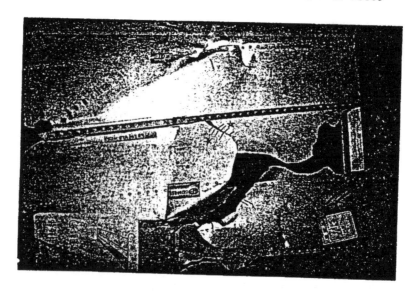

53   Scratches on vertical stabilizer front spar near FS445

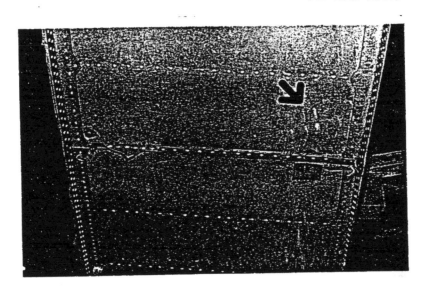

54   Scratches on vertical stabilizer front spar near FS420

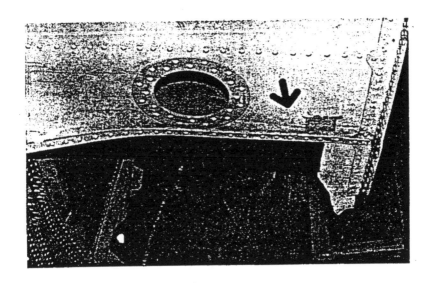

55   Scratches on vertical stabilizer front spar near FS220

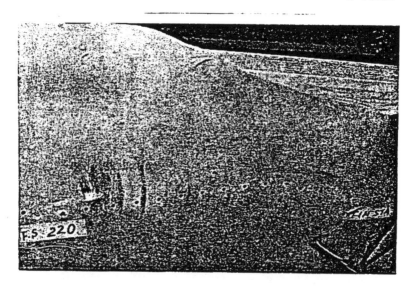

56   Scratches on vertical stabilizer front spar
     near FS169

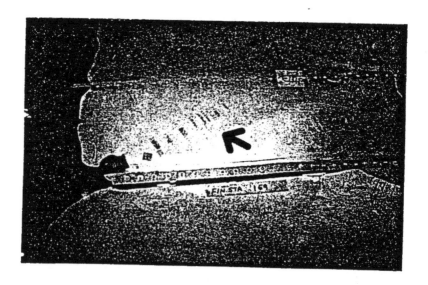

57   Scratches on vertical stabilizer front spar near FS143

58   Black substance adhering to right side skin of vertical
      stabilizer (1)

59 Black substance adhering to right side skin of vertical
    stabilizer (2)

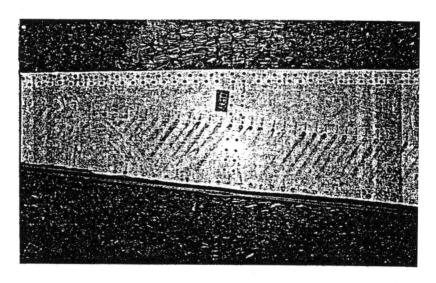

60 Fractured left horizontal stabilizer leading edge

313

61   Fractured right horizontal stabilizer leading edge

62   Fractured right horizontal stabilizer tip

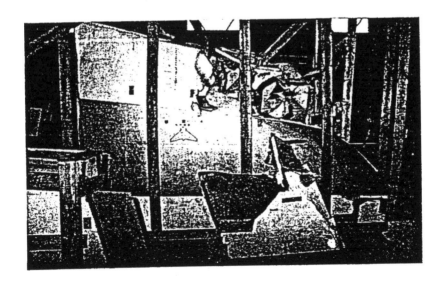

314

63   Fractured left horizontal stabilizer tip

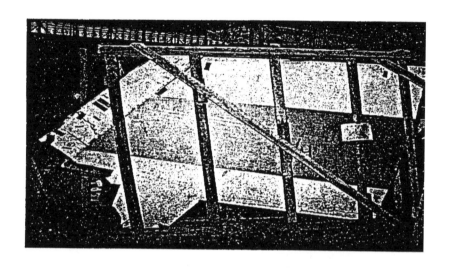

64   Aft pressure bulkhead part 1 (pressurized side)

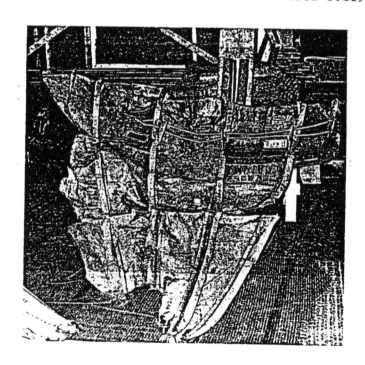

65   Aft pressure bulkhead part 1 (nonpressurized s

66   Aft pressure bulkhead part 2 (pressurized side)

67 Aft pressure bulkhead part 2 (nonpressurized side)

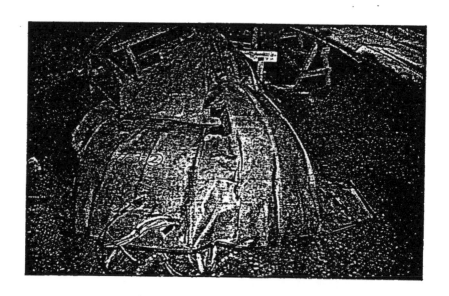

68 Aft pressure bulkhead part 2A (pressurized side)

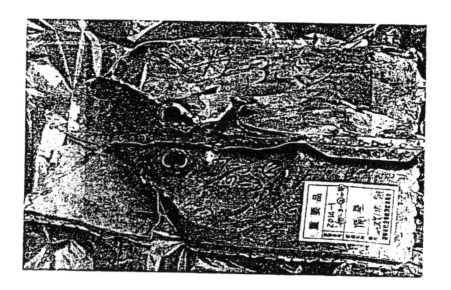

69   Aft pressure bulkhead part 2A (nonpressurized side)

70   Aft pressure bulkhead part 3 (pressurized side)

71　Aft pressure bulkhead part 3 (nonpressurized side)

72　Aft pressure bulkhead part 4 (pressurized side)

73　　Aft pressure bulkhead part 5 (pressurized side)

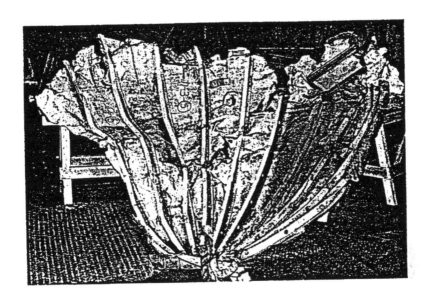

74　　Aft pressure bulkhead part 5 (nonpressurized side)

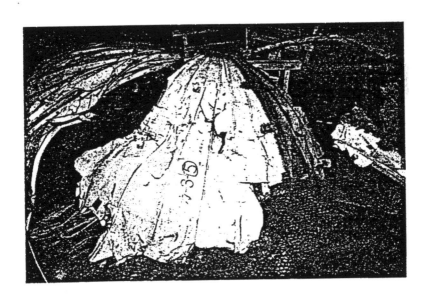

75　　Aft pressure bulkhead part 6 (pressurized side)

76　　Aft pressure bulkhead part 6 (nonpressurized side)

77　Buckling of aft pressure bulkhead (1)

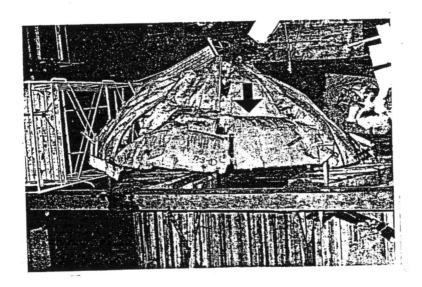

78　Buckling of aft pressure bulkhead (2)

79   Buckling of aft pressure bulkhead (3)

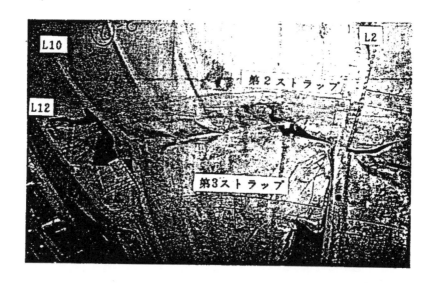

80   Buckling of aft pressure bulkhead (4)

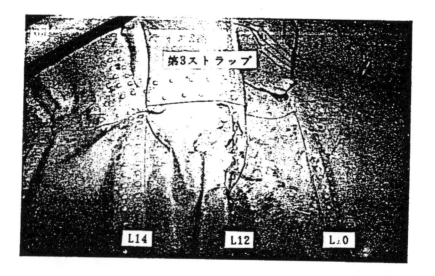

81   Buckling of aft pressure bulkhead (5)

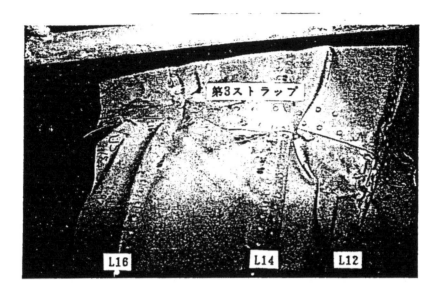

82   Buckling of aft pressure bulkhead (6)

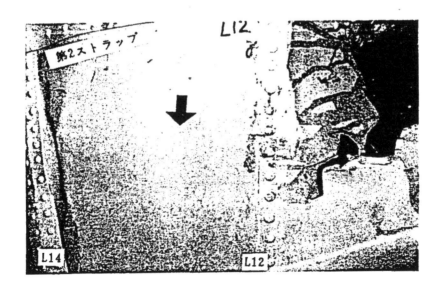

83   Buckling of aft pressure bulkhead (7)

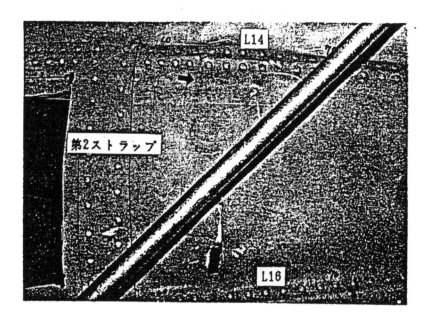

84 Aft pressure bulkhead L18 splice-lower web edge

85 Aft pressure bulkhead L18 splice-edge distance in vicinity of rivet No.29

86 Aft pressure bulkhead L18 splice-edge distance in vicinity of rivet No.84

87   Aft pressure bulkhead L18 splice-adherence of tabacco
nicotine in vicinity of rivet No.21 to No.24

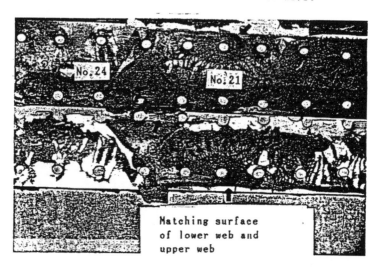

88   Aft pressure bulkhead L18 splice-adherence of tabacco
nicotine in vicinity of rivet No.39 to No.45

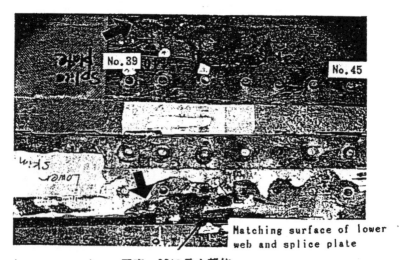

写真－92に示す部位

89 Aft pressure bulkhead L18 splice-adherence of tabacco nicotine in vicinity of rivet No.49 to No.55

Matching surface of lower web and splice plate

90 Aft pressure bulkhead L18 splice-adherence of tabacco nicotine in vicinity of rivet No.70 to No.72

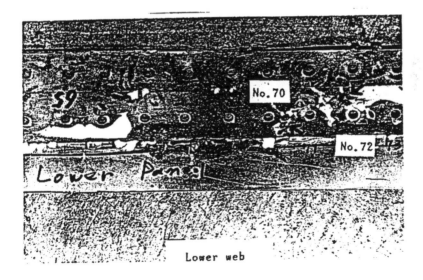

Lower web

91   Aft pressure bulkhead L18 splice-adherence of tabacco
      nicotine in vicinity of rivet No.75 to No.78

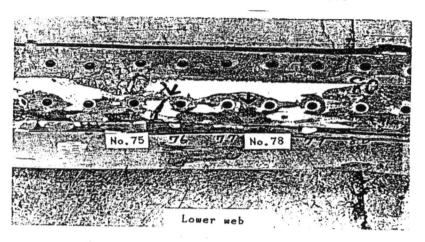

12   Aft pressure bulkhead L18 splice-adherence of tabacco
      nicotine in vicinity of rivet No.41

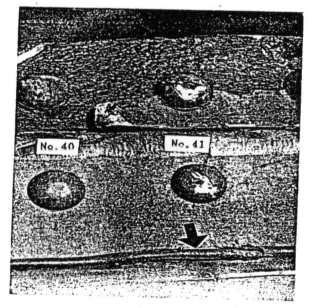

写真―88関連

93 Aft pressure bulkhead L18 splice-adherence of tabacco·
nicotine in vicinity of rivet No.50

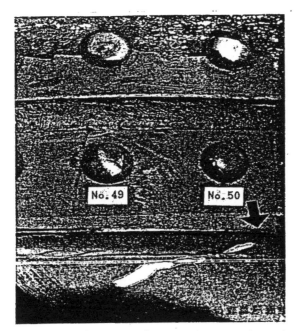

94 Fuselage frame at fuselage to vertical fin joint
(BS2436-2460)

Clump of head insulation materials found
reinforcement beam in fuselage frame.

330

95　Fuselage rupture at fuselage to vertical fin joint
　　(BS2484)

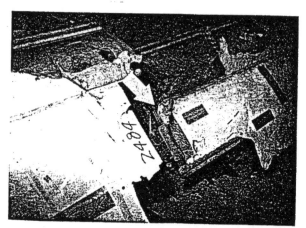

Heat insulation materials found in right skin. corner at base of aft rorque box.

96　Vertical stabilizer aft torque box-root of skin on
　　left side

Film covering heat insulation materials found
tangled in antenna cable, etc.

97 Central part of horizontal stabilizer center section

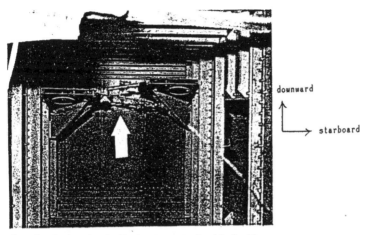

downward

starboard

Heat insulation found adhering to control cable inside.

98 Insulation materials adhering to fragments of ceiling of
    rearmost cabin lavatory (lavatory R)

332

99   Fracture of horizontal stabilizer jack screw (crash site)

100   Fracture of horizontal stabilizer jack screw
      (condition before teardown).

101 Damage to magnetic tape

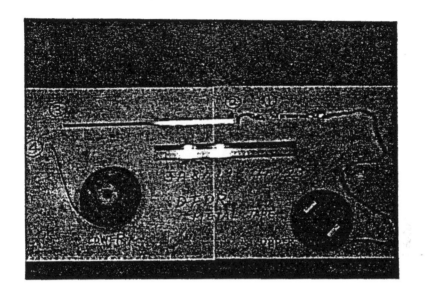

写真の中の③④は当該飛行以外の記録部分の損傷であり、
また、テープが白くなっている箇所はフラッシュ・ライト
のためである。

334

Photo-102 Microstructure of upper web skin

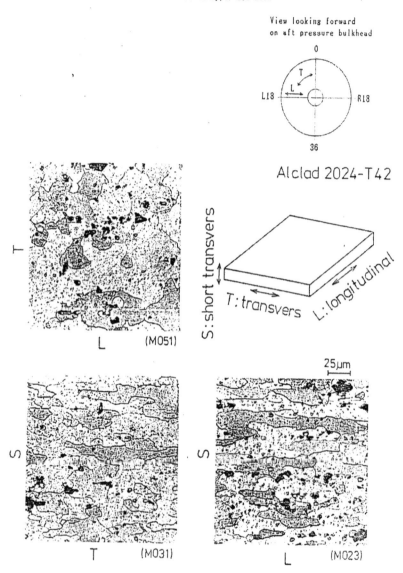

View looking forward
on aft pressure bulkhead

Alclad 2024-T42

335

336

The image cannot be displayed. Your computer may not have enough memory to open the image, or the image may have been corrupted. Restart your computer, and then open the file again. If the red x still appears, you may have to delete the image and then insert it again.

338

Photo-106 Microstructure of rivet

2017-T3

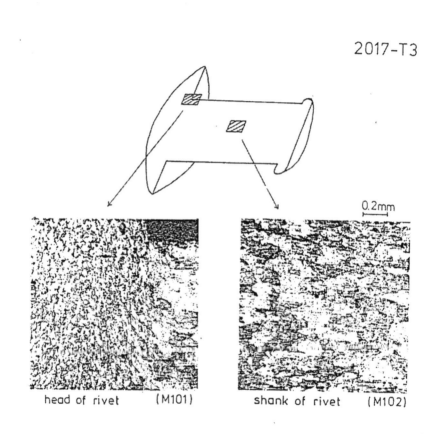

head of rivet   (M101)   shank of rivet   (M102)

0.2mm

339

Photo-109 Fracture surface of rivet hole No.34 inboard. Typical fatigue fracture facet. Fine striation patterns show stable crack propagation due to cyclic loading. The spacing of the striation gives the rate of propagation being 0.23μm per cycle at this point, 0.28mm from hole egde. Crack grew from left to right on the photo.

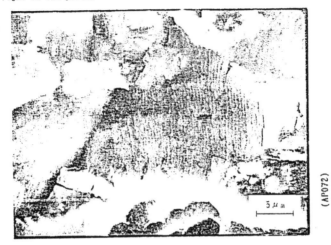

(AP072)

Photo-110 Fracture surface of rivet hole No.34 inboard. Striation spacing increases as crack growth rate increases, at 3.05mm from hole egde near the transition point shown photo-107.

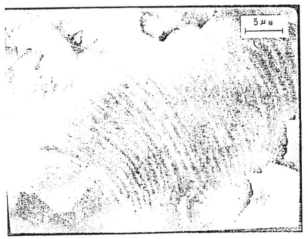

(AP120)

340

Photo-111 Fracture surface of rivet hole No.47 outboard. Fine striations observed at 0.32mm from egde of rivet hole No.47 outboard. Crack grew from right to left on the photo.

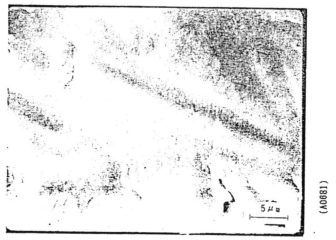

(A0681)

Photo-112 Fracture surface of rivet hole No.53 outboard. Clear striations observed at 1.00mm from egde of rivet hole No.53 outboard. Direction of crack growth is from lower right to upper left on the photo, as a result of local bending load.

(A0721)

341

Photo-113 Fracture surface of rivet hole No.66 outboard. Direction of crack growth is from upper right to lower left on the photo at 0.80mm from egde of rivet hole No.66 outboard.

Photo-114 Fracture surface of rivet hole No.90 inboard. Direction of crack growth is from left to right on the photo at 2.60mm from egde of rivet hole No.90 inboard.

Photo-115 Fracture aspect of No.1 strap. Lower fragment of the upper strap, aft view.

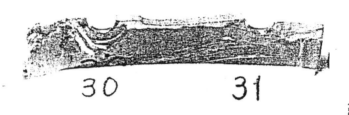

30   31

(■765)

Photo-116 Fracture aspect of No.2 strap. Lower fragment of the upper strap, aft view.

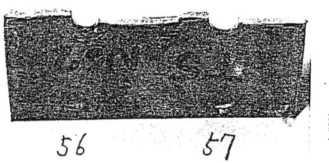

56   57

(■766)

343

Photo-117 Fracture aspect of No.3 strap. Lower fragment of the upper strap, aft view.

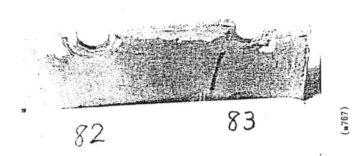

(m767)

Photo-118 Fracture aspect of No.4 strap. Lower fragment of the upper strap, front view.

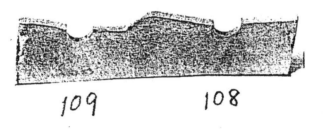

(m768)

344

Photo-119 Fracture aspect of stiffener L18, at rivet hole No.30.

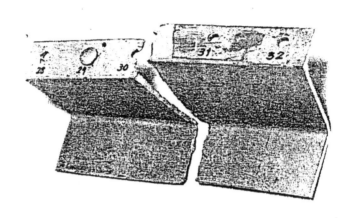

(㎜750)

Photo-120 Fracture aspect of stiffener L18, at rivet hole No.83.

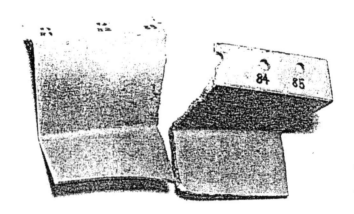

(㎜753)

345

Photo-121 Close-up view of stiffener L18, revealing shear mode fracture, at rivet hole No.30 outboard.

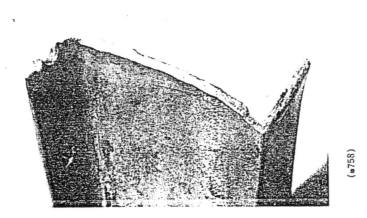

(m758)

Photo-122 Close-up view of stiffener L18, revealing shear mode fracture, at rivet hole No.83 outboard.

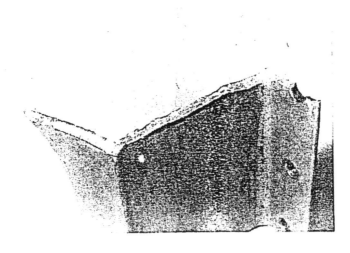

(m760)

346

Photo-123 A part of failure line in lower web through rivet-holes 84-?
Observation of upper fragment, aft view.

hole	hole	hole	hole
87	86	85	84
↓	↓	↓	↓

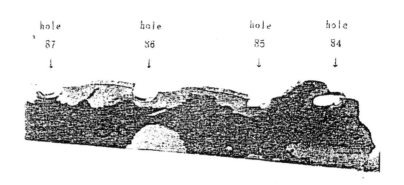

Photo-124 The accident aircraft flying over Okutama.

ATTACHED ATTACHMENTS

]

Attachment 1   Repair of damage caused by Accident at Osaka International Airport,
in June 1978

JA8119 received damage to part of its airframe during landing at Osaka
International Airport in June 1978. The aircraft was ferried to Tokyo
International Airport, where repairs were carried out.
The following investigation was conducted on the repair work of damage caused by
the accident:

1   Summary of the Accident at Osaka International Airport(*)
The aircraft, when landing at Osaka International Airport at approximately
1501 hours June 2, 1978 as JAL scheduled flight number 115 (Tokyo to Osaka), was
substantially damaged by contact of its lower part of the aft fuselage with the
runway, but no fire occurred. In this accident two passengers were seriously
injured and 23 passengers were slightly injured.
The total flight hours of the aircraft up to this accident was 8,832:25 hours.
(*1)   refer to Aircraft Accident Report on JAL's JA8119,
Boeing 747SR—100 (dated February 27, 1979)

2   Damage to the Aircraft
The aircraft was inspected in accordance with part of the Hard Landing
Inspection Phase 1 and 2 in JAL's Maintenance Regulations, and a more detailed
inspection was conducted on the damaged portions.

2.1   Major damage was as follows:
(see Photo—1 and —2, and Attached Figure—1 and —2, of Attachment 1)

(1)   Horizontal stabilizer control system
    (a) frame lower half chord and web of BS2460 and 2484   damaged

    (b) BS2484—2598 lower shear panel   cracked for
    about 2.1 meters

(2)   Lower chord section and web of horizontal   ruptured
stabilizer hinge support structure bulkhead (BS2598)

(3)   Aft pressure bulkhead dome (4 to 8 O'clock) webs   deformed

(4)   Lower section of frame BS2126, 2280, 2300 and 2340   deformed and/or
cracked

(5)   Right lower portion of frame BS2377, 2397 and 2412   deformed

(6)   Lower section of frame BS2436, 2506—2577   deformed and cracked

(7)   Lower section of frame BS2618, 2638 AND 2658   deformed and cracked

(8)   Both sides of APU door frame   cracked

—1—

(9)	Bottom frame and skin of tail cone aft section (BS2742—2792)	ruptured
(10)	Lower section of bulkhead BS2658	ruptured
(11)	Aft drain mast	ruptured
(12)	APU battery compartment door	deformed
(13)	Bottom surface skin of fuselage BS2100—2792	scratched and attrited
(14)	Both wing gear equalizer rod and truck beam Both wing gear equalizer rod and lower part of shock strut inner cylinder	damaged by contact "
(15)	APU aft mount assembly	deformed

3 After provisional repairs and maintenance were done by JAL at Osaka International Airport, the aircraft was ferried to Tokyo International Airport, on June 15, 1978.

4 It was decided the repairs of the aircraft be conudcted at Tokyo International Airport by the Boeing Company, the manufacturer of the the aircraft, and a repair contract (＊2) was concluded between JAL and the Boeing Company.

(＊2) The following letter of agreement was exchanged in connection with the contract:

Repair Agreement No.6—1171—7—2757, dated June 10, 1978
A partial revision was made later on details of this agreement.

4.1 The outline of agreed items on the repairs was as follows:
4.1.1 Boeing will accomplish the repair of the aircraft in JAL hangar facility at Tokyo International Airport.

4.1.2 Major repairs are as follows:
 (1) remove and replace of some of component materials of Section 46 (Fuselage of BS1480—2360)
 (2) remove and replace of some of component materials of Section 48 (Fuselage of BS2360—2792) (＊3)
 With regard to the aft pressure bulkhead, the work involve_ replacement of the lower half (including the collector ring), removal/replacement of APU for inspection, etc.

 (3) replacement of some parts of the main landing gear
 (4) hard landing check, fuselage pressure test, and other necessary system functional tests.
  (＊3) Replacement of the pressure relief door is included, although it is not

−2−

prescribed explicitly in the agreement.

4.1.3 Boeing will procure necessary parts and materials as determined by Boeing.

4.1.4 Boeing performs removal of certain equipment for functional check by JAL and reinstalls it on the airplane.

4.1.5 Boeing submits to JAL results of the repairs and inspections in FAA Approval Form 337 (＊4).

(＊4) FAA Approval Form 337 is a format for the report to be submitted to FAA when repair/alteration work has completed by a FAA-approved repair station, for the purpose of obtaining legal authorization for returning the repaired aircraft to operation in the USA.

4.1.6 Boeing will perform the work and services in accordance wih engineering and repair techniques established under FAA approved procedures to be inspected by Boeing personal to Boeing standards.

The repair plan above is based on the idea that major structural parts which were damaged be replaced by production parts for use in new aircraft, with the same production joint as for the new aircraft.

5 Prior to start of the repairs, on June 15, 1978 the application for the inspection of repair or alteration was submitted to Ministry of Transport from JAL.

6 In parallel with the maintenance work in progress, No.5C maintenance and modification work covering more than 50 items were conducted by JAL.

7 The outline of the repairs were as follows:
7.1 The repairs were conducted by a repair team dispatched from the Boeing Company, and composed of more than 40 persons involving engineers, inspectors and other members.

7.2 The repairs were conducted during a period of June 17 to July 11, 1978, in which June 24 to July 1 was for the aft pressure bulkhead.

7.3 The repairs for the aft pressure bulkhead (including other related work) were conducted as follows:
(1) Besides the usual jack support, jacks with a load meter (two each for the left and right, 4 in total) were supported at BS2200 and 2509.5 and the jack loads (＊5) were monitored and adjusted so as to prevent deformation to the fuselage after removal of a portion of the lower section of the aft fuselage for the repair work.
(＊5) The jack load was adjusted to a preset prescribed value, but no measurement was made of deformation in the supported condition.

(2) The lower half (lower than WL274, and including Y chord) of the aft

pressure bulkhead and the collector ring were removed.

(3) In the work to attach the new lower half of the aft pressure bulkhead, firstly, the lower half of the bulkhead was attached to the airframe at the Y chord portion, then, to connect it to the upper half of the aft pressure bulkhead on the airframe side, rivet holes were bored along the web edge of the lower half of the bulkhead, making them match the existing rivet holes of the upper half bulkhead.

(4) In the inspection by the inspector of the repair team after the completion of the work above, edge margin of less than value specified in the structural repair manual was found around the rivet holes for almost all area of L18 joint on the left side of the lower half of the aft pressure bulkhead.

(5) To compensate for the discrepancy above, a rework disposition was given from the engineer of the repair team that a splice plate be inserted, as shown on the left side of Attached Figure—3 of Attachment 1, between webs insufficient in edge margin.

(6) Irrespective of such rework instructions having been issued, in the actual repair work, a short splice plate and a filler were used as shown on the right side of the attached figure above, instead of a single splice plate, with the result that the connection for two bays between the 1st strap and the 3rd strap on the left side became a one-row riveted connection, instead of the two-row riveted web connection to be made between the upper half and the lower half of the aft pressure bulkhead. The splice plate and the filler were manufactured from the removed old bulkhead.

This work was carried out on June 26, and completion inspection by the inspector of the repair team on June 27, but the inspector could not find the above results.

(7) After the lower half of the aft pressure bulkhead was installed, the collector ring was then installed.

(8) In the inspection by the inspector of the repair team, oil canning was discovered at six locations on webs of the aft pressure bulkhead, as shown in Attached Figure—4 of Attachment 1, out of which three were within the allowance of the 747 Structure Repair Manual, but on the other three the following repairs were conducted:

As to the oil can on the web between the 1st strap and the 4th strap on the lower edge on the right side of the upper half of the bulkhead, it was planned to apply a doubler to cover this portion, and actually the doubler as shown in the figure was used for two bays. The oil can between the 3rd strap and the 4th strap was judged afterwards as within the allowance of the Repair Manual. The doubler was manufactured from the removed bulkhead, and was fixed by rivets at 1.5 inch intervals.

As to two small oil can area near the outer margin on the right side of the lower half of the bulkhead, the corrective action was made by riveting a short strap andan L-shaped angle.

(9) An investigation of the wreckage indicated that the edge margin was less than drawing requirement on some portions of the rivet row between the 3rd strap on the left side and the collector ring in the juncture of the upper half and the lower half of the bulkhead (refer to 2.15.1.5(5)).

7.4 As a test relating to the repair of the aft pressure bulkhead, a pressure leak test was conducted on July 9 to investigate the leakage of pressurized air from the repaired portions. In the test, the decrease in pressure with time was measured, the inner pressure being applied up to at 4 psi in accordance with the Boeing's standard. It was ascertained that the pressure decrease time was virtually within the limit value. The production step to apply a 12 psi load was not accomplished since it was not on FAA requirement.

8 Test flights were carried out on July 10 and 11 by JAL with attendance of airworthiness engineers of Civil Aviation Bureau. The test flights were made with respect to therepairs conducted under the charge of the Boeing Company.

In the test flights, no discrepancies were found of the structural repairs conducted under the charge of the Boeing Company.

9 Inspection of the structural repairs conducted under the charge of the Boeing Company was made in accordance with the standard of the company. Records of the repairs and inspections were described in FAA Form 337 and confirmation of its completion was made as of July 11.

1 0 The acceptance inspection by JAL was conducted as follows:
JAL carried out, as the acceptance inspection of the repairs conducted under the charge of the Boeing Company, confirmation on whether each repair item had been accomplished as contracted, attendance at system function tests after the repairs, and confirmation of functions by test flight, and check on work records submitted by the Boeing Company, and accepted on July 11.

1 1 Inspection by Civil Aviation Bureau was conducted as follows:
Civil Aviation Bureau on application from JAL of inspection on repair or modification in accordance with the Civil Aviation Law, made inspection on the repair plan, the process of repair and the condition after completion of the work.

This involves checks by the airworthiness engineers of CAB on the repair plan through reviewing the drawings submitted from the applicant, checks on the repair process based on work records, as well as inspection on the condition after completion of the work such as general external inspection, functional tests on the ground and flight test.

Check for drawings was made on the portion jointed with a splice plate of the structural material, which had been divided into two halves for convenience of air transport, for the replaced portion of the side longeron of section 48 of the aft portion of the fuselage. With regard to the repairs of L18 splice of the aft pressure bulkhead, confirmation of the work records was made after the repair work was completed in the same manner as other repaired portions.

At the first test flight, attended by the airworthiness engineers, discrepancies for travel of the horizontal stabilizer, which had been removed for maintenace, etc. were found. So, flight was again carried out after replacing stabilizer jack screw, etc.

During the test flight, no discrepancies of the aircraft structure were found.

As of July 12, the aircraft was judged to have passed the inspection of repair or alteration, subsequent to the issuance of the certificate from the Boeing Company in accordance with FAA procedures and the completion of the acceptance inspection by JAL on the repairs by the Boeing Company.

355

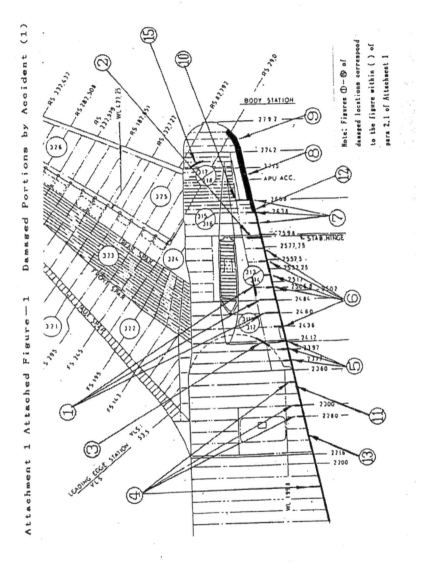

Attachment 1 Attached Figure—1 Damaged Portions by Accident (1)

-7-

356

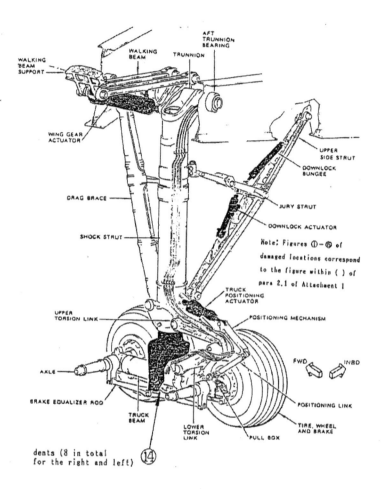

Note: Figures ①-⑮ of damaged locations correspond to the figure within ( ) of para 2.1 of Attachment 1

dents (8 in total for the right and left) ⑭

357

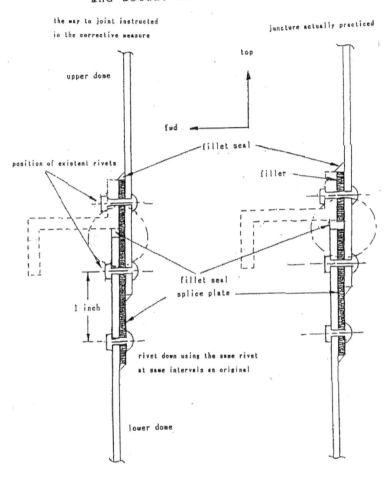

the way to joint instructed
in the corrective measure

juncture actually practiced

top

upper dome

fwd

fillet seal

position of existent rivets

filler

fillet seal
splice plate

1 inch

rivet down using the same rivet
at same intervals as original

lower dome

-9-

358

Attachment 1 Photo-2
Lower portion of the APU firewall

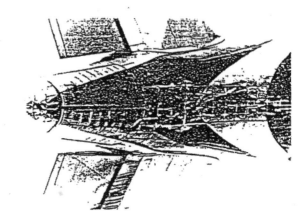

Attachment 1 Photo-1
Under surface of the empennage

Attachment 2 Status of Operations, Maintenance and Discrepancies of the
Accident Aircraft after the repairs in 1978

1. Status of Operations
1.1 Flying hours and number of flights of the accident aircraft were as follows:

Flying hours after No.5C maintenance in July 1978   16,195:59 hours
Number of flights   "   12,319
Total flying hours after manufacture   25,030:18 hours
Total number of flights   "   18,835

1.2 Main flight routes of the aircraft for domestic flight were as follows:
Between:

Tokyo — Okinawa   Sapporo — Osaka   Osaka — Fukuoka
Tokyo — Fukuoka   Sapporo — Fukuoka Osaka — Okinawa
Tokyo — Sapporo
Tokyo — Osaka

1.3 Main flight routes of the aircraft for international flight were as follows:
Between:
Osaka — Guam

1.4 In operations during this period, neither irregular operations nor
inappropriate matters to be mentioned occurred except for those described in paras.
1.5 and 1.6 below.

1.5 An irregular operation at Chitose Airport on August 19, 1982
When the aircraft made a go around on Runway 18L at Chitose Airport on
August 19 1982, No.4 engine pod contacted the runway. The aircraft thereafter
changed runway to 36R and landed.
(1) Damaged parts by this irregular operation were as follows:
(a) three bends on the fan reverser door link (5—7 O'clock positions)
(b) wear damage to the lower side of the fan cowl
(c) wear damage to the lower side of the engine primary reverser door

(2) The aircraft, after a provisional capair was conducted, was ferried to
Tokyo International Airport, where No.4 engine, and the side cowls both right and
left and the fan cowl of the engine were replaced.

1.6 An investigation was conducted on the flight records of the aircraft (the
cockpit flight log and the cabin flight log) in the latest half year (February to
August, 1985) for flight discrepancies in terms of the items below:
(1) vib.ation, disturbance and irregular sound of airframe
(2) faults such as structural deformation of the aft fuselage or the aft
passenger cabin
(3) malfunctions of the vertical fin and the rudder control systems
(4) malfunctions of the horizontal stabilizer, the elevator control systems, and
the stabilizer trim control system
(5) malfunctions of pressurization, air-conditioning, oxygen supply, and alert
system

(6) malfunctions of APU and its control system
(7) others (lavatory door)

1.6.1 Results of the investigation were as follows. and it was found that corrective measures had been taken for each discrepancy.
(1) Vibration. disturbance and irregular sound of airframe (15 cases)
There were 15 cases caused by air leak from the door seal. the cooling blower and for other reasons.

(2) Faults such as structural deformation of the aft fuselage or the aft passenger cabin
None

(3) Malfunctions of the vertical fin and the rudder control system (2 cases)
In flight 902 of June 18. there was a discrepancy that with the upper rudder at the neutral position the lower rudder indicated 2° left on the ground as well as in flight. A check made at Tokyo International Airport showed that the difference between the upper and the lower rudder. and the error of the indicator were within the allowances. Inspection on the seal between the upper and the lower rudder was carried over until the aircraft parked at Tokyo International Airport after it was operated thereafter three times as scheduled flight on the same day. The inspection was conducted upon termination of flight 130 at Tokyo International Airport. As a result of the inspection. the rudder position indicator was replaced because the indicator's pointer caught. In addition, the functions and neutral position of the rudder were checked and lubrication oil was applied on the contact surface of theseal between the upper and the lower rudder.

Furthermore. a discrepancy was reported on flight 101 of July 15 that with the rudder pedal and the rudder trim both in neutral position. the lower rudder was not brought into the neutral position on the rudder indicator. Test of the yaw damper. functional test of the rudder and inspection on the lower rudder position were carried out.

(4) Malfunctions of the horizontal stabilizer. the elevator control system. and the stabilizer trim control system.
None

(5) Malfunctions of pressurization. air-conditioning. oxygen supply and alert system (7 cases).
There were 6 discrepancies reported of the low pressure of the oxygen bottle for crew (the oxygen bottles replaced). and a discrepancy reported that the autopilot warning horn sometimes became unresettable (The flight mode annunciator on copilot side was replaced).

(6) Malfunctions of APU and its control system (2 cases)
There were two discrepancies that it was impossible to start APU because APU door light was on (APU door actuator replaced). and that the APU door did not move normal (APU door actuator replaced)

(7) Others (Lavatory doors) (33 cases)
There were 33 cases of discrepancy on lavatory doors reported. The cases were related to opening or closing of the door and locks, except for 2 cases. The breakdown of cases relating to opening or closing of the door by the location of the lavatory was: 19 cases for location S, 8 for location Q, one for location R, 3 for location B, one for location J, and one for location U1 (refer to Attached Figure of Attachment 2 for location of lavatory).

1.6.2 Investigation on malfunctions of the lavatory at location S
JAL conducted the following investigation on malfunctions of the lavatory at S location:
The malfunction concerning opening and shutting of the door of the lavatory at location S occurred only on Osaka—Guam route, and it has been also reported by other aircraft operating on the same route. The status of the occurrence during October 1 to December 31, 1985 on three representative aircraft were as follows:

Registration mark	Number of cases of malfunction	Measures taken
JA8121	5 (*1)	Trim of lower edge 2 cases, tightened fastener 1 case, inspection 2 cases
JA8117	11 (*2)	Trim of lower edge 1 case, tightened fastener 4 cases, latch adjusted 2 cases, inspection 1 case, others 3 cases (*3)
JA8126	1 (*4)	Others 1 case

(*1) one case occurred 20 minutes after take-off.
(*2) one case occurred 10 minutes after take-off, returned normal at 10,000 feet.
(*3) in two cases, magazines and newspapers were relocated.
(*4) occurred only on the ground.

The lavatory at location S is constructed of a module, connected with the adjacent T location lavatory at the upper and the forward portion, and connected with the aft coat room at the upper portion by rod. And the S location lavatory is easily affected by deformation of the coat room, because the aft coat room's side panel is near the S lavatory's door jamb.

On the Osaka—Guam flights ordinarily the following passenger cabin service supplies were loaded in the aft coat room at the time of departure from Osaka:

Leftside coat room | three pillows about 2 lbs on shelves, dry ice 88 lbs under shelves, about 90 lbs in total

Rightside coat room | ear phone 550 pieces 66 lbs on shelves, newspaper 55 lbs and magazines 200 copies 114 lbs under shelves, about 240 lbs in total

The loading of the cabin service supplies on the flight had been put into practice since several years before, and the amount carried increased in mid of the period. The load limit of the aft coat room is prescribed by the Boeing Company as 110 lbs on shelves and 200 lbs at the coat rods, and the loading under shelves are prohibited.

The gap between the door and the jamb of the S lavatory was measured on the ground simulating loading conditions of the supplies above, with a cabin pressurization of 6.5 psi, using JA8117 on which malfunctions were often reported of the S location lavatory. The test results indicated that the gap becomes small when the supplies are loaded, or the cabin ispressurized, and much smaller when both are applied at the same time, and the doorbecomes uneasy to open or shut. If there is no loading in the aft coat room, the opening and shutting of the door is not affected by the pressurization in the cabin.

In a flight of JA8117 on the Osaka—Guam route, an investigation was made on the influence to the door gap of the supplies loaded in the aft coat room and the cabin pressurization. The results obtained was the same as the tests results on the ground.

The same investigation was carried out on the T location lavatory located symmetrically to the S location lavatory, but no influences to opening or shutting of the door were found, possibly because the way the door jamb of the T location lavatory is loaded is different from the above case due to difference in weight, shape and loaded place of the articles loaded in the coat room.

JAL based on above results, further made sure of prohibition of loading of articles under shelves in the coat room throughout the company.

According to the JAL, 5 aircraft on Guam flight during April through September 1986 were checked, and there were no discrepancies of the door of the S location lavatory

1.7 Pressurization of Passenger Cabin in Flight

Pressurized structures of Boeing 747SR is designed in accordance with establised standards on such premise that the maximum pressure differential of 9.0 psi applies in normal operations. The cabin pressure selector switch to set up the cabin pressure pressurization level can be selected to either 8.9 psi or 6.9 psi as an established value (the maximum pressure differential). The selector switch can be selected to 6.9 psi in case that cruising altitude is low (short range flight), and to 8.9 psi in case the cruising altitude is high (long range flight).

However, JAL had operated the aircraft always with the selector switch set to 8.9 psi, in which case the pressure differential in operation would be 8.74 psi at altitude 35,000 ft, and 7.36 psi at altitude 18,000.

JAL made a study, at the time of the introduction of Boeing 747SR, on the fatigue life of the pressurized fuselage under its standard operational mode estimated. As a result of the study, JAL estimated that the fatigue life would be about 6 % shorter in case the cabin pressurization selector switch is set always to 8.9 psi than it is in case the switch is selected either 8.9 psi or 6.9 psi depending on the cruising altitude.

2. Inspection and Maintenance
2.1 Set-up of Maintenance Procedures for Boeing 747
Generally speaking, with regard to the maintenance procedure for a large transport category civil aircraft developed in the USA, the regulatory authorities that issued the type certificate of the aircraft would make up fundamental reference materials for the inspection and maintenance with cooperation of the aircraft manufacturer and leading air carriers. Based thereon, the manufacturer prepares more detailed reference materials.

Aircraft operators of each country, based on these reference materials, set forth their own manuals on inspection and maintenance taking into consideration their own systems, technology, facilities, etc. and put them into effect, with the approval of the regulatory authorities of the country.

2.2 Inspection and maintenance system of Boeing 747LR
In Boeing 747 series, 747LR—100 (for long range, hereinafter referred to as "LR" to distinguish it from SR) was firstly developed, and brought into operation in 1970 in the USA. Prior to the inauguration, ATA (American Transport Association) established the 747 Maintenance Steering Group with the cooperation of the FAA, and major aircraft manufacturers and leading air carriers, and drew up in 1968 the handbook "MSG—1" to be basic to inspection and maintenance procedures of Boeing 747. JAL participated in the work to drew up the document. Subsequently, the FAA established MRB (Maintenance Review Board) for 747 with the co-operation of the Boeing Company and air carriers, and draw up the MRB Report which should provide a guide line in case an operator introduces the aircraft. JAL was also a member of this board. Meanwhile, the Boeing Company, adding Boeing's recommeded items to MRB Report, prepared the MPD (Maintenance Planning Document) as reference materials to the operators of 747 which set forth their own maintenance regulations.

Based on thse materials JAL estab.ished their maintenance regulations of 747LR, pursuant to their introduction of the aircraft, and laid down the following manuals as attachments to the maintenance regulations which prescribe in details items of maintenance, substantial methods of maintenance and other related matters of 747LR. The regulations and the attachments have been revised as necessary thereafter with reference to the operational experience of many air carriers.
Maintenance System Manual (MSM)
Maintenance Requirement Manual (MRM)

Aircraft Release Specification (ARS)
Aircraft Maintenance Manual (AMM)
Structual Repair Manual (SRM)
Power Plant Overhaul Manual (POM)
Component Overhaul Manual (COM)
Standard Process Manual (SPM)
Material Handling Manual (MHM)

2.3 Inspection and Maintenance System of Boeing 747SR
The maintenance system for SR is fundamentally the same as that for LR.
However, due to difference in part of the structure as well as in way of
operation, there is difference between them on some items of the maintenance
regulations and the attachment manuals thereto.

The Boeing Company issued in 1983 the SID (Supplemental Structural Inspection
Document), with reference to methods of MSG—3 and by applying the concept of the
newly developed damage tolerant design, for the purpose of the life extension of
the LR aircraft, while ensuring the safety and reliability of LR aircraft already
in use. Based on this SID, JAL supplemented the maintenance items of the LR
aircraft with the SID maintenance items in 1984.

The above-mentioned SID does not require its application to SR aircraft, but
JAL applied the SID to their SR aircraft, and 95 items were added to the
maintenance items of SR at the same time as LR in 1984, for the reasons that the
pressurized structure of the fuselage of SR is fundamentally the same as for LR,
and that the means to operate the pressurization is almost the same.

The SID of the Boeing Company for SR was published in April 1986, but JAL
did not alter the SID maintenance items which had been brought into effect.

2.4 Maintenance Procedures of the Accident Aircraft
For Boeing 747SR-100 aircraft involving the accident aircraft, JAL adopted
the following divisions (＊5) of maintenance, and items of maintenance work
prescribed in their maintenance regulations and attachment manuals thereto have
been conducted by the division.

(＊5) Although there are maintenance items corresponding to "B" maintenance for B747SR and B747LR, in case of SR the work items corresponding thereto are dispersed in "A" maintenance.

Maintenance Division	Major work contents
T (for every flight)	Pre-flight Inspection: Overall external inspection, fuel supply, lubrication oil check, tyre pressure check, and dealing with flight squawks
A (for every 250 hours)	Inspection for external conditions: Inspection on conditions of engines and their accessories, landing gear, movable surface, fuselage, wings, cockpit, and passenger cabin, and dealing with flight discrepancies
C (for every 3,000 hours)	Detailed Inspection: Function test of systems, operation test, inspection on status of piping, wiring and cables, scheduled replacement of landing gear, inspection on airframe structure, and dealing with flight discrepancies
H (for every 3~4 years)	Planned modification of aircraft, recoating of the exterior, etc

Inspection items newly added pursuant to the application of the SID are incorporated into "C" maintenance or "H" maintenance above depending on its inspection interval required.

2.4.1 T Maintenance
"T" maintenance includes post-landing check, check at intermediary stops, and pre-flight check. An overall exterior check is made visually for detection of significant defects such as oil leak. In the post-landing check, the cockpit flight log and the cabin flight log are reviewed for flight squawks, and if any, inspection and repairs are conducted for the portions concerned.

The post-flight check is usually made by three personnel in about 50 minutes.

2.4.2 A Maintenance
This maintenance is usually done within 250 flying hours. As shown in the table above, it is an inspection and maintenance mainly by visual check on parts operating in flight such as engines, landing gear, control systems, and includes internal checks under the conditions that easily openable or removable doors and covers are kept opened. As to structures, only overall external visual inspection is made. Maintenance, repair, or replacement is made on faults discovered by inspection.
"A" maintenance is usually carried out by a team of 12 personnel for about 7 hours.

2.4.3 C maintenance

This maintenance is usually conducted within 3,000 flying hours. It consists mainly of inspection and maintenance of airframe structure, and check on functions and maintenance of each system, including detailed check on each part. Among the maintenance items, there are some items which are effected once at intervals of several "C" maintenances.

The structural inspection is done mainly by visual check from the outside, as well as from the inside with doors and covering removed. The means of the visual checks is described in detail in para. 2.6.(1).

The man-hour required for C maintenance varies with the number of times C maintenance was conducted to the aircraft, but the recent statistics of several cases on SR indicated 7—12 days by 60—90 people.

(1) The maintenance items relating to the aft pressure bulkhead are conducted in accordance with the following work cards:

Name of work card (card number)	Contents of work	Work interval
STR INSP—L.H/R.H FUSE EXTERIOR (7TK8251) (7TK8252)	exterior inspection on skin and stringer splice above stringer S—6 in BS2360 crown area (G2)(＊6)	every 4C
INT INSP—CBN AFT END STR (7SK7303)	interior inspection on skin and stringer splice above stringer S—6 in BS2360 crown area (G2)	sampling 16%/20,000 hours
STR INSP—L.H/R.H FUSE EXTERIOR (7TK8091) (7TK8092)	inspection on BS2360 pressure bulkhead and its installation status as well as the surrounding fuselage skin (G2)	every time
INT INSP—TAIL COMPT STR FWD (7SK7301)	internal inspection of forward portion of empennage structure(G2) ① BS2360 pressure bulkhead and fitting bolts ② backside stringer splices of BS2360 bulkhead from S—12L to S—12R	sampling 20%/20,000 hours
INSP&CORR PREV— TAIL COMP STR(SR) (7TS8375)	corrosion inspection on lower portion of aft surface of pressure bulkhead (20 inches high from bottom) and spray of T—9(corrosion preventive)	every 2C
INT INSP—FUSE BS 2360 PRESS DOME (7EK3381)	inspection on all circumference of Y chord and webs of BS2360 pressure bulkhead (around Y chord	SID item 30,000 cycles

—19—

and rear flange of web fixture)(G2)

INSP – AFT LAV UNDER STRUCTURE (7ZK2090)	corrosion inspection on structures under floor from No.5 door to aft pressure bulkhead, and spray of T9	every 6 years
CORR INSP – EMP INTERIOR (7TK7362)	corrosion inspection on inside of fuselage aft of pressure bulkhead (BS2360 – 2484)	every time

(＊6) For mark G, refer to visual inspection level in para.2.6.(1)

The work of the work cards 7SK7301, 7SK7303 and 7EK3381, sampling and SID items, had not been conducted for the accident aircraft, because its implementation date has not become due.

With regard to the aft pressure bulkhead, corrosion inspection on the lower segment of the bulkhead and inspection on Y chord are emphasized with special mention, but mutually spliced portions between webs of the bulkhead such as L18 joint where cracks were caused in the accident aircraft are not designated as special inspection points, and the inspection thereof is involved in the overall visual inspection of the aft pressure bulkhead (＊7).

(＊7) Such inspection method is considered to have been adopted, because a sufficient margin of strength was provided in the mutually spliced portions of webs from the structural design viewpoint, and there were no instances in the structural inspection of 747 aircraft where such critical defects as cracks were discovered at the portions, etc, therefore general visual inspection mainly for corrosion would be sufficient.

(2) With regard to maintenance items relating to structures of the empennage (section 48), the number of the inspection items in accordance with the maintenance regulation is 39 (including 7 inspection items on SID), and the number of the work cards used for this maintenance is 24 (including 7 work cards on SID).

(3) With regard to maintenance items relating to the vertical fin and the rudder, the number of the inspection items in accordance with the maintenance regulation is 37 (including 7 inspection items on SID), and the number of the work cards used for this maintenance is 22 (including 7 work cards on SID).

2.4.4 H Maintenance

"H" maintenance is for such work as large-scale modification of aircraft and recoating of the exterior, and is carried out at 3—4 years intervals as required. different from "A" maintenance or "C" maintenance conducted on a scheduled basis. In case of 747 aircraft, "H" maintenance is ordinarily made at the same time as the scheduled "C" maintenance, not being affected independently.

2.5 Status of Maintenance Work conducted for the Accident Aircraft

2.5.1 "C" and "H" maintenance carried out after the repair in July 1978 are as follows:

No.	Effected period	Total flying hours	Total No of flight	Remarks
5C	'78.06.15—07.10	8,834:19	6,516	conducted the same time as repair for the accident at Osaka
2H	'78.11.28—12.12	9,785:06	7,298	
6C	'79.05.21—05.28	10,927:55	8,220	
7C	'80.06.04—06.16	13,406:50	10,205	
8C	'81.06.23—07.10	15,698:07	12,019	No.3H maintenance was conducted the same time
9C	'82.06.22—07.04	17,744:35	13,633	
10C	'83.10.28—11.09	20,719:43	15,823	
11C	'84.11.20—12.05	23,329:47	17,595	No.4H maintenance was conducted the same time

2.5.2 "A" maintenance effected after No.11C maintenance are as follows:

No.	Effected period	Total flying hours	Total No of flight
1A	'85.01.08	23,535:47	17,757
2A	" .02.17	23,767:53	17,936
3A	" .03.27	23,896:24	18,104
4A	" .04.29	24,219:19	18,267
5A	" .05.29	24,443:14	18,427
6A	" .06.23	24,636:36	18,563
7A	" .07.21	24,849:00	18,713

2.5.3 In "C" maintenance and "A" maintenance conducted since July 12, 1978 up to present, there were recorded no faults to be remarked.

2.5.4 Records of "C" maintenance (No.5—11) since 1978 as well as "A" maintenance since January 1985 were reviewed for faults on the following items:
   (1) Faults such as structural deformation and corrosion, of the aft fuselage and the aft passenger cabin (including deformation of doors, lavatories, shelves,etc.)
   (2) Faults such as structural deformation and malfunction of the vertical fin
   (3) Faults such as structural deformation and malfunction of the horizontal

stabilizer
(4) Faults of rudder and elevator as well as horizontal stabilizer trim control system
(5) Faults of APU and APU control system
(6) Faults of pressurization and air-conditioning system

Results of the investigation on the above items were as follows:
(1) Faults such as structural deformation and corrosion, of the aft fuselage and the aft passenger cabin (including deformation of door, lavatories, shelves, etc) (14 cases)

The breakdown was air leak from L—5 and R—5 door frames 4 cases, corrosion on fuselage skin 9 cases, other 1 case. The leak and the corrosion were dealt with by rectification of the door seal and anti-corrosion treatment, respectively.

(2) Faults such as structural deformation and malfunction, of the vertical fin (16 cases)
There are 12 cases of corrosion on the skin of the vertical fin, hydraulic piping of the rudder etc, for each of which anti-corrosion treatment was given.

At the time of No.8 and No.9C maintenance there were 3 cases of limit-out from the neutral position of the upper and the lower rudder, for which adjustment was made.

At the time of No.9C maintenance was found leak of hydraulic fluid from PCP for the upper rudder, and the PCP was replaced.

(3) Faults such as structural deformation and malfunction, of the horizontal stabilizer (18 cases)

18 cases of corrosion were discovered on the horizontal stabilizer, the internal structures, etc, and anti-corrosion treatment was taken for them.

(4) Faults of rudder and elevator as well as horizontal stabilizer trim control system (2 cases)

At the time of No.6C maintenance, rust was found on the rudder trim cable (rust was dealt with), and at the time of No.11C maintenance was found damage to the clump of the horizontal stabilizer driving motor and break seal drain tube (clump replaced).

(5) Faults of APU and APU control system (7 cases)
There were fuel leak from the APU low pressure filter housing (O ring replaced), emission of smoke from APU starting terminal (APU starter replaced), cracking in APU exhaust inner liner (inner liner replaced), high temperature and low air pressure of APU exhaust gas (air flow sensor, load control valve and breed valve replaced), cracking in APU turbine case (repaired), damage to APU exhaust liner (liner replaced), and attrition of APU fire sensing elements at support clump (elements replaced or repaired), one case for each fault.

(6) Faults of pressurization and air-conditioning system (6 cases)

There were 2 cases of damage to air-conditioning ducts (repaired), 2 cases of strange sounding from air-conditioning ducts (inside of duct washed), and 2 cases of damage to ACM (Air Cycle Machine) fan blade(ACM replaced).

2.6 Discovery of Faults by Visual Inspections

(1) As to the method and the level of the visual inspection, the following are set forth in Attachments to the Maintenance Regulations, and the inspection is carried out in accordance with them:

Level of vis. insp.	Outline	example of application
G1 (Macroscopic inspection)	An inspection method to detect defects and their symptoms by overall observation for a certain area. Defects or symptoms expected to be discovered at first by this inspection are macroscopic abnormality in structural materials; for example, waving, warp, wrinkle, crush, deformation, crack, separation, wrong combination, leakage of fuel, extensive corrosion, etc.	the overall exterior of airframe; fairing; doors of cargo compartment; honeycomb structure
G2 (Microscopic inspection)	An inspection method to detect local defects and their symptoms by detailed observation on a particular area. For this reason usually a visual distance is necessary. Defects or symptoms expected to be discovered by this inspection are microscopic abnormality caused in structural materials or elements; for example, as crack, bent, groove, abrasion, loosened joint, corrosion, errosion, solution, wear, rubbing, crazing of window glass, partial lack, electric discharge, blot of fuel due to leak from fuel tank, etc. In this inspection, substances which screen the inspected portions prescribed in the procedure from observation must be removed. However, component parts need not be removed unless otherwise specified in the maintenance procedure. The inspected portions must be in proper conditions for detection of microscopic defects. Therefore, prior to the inspection, cleaning must be conducted unless the inspection is made for corrosion, rust, or blot of liquid.	major structural blocks juncture between wings and fuselage juncture between main gear and fuselage
G3 (special inspection)	Indicate use of a special inspection method in addition to visual inspection. Detailed inspection by dye penetrate, torque check, etc and special inspection methods such as X rays, magna-flux and	cockpit window frame (X rays)

ultrasonic detection are designated in this case.

This inspection is used in case the portion or the defect is invisible by the visual inspection, or used as an equivalent method in case removal of a number of parts becomes necessary to do a visual inspection.

Corrosion inspection

An inspection with the main objective of discovering corrosion on or behind structural material by checking appearances caused on the the surface of the material by corrosion. In the inspection, special care is taken to irregularities such as surface corrosion, bulge at seams of structural materials due to corrosion, cracks, waving, dents on or lack of faterner's head.

The inspection is made adapted for the shape of the material inspected, location to be installed, and method to be used for installation. During this time, inspection for defect in general is also carried out in parallel.

(2) Division of levels of the visual inspection has not been specified for aircraft prior to 767 aircraft by the Boeing Company. The following are inspection methods prescribed in MSG—3 and MRB report of the 767 aircraft listed for reference:

Inspection method	Boeing standards
Walkaround	Observations from the ground to detect obvious discrepancies such as fuel leaks
General Visual (GEN)	Visual check of exposed areas of wing lower surface, lower fuselage, doors and door cutouts, and landing gear basys.
Surveillance (SURV)	Visual examination of defined internal or external structural areas from a distance considered necessary to carry out an adequate check. External includes structure visible through quick-opening access panels or doors. Internal applies to obscured structure requiring removal of fillets, fairings, access panels or doors, etc., for visibility (*8).
Detailed (DET)	Close intensive visual inspections of highly defined structural details or locations searching for evidence of structural irregularity (*8).
Special	Inspections of specific locations or hidden details using specified nondestructive inspection (NDI) procedures.

(*8) Using adequate lighting and where necessary, inspection aids such as mirrors, etc., surface cleaning and access procedures may be required to gain proximity.

372

(3) In JAL, inspection and maintenance work has been carried out, considering
visual inspection levels G1, G2 and G3 as virtually equivalent to inspection
methods General Visual, Surveillance and Detailed, and Special in the Boeing
Company standards, respectively.

Attachment 2   Attached Figue
Denominations and Locations of Lavatories

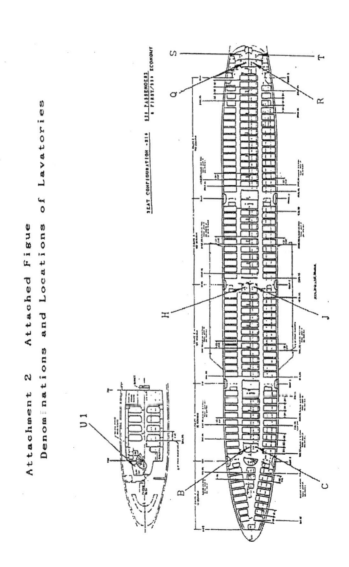

Communication Records with ATC Facilities

Station			Frequecny
DELIVERY	=	Clearance Delivery, Tokyo Aerodrome Control Tower	121.8 MHz
GROUND	=	Ground Control, Tokyo Aerodrome Control Tower	121.7 MHz
TOWER	=	Tokyo Aerodrome Control Tower	118.1 MHz
DEPARTURE	=	Departure Control, Tokyo Terminal Control	126.0 MHz
ACC	=	Tokyo Area Control Center	123.7 MHz
JL123	=	Japan Air Lines Flight 123	

Time	Station	Communication
1753:17	JL123	Ah, TOKYO CLEARANCE, JAPAN AIR 123.
	DELIVERY	JAPAN AIR 123, CLEARANCE.
1753:24	JL123	JAPAN AIR 123, this is Spot 18, we have Yankee, 5 minutes to Osaka, propose 240 via departure URAGA 6 SAGARA TRANSITION, please.
1753:34	DELIVERY	123, advise when ready.
1753:36	JL123	Roger.
1759:38	JL123	CLEARANCE DELIVERY, JAPAN AIR 123, ready to start over.
1759:42	DELIVERY	JAPAN AIR 123, start engine, cleared YAMATO, correction, SHINODA VOR via URAGA 6 DEPARTURE SAGARA TRANSITION SEAPERCH, flight planned route, maintain flight level 240, squawk 2072, DEPARTURE 126.0
1759:56	JL123	Roger, JAPAN AIR 123, cleared to SHINODA VOR via URAGA 6 DEPARTURE SAGARA TRANSITION SEAPERCH, flight planned route, maintain 240, squawk 2072, over.
1800:10	DELIVERY	Read back is correct. Contact GROUND CONTROL 121.7 for push back, good night.
1800:14	JL123	Good night.
1801:00	JL123	GROUND CONTROL, JAPAN AIR 123, spot 18, we have Yankee, request push back.
1801:05	GROUND	JAPAN AIR 123, GROUND, roger, stand by, for about 2 minutes, another Boeing 747 behind of you.
1801:10	JL123	Roger.
1803:40	GROUND	JAPAN AIR 123, Runway 15L, push back approved.
1803:43	JL123	Roger. JAPAN AIR 123, 15L.
1807:30	JL123	GROUND, JAPAN AIR 123, request taxi, ah, request C7 take off.
1807:36	GROUND	JAPAN AIR 123, roger, Runway 15L, taxi to C7 A4 A Runway.
1807:43	JL123	A4, A Runway to C7, JAPAN AIR 123.

1809:15	GROUND	JAPAN AIR 123. contact TOWER 118.1
1809:19	JL123	Roger.
1809:25	JL123	TOWER, JAPAN AIR 123 with you, we are C7.
1809:28	TOWER	JAPAN AIR 123, roger, hold short of Runway 15L.
1809:32	JL123	Roger, hold short.

1809:41	TOWER	JAPAN AIR 123, taxi into position and hold Runway 15L.
1809:45	JL123	Into position and hold 15L, JAPAN AIR 123.
1811:20	TOWER	JAPAN AIR 123, fly runway heading, wind 220, 16, cleard for take off, Runway 15L.
1811:26	JL123	Cleared for take off, 15L, fly runway heading, JAPAN AIR 123.

| 1812:23 | TOWER | JAPAN AIR 123, contact TOKYO DEPARTURE. |
| 1812:24 | JL123 | Roger, JAPAN AIR 123. |

1812:30	JL123	TOKYO DEPARTURE, JAPAN AIR 123, maintaining runway heading passing 8, ah, 800.
1812:35	DEPARTURE	JAPAN AIR 123, DEPARTURE, radar contact, turn right, heading 180, vector to URAGA, climb and maintain 13,000.
1812:42	JL123	Turn right heading 180, ah, maintain 13,000.

| 1815:55 | DEPARTURE | JAPAN AIR 123, turn right heading 200. |
| 1815:57 | JL123 | Roger, 200, JAPAN AIR 123. |

1816:22	DEPARTURE	JAPAN AIR 123, 2 miles right of course, resume normal navigation, climb and maintain flight level 240, cancel altitude restriction, contact TOKYO CONTROL, frequency 123.7.
1816:35	JL123	Roger, own navigation direct, ahhhhh, MIHARA and climb and maintain 240, contact 123.7.
1816:46	DEPARTURE	Correct.

1816:55	JL123	TOKYO CONTROL, JAPAN AIR 123, passing 9,400 for 240 and direct to MIHARA. If available, request direct to SEAPERCH, over.
1817:15	ACC	JAPAN AIR 123, TOKYO roger, stand by radar vector.
1817:17	JL123	Roger.

| 1818:33 | ACC | JAPAN AIR 123, cleared direct SEAPERCH via present position direct. |
| 1818:38 | JL123 | Present position direct SEAPERCH, — — —123. |

Communication Records with Company

Station		Frequecny
JL HANEDA	= Flight Operations Department of Tokyo Airport	131.85 MHz
	Branch of JAL (Ground)	
JL TOKYO	= Flight Operations Department of Tokyo Airport	131.90 MHz
	Branch of Japan Air lines (En—route)	
JL 123	= Japan Air Lines Flight 123	

Time	Station	Communication
1736:30	JL123	JAPAN AIR 123.
1736:33	JL HANEDA	JAPAN AIR 123, go ahead.
1736:35	JL 123	Well · ·, SELCAL please, it's CJDE.
1736:40	JL HANEDA	123, loud and clear, SELCAL stand by.
1736:43		(the sound of SELCAL)
1736:47	JL 123	Well · ·, checked ok. Well · ·, Do you have any information on the route of Flight 121.?
1736:54	JL HANEDA	Yes, well · ·, Flight 121, well, · concerning information on the route, well · ·, let me see. Although we tried to ask him, but as no reply has been received, he has not established radio contact with us.
1737:05	JL 123	Yes, much obliged.
1737:07	JL HANEDA	Yes, well, by the way, 123, you have dangerous goods on baord. They're RRW and RRY, ask the Cargo Section of their location.
1737:14	JL 123	Yes, yes.
1820:51	JL 123	Ah, JAPAN AIR TOKYO, JAPAN AIR 123.
1820:55	JL TOKYO	123, JAPAN AIR TOKYO, go ahead.
1820:58	JL 123	Off at 12, over.
1821:00	JL TOKYO	123, copied ok, good day.

Attachment 5

DFDR Record

So far as "Attachment 5 DFDR Record" is concerned, only the part
attached herewith is translated. Other parts not translated are
explanatory sentences, DFDR record (explanation written in both
Japanese and English), and please refer to Original Text.

Flight Conditions Recognized by DRDR Records

Time	Observations on DFDR [Numbers indicate DFDR pages.]

1811:32   The aircraft commenced take-off roll. [2]

1812:16   The aircraft lifted off. [1]

—1824:34   There is no indication of abnormal flight until the aircraft reached an altitude of 23,900 ft. Reduction of EPR at 1824:34 is not specifically abnormal. [1,2,3,4,5,6]

1824:35.7✱   LNGG showed 0.11G, and large impulsive force acted forward. Slight upward force began to act and VRTG increased gradually and slightly. [magnified plot]

(Remarks)✱   A sound "bang" is recorded on CVR at about 1824:35.

1824:36   Change occurred on LATG, and thereafter about 2 Hz oscillation began to be recorded, but it did not become larger and decayed gradually by 1837:40 after 1837:20. [magnified plot]

About 1824:36.13   HSTB showed abnormality exceeding normal limit, but no corresponding trim change in longitudinal motion was observed thereafter. [magnified plot]

1824:36.25   Significant pull up of CCP was observed at 1824:35.25 through this time. [magnified plot]

1824:36.28   VRTG showed abnormal jump of about —0.24G, and a big shock occurred downward at 1836.16 through this time. [magnified plot]

1824:36.7   PED was fully applied to the right and continued for about 1.5 seconds, but no corresponding movement of the aircraft was observed. Abnormality occurred on rudder control systems at 1824:36.2 through this time. [magnified plot]

About 1824:37 —about 1824:43   Corresponding to abnormal external force, airspeed decreased a little, and AOA and PCH increased, and large motion were observed on CCP, LNGG and VRTG. [magnified plot]

About 1824:38   PED was observed to return to original position, but no response shown by aircraft. [magnified plot]

1824:38.9   CMD of A/P went off. (Auto throttle was off from beginning to end.) [magnified plot]

1824:45 −1824:50	Considerable amonut of right CWP was observed. 【magnified plot】
1825:13	PED was returned to its neutral position, but no aircraft response was observed. 【2,1】
−1826	CWP was applied to the right. Right roll in and right turn were observed. Then left CWP was applied. The aircraft rolled out from right roll, and stopped to turn. No remarkable phugoid had been observed until this time. 【2,1】
About 1826	Remarkable phugoid and dutch roll motion began. The pilot tried to stop them by applying CCP and CWP, but in vain. Particularly, CWP application for dutch roll had been continued until immediately before the crash. 【2,1】
1826−1840	The aircraft maintained almost straight level flight as a whole. During this period, maximum amplitudes are recorded for RLL ±about 40° by dutch roll, and for CAS ±about 25 knots and for altitude ±about 1500 feet by phugoid. 【4】
1826−1831	There observed large and rapid variation on each EPR. These variations of EPR are not inconsistent with these in londitudinal acceleration. 【4】
1829−1831	EPR No.1 was slightly higher than EPR No.4. There observed right turn and right roll. 【4,1,2】
1834:36	Stepwise changes on PED and CCP were recorded, but no response followed. 【2,1】
1835−About 1837	Phugoid motion slightly damped due to EPR operation. 【2,1】
1839:32	Main landing gears were extended.
1839:51 −1845:21	EPR No.1 is higher than EPR No.4, and EPR No.2 than EPR No.3 respectively. The aircraft turned right about 420° from heading about 040°, becoming heading about 100°. During this period, averaged RLL was maximum 40° to the right. The maximum amplitude of RLL by dutch roll is ±25°. 【4,1,2】
1840−1848	The aircraft descended from about 22,000 ft to about 6,600 ft. 【1】
About 1840 −about 1842	EPR which was higher than that of take-off climb was recorded. The aircraft began to descend slightly, and phugoid motion damped rapidly. 【4,1】
1842:26	EPR was reduced to large extent, and rate of descent increased. 【4,1】

379

About 1845	EPR was further reduced to about 0.9, and average rate of descent became about 2,500 feet/min. 【4,5】
1845—1848	Phugoid motion had been completely disappeared. 【1】
1845:21— about 1849	The aircraft made a slow left turn from heading about 100° to about 300° . The maximum RLL during this turn was about 25° to the left, and maximum amplitude for RLL by dutch roll was about ±12° .【1,2】
About 1847:46(∗)	Extremely large CWP and PED were applied to make right turn, but in vain. 【2,1】

   (Remarks) ∗ According to CVR, recognizing mountains an instruction to turn right is recorded.

1848	The aircraft stopped descending in average with EPR increasing rapidly to about 1.6, but large phugoid motion was excited again. 【4,1】
About 1849	The minimum ALT during this motion was about 5,300 ft. 【1】
1849:36 —about 1853	Phugoid motion was damped by EPR control, but the aircraft began to climb again due to high power level. 【4,1】
1849:42	Minimum CAS became 108 kts, and AOA became 30.9° . 【1,3】
1851:06— 1855:26	Flaps began to be extended. It took 3 min. and 10 sec. for flaps to be extended to 5 units. Flaps reached 20 units in 1 min.and 2 sec thereafter. Leading edge flaps except left/right outer groups(No.1— No.5 and No.22—No.26) began to be extended at 1851:06, and the extension completed at 1852:39. 【3】
1852:52	EPR was reduced and average rate of descent became more than 3,000 ft/min. 【4,5】
1854:01— 1854:21	EPR No.3 and EPR No.4 were higher than EPR No.2 and EPR No.1 and left roll and left turn resulted. 【4,2】
1854:31—	At about the time when flap angle became 5 units, phugoid motion was excited and EPR control was carried out. 【3,1】
About 1854:32	Left and right EPR became nearly the same, and left RLL recovered almost to 0 deg, but phugoid was excited. Flap angle, at about this time, was about 6.6 units. 【4,2,3,1】
About 1854:50	Flap angle became 10 units. Right RLL increased and right turn began. 【3,2,1】

380

About 1855	CAS decreased and power was added. But, EPR of left side engines was slightly higher than that of right side, and right turn increased with increasing right roll. [2.1.4]
1855:12— 1855:40	Right turn increased as dutch roll continued around about 40° of averaged right roll. Phugoid motion did not stop. [2.1]
1855:42	Flap angle became about 25 units and flaps began to be retracted immediately. But the right RLL further increased to 50° — 60° . [3.2]
1855:57	PCH became about 15° nose down, and power was added abruptly. EPR 1 and 2 on the left were higher than EPR 3 and 4 on the right in spite of rapid right turn. ALT at this time was about 10,000 feet. [2.4.1]
1856:07	The aircraft began to descend rapidly and VRTG began to increase due to rapid increase of airspeed and rapid right turn. PCH was about 36° nose down and RLL was about 70° to the right. [1.2]
1856:11	The rate of descent became more than 18,000 feet/min. at about this time. [1.2]
1856:17	At ALT of about 5,000 feet. CAS exceeded 340 knots. Right RLL recovered to about 40° , and the pitch attitude was recovering toward nose up. [1.2]
1856:18— 1856:23.5	Power was added up to the maximum, the descent ceased, but VRTG maintained about 3G's. [4.1]
About 1856:2 —1856:27.92	Abnormal changes are recorded in various DFDR data. [1.2.3.4.5.]

ATTACHMENT 6

CVR RECORD

Note:

1. The lines indicated in this record are obtained by collating the time signal (Japan Standard Time) recorded in the ATC tape with the running speed of the CVR tape.

2. (CAP) indicates the captain, (COP) the copilot, (F/E) the flight engineer, (PUR) purser, (STW) the stewardesses including the assistant purser, and (PRA) pre-recorded announcements.

3. (ACC) indicates Tokyo Area Control Center, (APC) Tokyo Approach Control, (YOK) Yokota Approach Control, and (COM) the Japan Air Lines company radio.

4. ... indicates that the recording is indecipherable, and ____ that the recording is unclear.

5. ☐ indicates utterance is recorded simultaneously.

6. The following symbols are used in the text.

☆   HI-CHIME
SELCAL   SELECTIVE CALLING SYSTEM
■   FIRE WARNING
♦   STALL WARNING
GPWS   GROUND PROXIMITY WARNING SYSTEM

● Sound like "bang"

CABIN ALTITUDE WARNING or TAKE OFF WARNING

SELCAL

☆ ALTITUDE ALERT

Communication between other aircraft and ACC

Communication between other aircraft and COM

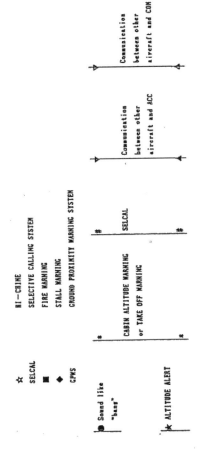

382

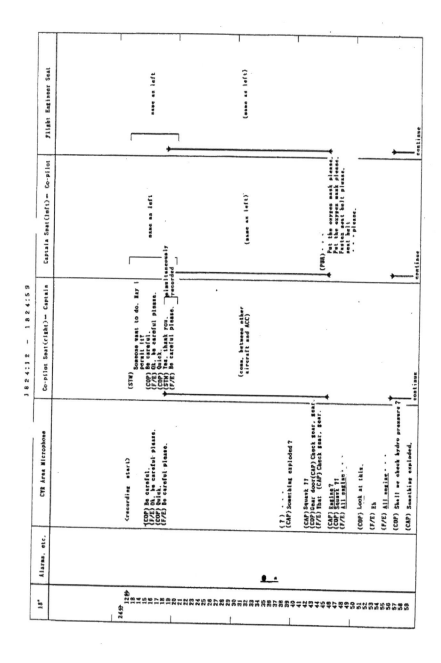

1 8 2 5 : 0 0 — 1 8 2 5 : 5 9

18*	Alarms, etc.	CVR Area Microphone	Co-pilot Seat(right) = Captain	Captain Seat(left) = Co-pilot	Flight Engineer Seat
25½ 00 01 02 03 04 05 06 07 08 09 10 11 12 13 14 15 16 17 18 19	*	(F/E) Gear (ive off.	(comm. between other aircraft and ACC)	(same as left) (PUR) Be sure to fasten your belt, please.	(same as left)
20 21 22 23 24 25 26 27 28 29 30 31 32 33 34		(F/E) Yes, roger. (CAP) Right turn (CAP) Right turn (COP) Pressure ? (F/E) Dropped. (CAP)Ah, TOKYO, JAPAN AIR 123 request from immediate u- trouble request return back to HANEDA descend and maintain 220 over.	(CAP)Ah, TOKYO, JAPAN AIR 123 request from immediate u- trouble request return back to HANEDA descend and maintain 220 over.	(PRA) Fasten your seatbelt. Put out your cigarettes. This is an emergency descent.	
35 36 37 38 39 40 41 42 43 44 45 46 47 48 49		(CAP)Radar vector to OSHIMA, please. (CAP)Going to right turn, over.	(ACC)Roger, approved as you request (CAP)Radar vector to OSHIMA, please. (ACC)Roger, you want right or left turn ? (CAP)Going to right turn, over. (ACC)Right, right heading 090 Radar Vector to OSHIMA. (CAP)090.	(same as left) (PRA) - - - (PRA) - - -	same as left
50 51 52 53 54 55 56 57 58 59	continue	(CAP)090. (CAP) Don't bank so much. (COP) Yes, (CAP) Don't bank no such. (COP) Yes. (CAP) What's is that ?		(PRA)Fasten your seatbelt. Put out your cigarettes. This is an emergency descent.	

384

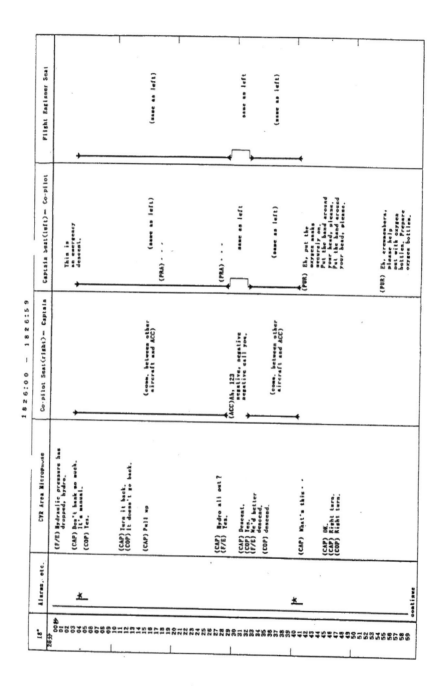

1826:00 - 1826:59

18"	Alarms, etc.	CVR Area Microphone	Co-pilot Seat(right)- Captain	Captain Seat(left)- Co-pilot	Flight Engineer Seat
26% 00%					
01				This is	
02				an emergency	
03	★	(F/E) Hydraulic pressure has		descent.	
04		dropped, hydro.			
05		(CAP) Don't bank so much.			
06		It's manual.			
07		(COP) Yes.			
08					
09					
10					
11		(CAP) Turn it back.			
12		(COP) It doesn't go back.			
13					
14				(same as left)	(same as left)
15		(CAP) Pull up	(comm. between other		
16			aircraft and ACC)	(PRA) · · ·	
17					
18					
19					
20					
21					
22					
23					
24					
25					
26					
27		(CAP) Hydro all out?		same as left	same as left
28		(F/E) Yes.	(ACC)Ah, 123		
29			negative, negative		
30			negative call you.	(PRA) · · ·	
31		(CAP) Descent.			
32		(COP) Yes.			
33		(F/E) We'd better			
34		descend.			
35		(COP) descend.	(comm. between other	(same as left)	(same as left)
36			aircraft and ACC)		
37					
38					
39					
40	★	(CAP) What's this· ·		(PBR) Eh, put the	
41				oxygen masks	
42				securely on.	
43		(CAP) OK.		Put the band around	
44		(CAP) Right turn.		your head, please.	
45		(COP) Right turn.		Put the band around	
46				your head, please.	
47					
48					
49					
50				(PBR) Eh, crewmembers,	
51				please help	
52				out with oxygen	
53				bottles. Prepare	
54				oxygen bottles.	
55					
56					
57					
58					
59		continue			

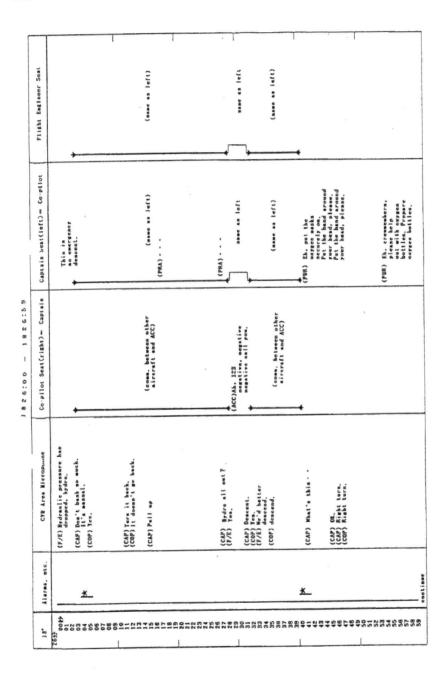

1826:00 - 1826:59

18″	Alarms, etc.	CVR Area Microphone	Co-pilot Seat(right)— Captain	Captain Seat(left)— Co-pilot	Flight Engineer Seat
00		(F/E) Hydraulic pressure has dropped, hydro.		This is an emergency descent.	
01					
02					
03		(CAP) Don't bank so much. It's manual.			
04					
05	✳	(COP) Yes.			
06					
07					
08					
09					
10		(CAP) Turn it back.			
11		(COP) It doesn't go back.			
12					
13					
14		(CAP) Pull up			
15			(comm. between other aircraft and ACC)	(same as left)	(same as left)
16					
17					
18					
19					
20					
21					
22					
23					
24					
25				(PRA) - - -	
26		(CAP) Hydro all out?	(ACC)Ah, 123 maritime, negative negative call zou.		
27		(F/E) Yes.			
28					
29					
30		(CAP) Descent.	(comm. between other aircraft and ACC)	(same as left)	same as left
31		(COP) Yes.			
32		(F/E) We'd better descend.			
33					
34					
35		(COP) descend.		(PRA) - - -	
36					
37					
38					
39					
40	✳	(CAP) What's this · ·		(same as left)	(same as left)
41				(PUR) Eh, put the oxygen masks securely on. Put the band around your head, please. Put the band around your head, please.	
42					
43		(CAP) OK.			
44		(CAP) Right turn.			
45		(COP) Right turn.			
46					
47					
48					
49					
50					
51					
52				(PUR) Eh, crewmembers, please help out with oxygen bottles. Prepare oxygen bottles.	
53					
54					
55					
56					
57					
58	continue				
59					

1 8 2 7 : 0 0 — 1 8 2 7 : 5 9

15"	Alarms, etc.	CVR Area Microphone	Co-pilot Seat(right) — Captain	Captain Seat(left) — Co-pilot	Flight Engineer Seat
2735 00H					
01					
02					
03			(ACC)JAPAN AIR 123		
04			confirm you are		
05			declare emergency		
06			that's right?		
07				(PRA) · · · same as left	same as left
08					
09			(CAP)That's affirmative.		
10					
11			(ACC)123 roger.		
12				(PRA) · · ·	
13			(ACC)And request		
14			your nature		
15			of emergency.		
16					
17				(PRA)Attention.	
18				Emergency	
19				descent.	
20				Put the mask	
21				over the face.	
22				Fasten your	
23				seatbelt.	
24				Put out	
25				your cigarettes.	
26				This is	
27				an emergency	
28				descent.	
29					
30				Attention.	
31		(CAP) Hydro 2		Emergency	
32		(F/E) Yes.		descent.	
33				Put the mask	
34				over the face.	
35				Fasten your	
36				seatbelt.	
37				Put out	
38		(F/E) Hydro pressure all loss.		your cigarettes.	
39				This is	
40		(CAP) All loss?		an emergency	
41		(CAP) No loss.		descent.	
42		(F/E) All loss,			
43		(CAP) All loss? (F/E) Yes.		Attention.	
44				Emergency	
45		(CAP) The company, eh · · ·		descent.	
46		ask eh.		Put the mask	
47		Please.		over the face.	
48		I request		Fasten your	
49		to the company		seatbelt.	
50		please.		Put out	
51				your cigarettes.	
52				This is	
53				an emergency	
54				descent.	
55					
56				Attention.	
57				Emergency	
58				descent.	
59				Put the mask	

continue

387

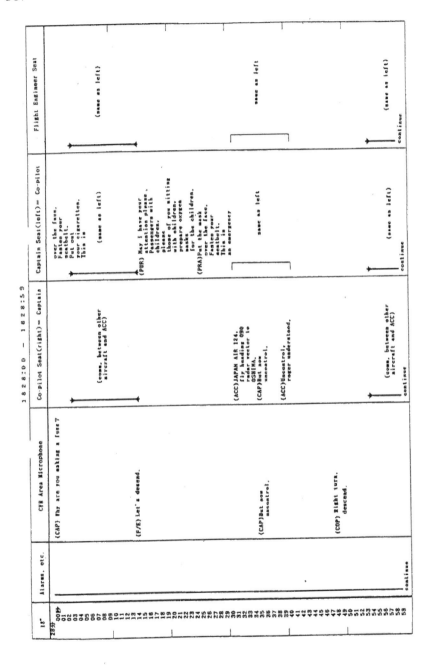

1 8 2 8 : 0 0 — 1 8 2 8 : 5 9

18"	Alarms, etc.	CVR Area Microphone	Co-pilot Seat(right) — Captain	Captain Seat(left) — Co-pilot	Flight Engineer Seat

(CAP) Why are you making a fuss?

(F/E) Let's descend.

(CAP) But now uncontrol.

(COP) Right turn. descend.

(comm. between other aircraft and ACC)

(ACC) JAPAN AIR 124, fly heading 090 radar vector to OSHIMA.
(CAP) But now uncontrol.
(ACC) Uncontrol, roger understood.

(comm. between other aircraft and ACC)

over the face.
Fasten your seatbelt.
Put out your cigarette.
This is

(same as left)

(PUR) May I have your attention please. Passengers with children, please, those of you sitting with children, prepare oxygen masks for the children.
(PRA) Put the mask over the face. Fasten your seatbelt. This is an emergency!

same as left

(same as left)

(same as left)

same as left

(same as left)

continue

388

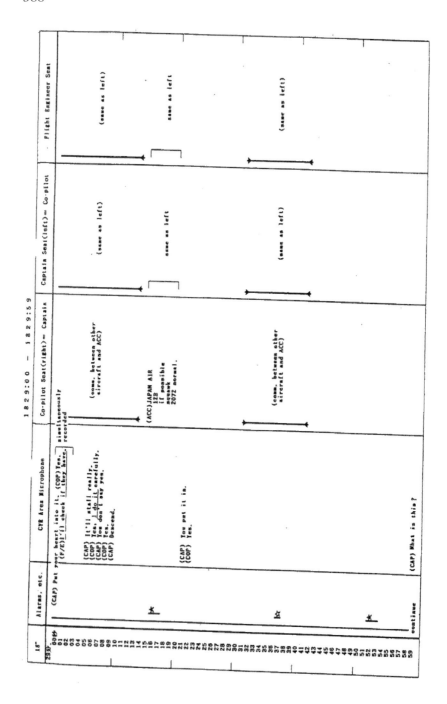

389

1 8 3 0 : 0 0 - 1 8 3 0 : 5 9

18"	Alarms. etc.	CVR Area Microph...	Co-pilot Seat(right)= Captain	Captain Seat(left)= Co-pilot	Flight Engineer Seat
30:00					
		(CAP)...			
				(comm. between other aircraft and CON)	(same as left)
		(F/E) How about the oxygen pressure? Have the oxygen masks dropped?			
		Oh, I see. Well, oxygen pressure Ah put that P0. bottle firmly please.	(comm. between other aircraft and ACC)		
		(CAP)...		(same as left)	(same as left)
		(F/E) As the oxygen masks have dropped			
	continue				

1 8 3 1 : 0 0 — 1 8 3 1 : 5 9

＂	Alarms. etc.	CVR Area Mirror	Co-pilot Seat(right)= Captain	Captain . (left)= Co-pilot	Flight Engineer Seat
31:00					
01					
02					
03					
04			(ACC)JAPAN AIR 123 ah, can you descend?		
05					
06					
07	✷	(CAP)Ah, roger	(CAP)Ah, roger now descending.		
08		(F/E)The oxygen masks have dropped.			
09			(ACC)All right		
10			(CAP)say altitude now.		
11		(COP)Yes,			
12		(CAP)240,			
13					
14			(ACC)Right, your position 72 miles, ah, MAGOTA, you head to NAGOYA?	same as left	same as left
15					
16					
17					
18					
19					
20					
21	✷	(CAP)Ah, negative ... request back to HANEDA.	(CAP)Ah, negative ... request back to HANEDA.		
22					
23					
24					
25					
26			(ACC)All right, ah You may speak in Japanese from		
27					
28					
29					
30			(CAP)now Oh.		
31			(CAP)Yes, Yes.		
32		(CAP) Yes, yes.			
33					
34					
35	✰	(COP) To where?			
36		(CAP) Oh—. Oh Oh			
37					
38					
39					
40					
41		(F/E)Yes. What is it?			
42					
43					
44					
45					
46		(CAP) Can you hold?			
47		(F/E) Is it to the rear?	(comm. between other aircraft and ACC)	(same as left)	(same as left)
48					
49		(F/E) Eh, What has been broken?			
50					
51					
52					
53					
54					
55		(F/E) Where?			
56					
57					
58		(CAP) Ah, ah, ah			
59					

continue   continue   continue   continue   continue

1 8 3 2 : 0 0 - 1 8 3 2 : 5 9

i8*	Alarms, etc.	CVR Area Microphones	Co-pilot Seat(right)= Captain	Captain Seat(left)= Co-pilot	Flight Engineer Seat
32:39					
00*					
01					
02					
03		(F/E) So, it's the baggage compartment.			
04					
05		The frontmost to the rear.			
06					
07		Yes, I understand.			
08					
09					
10					
11		(F/E) Listen, the baggage in the baggage compartment, the very rearmost part.			
12					
13					
14					
15					
16		The storage space for baggage has collapsed. I think we'd better descend.			
17					
18					
19					
20					
21					
22					
23			(comm. between other aircraft and ACC)		
24					
25				(same as left)	(same as left)
26					
27					
28					
29					
30					
31		(F/E) All passengers are using masks.			
32					
33					
34					
35					
36				(comm. between other aircraft and COM)	
37					
38					(same as left)
39					
40					
41					
42					
43					
44					
45					
46					
47					
48					
49					
50					
51					
52					
53					
54					
55					
56					
57					
58					
59					

continue

1833:00 - 1833:59

18"	Aircraft, etc.	CVR Area Microphone	Co-pilot Seat(right) = Captain	Captain Seat(left) = Co-pilot	Flight Engineer Seat
33'00		(COP) Shall we descend, a little?			
01					
02					
03					
04					
05					
06					
07					
08					
09					
10					
11					
12					
13					
14					
15					
16					
17		(F/E) Will you confirm oxygen?			
18					
19					
20					
21					
22		(F/E) The R5 at?		(same as left)	(same as left)
23					
24		Yes, I understand.	(COM)SELCAL	(COM)SELCAL	(COM)SELCAL
25			(comm. between other aircraft and COM)	(same as left)	
26		Yes, I understand.			
27					
28		Yes, I understand.			
29					
30					
31					same as left
32					
33					
34				(COM)JAPAN AIR 123	
35		(F/E) Captain.		JAPAN AIR	
36		(CAP) Yes.		TOKYO	
37		(F/E) The R5 seats have stopped;		How do you read.	
38					
39		.....			
40		I think we'd better make an emergency descent.			
41					
42		(CAP) Yes.			
43					
44					
45					
46		(F/E) Shall we use masks too?			
47					
48		(CAP) Yes.	(COM)SELCAL	(COM)SELCAL	(COM)SELCAL
49		(COP) We'd better.	(comm. between other aircraft and COM)	(same as left)	(same as left)
50		(CAP)			
51					
52					
53					
54		(F/E) If possible I think it'd better to use oxygen masks.			
55					
56					
57					
58		(CAP) Yes.			
59			continue	continue	continue

1 8 3 4 : 0 0 — 1 8 3 4 : 5 9

18"	Alarms, etc.	CVR Area Microphones	Co-pilot Seat(right)= Captain	Captain Seat(left)= Co-pilot	Flight Engineer Seat
3437					
00					
01					
02					
03					
04					
05					
06					
07					(COM)SELCAL
08					
09	*				
10		(COP) Please communicate through			same as left
11		company radio. Please communicate			
12		through company radio.			
13					
14		(F/E) Yes, I understand.		(COM)JAPAN AIR 123	
15				JAPAN AIR	
16				TOKYO	
17		(F/E) Eh		How do you read.	
18		where?			
19		(CAP) Stick with it.			
20					
21					
22				(COM)JAPAN AIR 123	same as left
23				JAPAN AIR	
24				TOKYO	
25				How do you read.	
26					
27					
28					
29					
30					
31					
32					
33					
34					
35					
36					
37				(COM)SELCAL	(COM)SELCAL
38		(F/E) Eh			
39		Where now?			
40	#	company			
41					
42					
43					
44					
45					
46					
47				(COM)JAPAN AIR 123	
48				JAPAN AIR	
49		(COP) Yes.		TOKYO	
50		We are		How do you read.	
51		making a descent.			
52					
53		(F/E) Japan Air			
54		where?			
55		(CAP) From where?			
56					
57					
58					
59					

continue

1 8 3 5 : 0 0 - 1 8 3 5 : 5 9

18'	Airms. etc.	CAM Area Microphone	Co-pilot Seat(right)= Captain	Captain Seat(left)= Co-pilot	Flight Engineer Seat
353°				same as left	same as left
00		(COP) Osaka.		(same as left)	(same as left)
01		(CAP) Call Japan Air.			
02		(F/E) Japan Air			
03		Osaka ?			
04		(COP) Japan Air Tokyo			
05		(F/E) Japan Air Tokyo			
06		(CAP) Japan Air			
07		where ?			
08		(F/E) Japan Air Tokyo.			
09			(F/E)Japan Air Tokyo		
10				(F/E) Japan Air	
11			(comm. between other	Tokyo	
12		(F/E) Japan Air	aircraft and ACC)	oh,	
13		Tokyo		Japan Air	
14		oh,			
15		Japan Air		Ah,	
16					
17		Ah		123 over.	
18				(COM) Japan Air	
19		123 over.		123	
20				Japan Air	
21				Tokyo.	
22				Tokyo ACC	
23				monitored	
24				your emergency	
25				call at	
26				25	
27				30 minutes	
28				miles west	
29				of Oshima,	
30				is that	
31				right?	
32				(STK) ···seems to be; sir.	
33				(F/E) Eh, listen	
34		(F/E) Eh, listen		right now	
35		right now		eh,	
36		eh,		R5	
37		R5		door, eh	
38		door, eh		has broken.	
39		has broken.		Eh,	
40		Eh,		no	
41		no			
42				Eh,	
43		Eh,		right now	
44		right now		we're	
45		we're		descending.	
46		descending.		Eh.	
47		Eh.			
48					
49					
50				(COM) Roger.	
51		(CAP)···		Is it the	
52				captain's intention	
53				to return to	
54				Tokyo ?	
55				(F/E)Yes, what is it ?	
56					
57					
58		(F/E) Yes, What is it ?			
59					

continue

18:36:00 - 18:36:59

Time	Alarms, etc.	CVR Area Microphone	Co-pilot Seat(right)= Captain	Captain Seat(left)= Co-pilot	Flight Engineer Seat
1836 00 01 02 03 04 05 06 07 08 09 10 11 12 13 14 15 16 17 18 19 20 21 22 23 24 25 26 27 28 29 30 31 32 33 34 35 36 37 38 39 40 41 42 43 44 45 46 47 48 49 50 51 52 53 54 55 56 57 58 59	continue	(F/E) Eh, wait a moment, we're now making an emergency descent. eh. We'll contact you again in a little while. Again, We'll contact you again, so, eh. Keep monitoring us please. (CAP) . . . (COP) Well, . . . (COP) I don't understand well. (COP) We're now descending. (F/E) Eh,	(comm. between other aircraft and ACC) (same as left)	(COM) Can you return to Haneda ? (F/E) Eh, wait a moment, we're now making an emergency descent. eh. We'll contact you again in a little while. Again, We'll contact you again, so, eh. Keep monitoring us please. (COM) Roger. (STW) Passengers using oxygen now . . . use the oxygen, please, at that time, . . . please. (comm. between other aircraft and COM)	(same as left) (same as left)

1 8 3 7 : 0 0 - 1 8 3 7 : 5 9

18ᵐ	Alarms. etc.	CVR Area Microphone	Co-pilot Seat(right)— Captain	Captain Seat(left)— Co-pilot	Flight Engineer Seat
37ˢ					
00#					
01					
02					
03					
04		(CAP) Descend.			
05		(?) ...			
06					
07		(CAP) Never mind that.			
08					
09					
10		(CAP) Ah,ah,ah,			
11					
12					
13					
14					
15					
16					
17					
18					
19					
20					
21					
22					
23					
24		(CAP) Lower the nose.			
25			(comm. between other aircraft and ACC)	(same as left)	
26					
27					
28					
29					
30					
31					
32					
33					
34					
35					
36					
37		(CAP) Lower the nose.			
38		(COP) Yes.			
39					
40					
41					
42					
43					
44					
45					
46					
47					
48					
49					
50					
51					
52					
53					
54					
55					
56					
57					
58					
59	continue				

1 8 3 8 : 0 0 - 1 8 3 8 : 5 9

Time (15" 3827)	Alarms, etc.	CVR Area Microphone	Co-pilot Seat(right)= Captain	Captain Seat(left) = Co-pilot	Flight Engineer Seat
00–59		(CAP) Lower the nose. (COP) Yes.			
		(CAP) Lower the nose. (COP) Yes.			
		(CAP) Use both hand, both hand. (COP) Yes. (F/E) How about gear down? Gear drop. (COP) Shall we gear down?	(comm. between other aircraft and ACC)	(same as left)	
		(CAP) Doesn't work. Gear doesn't go down.	(comm. between other aircraft and ACC)	(same as left)	
	continue	(CAP) Lower the nose. (COP) Yes.			

1839:00 - 1839:59

18*	Airues. etc.	CVR Area Microphone	Co-pilot Seat(right)— Captain	Captain Seat(left)— Co-pilot	Flight Engineer Seat
39:2 00–59		(F/E) Shall I lower it slowly by alternate?			
		(CAP) Yes. wait a moment.	(comm. between other aircraft and ACC)	(same as left)	
		(CAP) ... lower ...	(comm. between other aircraft and ACC)	(same as left)	
		(COP) Yes.			
		(CAP) ...			
		(COP) Yes.			
		(F/E) Shall we use speed brakes?			
	continue	continue	continue	continue	

1 8 4 0 : 0 0 - 1 8 4 0 : 5 9

time	Alarms, etc.	CVR Area Microphone	Co-pilot Seat(right)= Captain	Captain Seat(left)= Co-pilot	Flight Engineer Seat
40:00		(CAP) Ah, lower the nose. (COP) Yes.			
01					
02					
03					
04			(conv. between other aircraft and ACC)	(same as left)	
05					
06					
07					
08					
09					
10		(CAP)····			
11					
12					
13					
14					
15		(CAP) Let's return ···			
16					
17					
18					
19					
20					
21		(F/E) I have lowered the gear. (COP) Yes.			
22					
23					
24					
25					
26					
27					
28					
29					
30					
31					
32					
33					
34					
35					
36					
37					
38					
39					
40		(CAP) Lower the nose. (COP) Yes.			
41					
42					
43			(ACC)JAPAN AIR 123 JAPAN AIR 123		
44					
45			Can you switch to frequency 134.97		
46					
47				same as left	
48					
49					
50			(ACC)JAPAN AIR 123 JAPAN AIR 123		
51					
52			TOKYO CONTROL, If you read me		
53			ideal, please.		
54				same as left	
55					
56					
57					
58					
59	continue				

1 8 4 1 : 0 0 — 1 8 4 1 : 5 9

18"	Alarms. etc.	CVR Area Microphone	Co-pilot Seat(right)= Captain	Captain Seat(left)= Co-pilot	Flight Engineer Seat
00					
01					
02					
03					
04					
05					
06					
07		(CAP) Lower the nose. Never mind that.			
08					
09					
10		(CAP) (ou'll) stall.			
11		(COP) ea.			
12					
13					
14					
15					
16		(CAP) You must use both hands to lower.			
17					
18					
19					
20					
21					
22			(comm. between other aircraft and ACC)	(same as left)	
23					
24					
25					
26					
27		(CAP) . . .			
28					
29					
30					
31					
32					
33					
34					
35					
36					
37					
38					
39					
40					
41					
42					
43					
44					
45					
46					
47					
48			(ACC)All station all station except JAPAN AIR 123 and	same as left	
49					
50					
51					
52					
53					
54					
55					
56					
57					
58					
59	continue				

1 8 4 2 : 0 0 - 1 8 4 2 : 5 9

18*	Alarms, etc.	CVR Area Microphone	Co-pilot Seat(right)— Captain	Captain Seat(left)— Co-pilot	Flight Engineer Seat
00			(ACC)contact TOKYO CONTROL contact TOKYO CONTROL 134 decimal 0 change frequency 134,0 and keep silent until further advised.	same as left	
20		(CAP) Lower the nose.			
		(COP) Yes.			
25			(comm. between other aircraft and ACC)	(same as left)	
40			(comm. between other aircraft and ACC)	(same as left)	
47		(CAP) Power.			
52		(CAP) Heavy.			
	continue				

1 8 4 3 : 0 0 – 1 8 4 3 : 5 9

18"	Alarm. etc.	CVR Area Microphone	Co-Pilot Seat(right)= Captain	Captain Seat(left)= Co-pilot	Flight Engineer Seat
43"					
00					
01					
02					
03					
04					
05					
06					
07					
08					
09					
10					
11					
12					
13					
14					
15					
16					
17					
18					
19					
20					
21		(CAP) Lower the nose.		(STW) Please remain in that condition and well please.	
22					
23					
24					
25				(STW) . . . (same as left)	
26					
27			(comm. between other aircraft and ACC)		
28					
29					
30					
31				(STW) . . . please.	
32					
33					
34					
35					
36					
37					
38					
39					
40					
41					
42					
43		(CAP) Heavy, lower the			
44		nose, a little more.			
45					
46					
47		(COP) Yes.			
48					
49					
50					
51					
52		(CAP) We're going down.			
53					
54					
55					
56					
57					
58					
59	continue				

403

1 8 4 4 : 0 0 — 1 8 4 4 : 5 9

1'	Alarms, etc.	CVR Area Microphone	Co-pilot Seat(right) — Captain	Captain Seat(left) — Co-pilot	Flight Engineer Seat
00					
01					
02					
03					
04					
05		(CAP) Heavy.			
06					
07					
08					
09					
10					
11					
12					
13					
14					
15					
16					
17					
18					
19					
20					
21					
22		(CAP) Is the wheel pushed all the way?			
23		(COP) All the way,			
24		it's all the way.			
25					
26					
27					
28					
29					
30					
31					
32					
33					
34					
35					
36					
37				(comm. between other aircraft and ACC)	
38					
39					
40					
41		(CAP) Ah, heavy.			
42					
43					
44					
45					
46		(F/E) How about the flap?			
47		Shall we extend it?			
48		(CAP) It's still too early.		(same as left)	
49		(F/E) It is still too early?			
50		(CAP) It's still too early.			
51		(COP) Are the gears down?			
52		(F/E) Gears are down.			
53		(CAP) Eh,			
54		(COP) Control is			
55					
56					
57					
58					
59	continue				

1 8 4 5 : 0 0 ~ 1 8 4 5 : 5 9

時"	Alarms, etc.	CVR Area Microphone	Co-pilot Seat(right)= Captain	Captain Seat(left)= Co-pilot	Flight Engineer Seat
45ʺ00					
01					
02					
03					
04					
05					
06					
07					
08					
09					
10		(CAP) Hold here･･･			
11					
12					
13					
14					
15					
16					
17					
18					
19					
20					
21					
22					
23					
24					
25					
26					
27					
28					
29					
30					
31					
32					
33					
34					
35					
36					
37				(TOK)JAPAN AIR ONE TWENTY THREE JAPAN AIR ONE TWENTY THREE YOKOTA APPROACH on guard. If you hear me. Contact YOKOTA 129.4.	
38					
39					
40					
41					
42					
43					
44					
45					
46		(CAP) Japan Air 123 uncontrollable	(CAP) Japan Air 123 uncontrollable		
47					
48		(F/E) Shall we contact?		same as left	(same as left)
49			(ACC)JAPAN AIR 123 go ahead.		
50		(CAP) Wait a minute.			
51		Control			
52		(F/E) where?		(comm. between other aircraft and CON)	
53					
54			(ACC)JAPAN AIR 123 roger understood understood and ah─.		
55				same as left	
56					
57					
58					
59	continue	continue		continue	continue

1 8 4 6 : 0 0 - 1 8 4 6 : 5 9

18*	Alarms, etc.	CVR Area Microphone	Co-pilot Seat(right)~ Captain	Captain Seat(left)~ Co-Pilot	Flight Engineer Seat
00* 01 02 03 04 05 06 07 08 09 10 11 12 13 14 15 16 17 18 19 20 21 22 23 24 25 26 27 28 29 30 31 32 33 34 35 36 37 38 39 40 41 42 43 44 45 46 47 48 49 50 51 52 53 54 55 56 57 58 59		(CAP) Lower the nose. (COP) Eh, we've come to Lake Sagami. (CAP) Yes. (CAP) Stay with us please. (CAP) Stay with us, please. (CAP) This may be hopeless. (CAP) Hey. · · · (COP) Yes. (CAP) Lower the nose more. (COP) Yes.	(ACC) JAPAN AIR 123 do you wish to contact Haneda? (CAP) Stay with us please. (ACC) Do you wish to contact? (CAP) Stay with us, please. (ACC) Yes, understood. standby, Please wait. (comm. between other aircraft and ACC)	(comm. between other aircraft and COM) same as left (TOK) JAPAN AIR ONE TWENTY THREE JAPAN AIR ONE TWENTY THREE YOKOTA APPROACH on radar. If you hear me, squawk 5423. (STN) · · · · (same as left)	(same as left) same as left (same as left)
continue	continue		continue	continue	continue

18:47:00 – 18:47:59

18"	Alarms, etc.	CVR Area Microphone	Co-Pilot Seat(right)— Captain	Captain Seat(left)— Co-pilot	Flight Engineer Seat
00				(STW)...	(same as left)
01					
02		(COP)... As aileron...			
03					
04					
05					
06			(comm. between other aircraft and ACC)	(same as left)	
07		(CAP)Ah, request radar vector to HANEDA ah KISARAZU.	(CAP)Ah, request radar vector to HANEDA ah KISARAZU.		
08					
09			(ACC)Roger, understood. Ah, the runway 22, keep heading 090.		
10				(YOK)JAPAN AIR ONE TWO THREE JAPAN AIR ONE TWO THREE YOKOTA APPROACH on ground. I you hear me. Contact YOKOTA 129.4.	
11					
12		(CAP)Roger.	(CAP)Roger.		
13					
14					
15		(F/E)The hydraulic quantity is all lost.			
16					
17			(ACC)Can you control the aircraft now?	same as left	same as left
18		(CAP) It's uncontrollable.	(CAP)It's uncontrollable. (ACC) Roger.		
19					
20					(same as left)
21				(comm. between other aircraft and COM)	
22				We are descending to lower altitude.	
23					
24				Soon you won't have to use the oxygen masks.	
25					
26					
27					
28					
29					
30			(ACC)JAPAN AIR 123 contact TOKYO COM ah TOKYO APPROACH		
31					
32					
33					
34		(CAP)... OK? (COP)Yes.	119.7, 119.7.		same as left
35		(CAP)119.7. Roger.		same as left	
36			(CAP)119.7 Roger.		
37					
38					
39		(CAP)Hey, mountain (F/E) Yes, please.			
40					
41		(CAP) Turn right.			
42				(STW) Passengers with babies.	
43		(CAP) Mountain (COP) Yes.			
44		(CAP) Take control, right.		keep your head on the back	
45		(CAP) Right turn.			
46				of the seat.	
47				Hold, please. Hold your babies firmly please.	
48					
49				is your belt fastened?	
50					
51		(COP) Right turn?		is your table up? Please check.	
52		(CAP)We'll hit a mountain! (COP) Yes.			
53					
54		(CAP) Right turn.			
55					
56					
57					
58		(CAP)Max. power.			
59				(comm. between other aircraft and COM)	(same as left)
	continue	continue		continue	continue

1 8 4 8 : 0 0 – 1 8 4 8 : 5 9

18"	Alarms, etc.	CVR Area Microphone	Co-pilot Seat(right)= Captain	Captain Seat(left)= Co-pilot	Flight Engineer Seat
4833					
00		(COP) Max. power.			
01		(F/E) Keep trying.			
02		(CAP) Ah, it doesn't need for two persons to do.		(com. between other aircraft and COM)	(same as left)
03					
04		(CAP) Left turn.			
05					
06					
07					
08		(CAP) Left turn. (COP)Yes.		(STM): in case, ah, a landing without notice . . .	
09		(CAP) Increase power.			
10		(CAP) Left turn, this time.			
11					
12		(CAP) Left turn.		(STM)JAPAN AIR ONE TWENTY THREE JAPAN AIR ONE TWENTY THREE YOKOTA APPROACH on guard. If you hear me, squawk 5423.	
13					
14					
15					
16		(CAP) Reduce power slightly.			
17					
18		(CAP) Ah, right right, lower the nose.			
19					
20					
21		(CAP) Lower the nose.			
22					
23					
24		(COP) Wheel is pushed all the way.			
25					
26				(same as left)	(same as left)
27			(com. between other aircraft and ACC)		
28	*				
29					
30					
31		(CAP) Then... '...'cess you?			
32		(COP) It's doesn't work.			
33					
34		(CAP) Lower the nose.			
35					
36		(CAP) Good.			
37					
38		(CAP) We'll go into the mountains. (COP) Yes.			
39					
40					
41		(CAP) isn't.			
42					
43				(same as left)	(same as left)
44			(com. between other aircraft and ACC)	(YOK)JAPAN AIR ONE TWENTY THREE JAPAN AIR ONE TWENTY THREE YOKOTA APPROACH on guard. If you hear me, Contact YOKOTA 129.4.	
45					
46	*				
47					
48		(COP) Shall I increase power?			
49		(CAP) Power, power.			
50			(CAP) <heavy breathing>		
51			*		
52			*		
53			*	same as left	same as left
54					
55		(CAP) Power.	(CAP) Power.		
56					
57					
58	continue				
59					

407

1 8 4 9 : 0 0 ~ 1 8 4 9 : 5 9

IS"	Alarms. etc.	CVR Area Microphone	Co-pilot Seat(right)= Captain	Captain Seat(left)= Co-pilot	Flight Engineer Seat
49¥¥ 00			(CAP) <heavy breathing>		
01			"		
02			"	same as left	same as left
03			"	(COM)SELCAL	(COM)SELCAL
04					
05					same as left
06					
07					
08					
09		(F/E) Let's increase power.			
10		Let's increase power.			
11		(CAP) Right turn.			
12					
13		(?) · · · ·			
14					
15					
16				(COM)JAPAN AIR 123	
17				JAPAN AIR	
18				TOKYO	
19				How do you read ?	
20					
21					
22				(TOK)JAPAN AIR ONE	
23				TWENTY THREE JAPAN AIR	
24				AIR ONE TWENTY THREE	
25				YOKOTA APPROACH on guard.	
26				If you hear me,	
27				direct headings for	
28				maintain niner	
29				thousands	
30				then contact	
31				YOKOTA	
32				129.4.	
33					
34					
35					
36					
37					
38					
39			(comm. between other		
40		(CAP) Ah, no good · · ·	aircraft and ACC)		
41		(CAP) Stall.			
42		(CAP) Max power, max power.			
43		max power.			
44				(same as left)	(same as left)
45		(CAP) Stall.		(COM)JAPAN AIR TOKYO	same as left
46		(CAP) Yes, the altitude has lost.		How do you read ?	
47					
48	♦			(TOK)JAPAN AIR ONE	
49				TWENTY THREE JAPAN	
50				AIR ONE TWENTY THREE	
51				YOKOTA APPROACH on guard.	
52				If you hear me,	
53				Contact YOKOTA	
54				129.4.	
55					
56					
57					
58					
59	continue				

continue

1 8 5 0 : 0 0 — 1 8 5 0 : 5 9

18*	Alarms, etc.	CVR Area Microphone	Co-pilot Seat(right)= Captain	Captain Seat(left)= Co-pilot	Flight Engineer Seat
50:00					
01					
02					
03					
04					
05		(COP) We're gaining speed.			
06		speed.			
07					
08		(CAP) Let's give it a try.			
09					
10					
11					
12					
13					
14					
15					
16					
17					
18					
19					
20					
21					
22					
23					
24					
25					
26		(CAP) Stick with it. (COP)Yes.			
27		(F/E) Max.			
28		(CAP) Lower the nose. (COP)Yes.			
29		(CAP) Stick with it. Stick with it.			
30		(COP) Now, I've fully pushed the control.			
31		(F/E) Max power.			
32					
33					
34					
35		(COP) We're losing speed.			
36		speed.			
37					
38					
39			(comm. between other aircraft and ACC)		
40				(same as left)	(same as left)
41					
42		(CAP) You'll have to control			
43		pitch with power.			
44		(F/E) Lower control is OK.			
45		Let's use power control.			
46		please. (CAP)Yes.			
47		(COP) Speed.			
48		220 knots.			
49		(F/E) Yes.			
50					
51					
52					
53					
54					
55					
56		(F/E) Yes.			
57		Don't lower the nose.			
58		It's is lowering. (COP)Yes.	(comm. between other aircraft and COM)		
59	continues		continue	continue	continue

1851:00 — 1851:59

18"	Alarms, etc.	CVR Area Microphone	Co-Pilot Seat(right)= Captain	Captain Seat(left)= Co-pilot	Flight Engineer Seat
51' 00					
01					
02					
03					
04		(CAP) We're losing altitude. (COP)Yes.			
05		(CAP) Raise, raise the nose.			
06					
07					
08		(COP) Flap? I, lower it?			
09		(F/E) She I, lower it?			
10		(CAP) it won't go down.			
11		(F/E) Yes, eh, by alternate,			
12		(CAP) Alternate, as expected, (F/E)Yes, it is by alternate, [simultaneously recorded]			
13					
14					
15					
16					
17					
18					
19					
20					
21					
22		(CAP) Lower the nose.			
23					
24		(CAP) The rest is OK,			
25		just do your			
26		own job, your			
27					
28					
29		(F/E) Both hands. (COP)Yes.			
30		(CAP) Lower the nose.			
31					
32					
33		(CAP) Yes power.			
34		(F/E) I'll increase power.			
35					
36					
37		(F/E) Flap is now being			
38		extended. (CAP)Yes.			
39			(comm. between other aircraft and ACC)	(comm. between other aircraft and COM)	(same as left)
40					
41		(CAP) Lower the nose.			
42					
43					
44					
45					
46					
47					
48		(CAP) Push.			
49					
50					
51					
52					
53					
54			(same as left)	(same as left)	(same as left)
55					
56					
57					
58		continue	continue	continue	continue
59					

1 8 5 2 : 0 0 — 1 8 5 2 : 5 9

18"	Alarms, etc.	CVR Area Microphone	Co-pilot Seat(right)— Captain	Captain Seat(left)— Co-pilot	Flight Engineer Seat
52"					
00#				(same as left)	(same as left)
01					
02					
03					
04					
05					
06					
07					
08					
09			(comm. between other aircraft and ACC)	(comm. between other aircraft and COM)	(same as left)
10					
11	#				
12					
13					
14					
15					
16					
17					
18					
19		(F/E)The flap is now being extended by alternate. (COP)Yes.			
20					
21		(CAP)Lower the nose.			
22		(COP)Yes.			
23					
24					
25					
26					
27					
28					
29					
30					
31					
32					
33					
34					
35					
36		(CAP)Lower the nose. (COP)Yes.			
37					
38			(comm. between other aircraft and ACC)	(YDK)···123···	(same as left)
39					
40					
41					
42					
43					
44					
45					
46					
47					
48					
49					
50		(COP) Shall I take control ⌐ simultaneously			
51		(CAP) Yes, please. ⌐ recorded			
52					
53					
54					
55					
56					
57					
58					
59					
	continue		continue	continue	continue

412

1 8 5 3 : 0 0 — 1 8 5 3 : 5 9

18°	Alarm, etc.	CVR Area Microphone	Co-pilot Seat(right)= Captain	Captain Seat(left)= Co-pilot	Flight Engineer Seat
53;5 00 01 02 03 04 05 06 07 08 09 10 11 12 13			(comm. between other aircraft and ACC)	(same as left) (TOK)...123... (comm. between other aircraft and COM)	(same as left) (same as left)
14 15 16 17 18 19 20		(CAP) Raise the nose. (CAP) Power. (COP) Power up.			
21 22 23 24 25 26 27 28 29 30		(CAP) Eh. uncontrol. Japan Air 123 uncontrol.	(ACC)JAPAN AIR 123 JAPAN AIR 123 TOKYO. (CAP) Eh. uncontrol, Japan Air 123 uncontrol. (ACC)123 roger.	same as left	same as left
31 32 33 34 35 36 37 38 39 40 41 42 43 44 45 46			(ACC)JAPAN AIR 119 123 JAPAN AIR 123 Switch frequency to 119.7, 119.7 please.	(TOK)123 YOKOTA APPROACH CONTROL on guard. If you hear me, squawk 54 23 contact YOKOTA 129 same as left	same as left
47 48 49 50 51 52 53 54 55 56 57 58 59	## continue	(CAP) Yes, yes, 119.7. (COP) Ah, yes. Number 2. (CAP) 119.7. (COP)Yes. (F/E) Shall we try? (COP) Yes.	(ACC)JAPAN AIR 123	(APC)JAPAN AIR 123 (COM)SELCAL (same as left)	(COM)SELCAL (same as left)

1 8 5 4 : 0 0 — 1 8 5 4 : 5 9

18"	Alarms, etc.	CVR Area Microphone	Co-pilot Seat(right)= Captain	Captain Seat(left)== Co-Pilot	Flight Engineer Seat
54'00			(ACC) If you can switch to 119.7.	same as left	same as left
01					
02					
03		(CAP) Yes, left, left turn.	(APC)if you reading, come up freq— ency	(APC)...mittime. If you reading.	
04					
05		(COP) Yes, left turn.			
06		(F/E) Yes 119	(F/E)119.7.	(F/E) Yes, 119	(F/E) Yes, 119
07		(CAP) Left turn.	(APC)one one niner		
08		(F/E) 119.7.	seven, or set are already		
09			openly any		
10			frequency		
11			TOKYO		
12			APPROACH out.		
13					
14					
15					
16					
17					
18		(F/E) Japan Air 123.	(F/E) Japan Air 123	same as left	same as left
19		Eh I've selected 119.7.	eh, we've selected 119.7.		
20					
21		(CAP) Request position.			
22		(F/E) Request position.			
23					
24		(F/E) Japan Air 123	(F/E) Japan Air 123		
25		request position.	Request position.		
26					
27					
28			(APC)JAPAN AIR 123 your		
29			position 5		
30			ah— 5		
31			45		
32			miles north		
33			west of		
34			HANEDA.		
35					
36					
37		(F/E) Northwest of Haneda	(F/E) Northwest of Haneda		
38		eh__(CAP)__	ah eh		
39		(F/E) ah ah	how many miles?		
40		how many miles?			
41			(APC) Yes, that is correct.		
42			On our radar		
43			you're 55		
44			miles NW		
45		(CAP) Lower the nose.	eh,		
46			25 miles		
47		(?) ...	th		
48			th the		
49		(COP)The wheel is all the way.	west		
50			of		
51			Kawaguro.		
52			over.		
53				(TOK)JAPAN AIR ONE	
54		(F/E) Yes, roger.	(F/E) Yes, roger.	TWO THREE JAPAN	
55		(F/E) They say we're		AIR ONE TWO THREE	
56		25 miles west		TOKOTA APPROACH on served	
57		of Kawaguro.		. . .	
58			(scan, between other aircraft and CDR)	
59	continue			(TOK)JAPAN AIR ONE	(same as left)
			continue	continue	continue

1 8 5 5 : 0 0 — 1 8 5 5 : 5 9

:18'	Alarms, etc.	CVR Area Microphone	Co-pilot Seat(right) = Captain	Captain Seat(left) = Co-pilot	Flight Engineer Seat
:55' 00# 01 02 03 04 05 06 07 08 09 10 11 12 13 14 15 16 17 18 19 20 21 22 23 24 25 26 27 28 29 30 31 32 33 34 35 36 37 38 39 40 41 42 43 44 45 46 47 48 49 50 51 52 53 54 55 56 57 58 59		(CAP) Can you extend flap. (COP) Yes, flap 10. (CAP) Raise the nose. (F/E) Yes, power. (CAP) Raise the nose. (CAP) Raise the nose. (CAP) Raise the nose. (COP) I've been holding for a long time. (COP) Power. (CAP) Rer. halt the flap. (?) Ah (CAP) Power. (CAP) Flap. stop crowding together. (COP) Flap up, flap up, flap up. (COP) flap up (CAP)flap up. (COP) Yes. (CAP) Power. (CAP) Power. (CAP) Flap. (F/E) It is up.	(APC) [I'll speak in Japanese]. We are ready for your approach at any time. And, coordinating with possible update in landing also. (F/E) Yes, power. (APC) Let's know your intention, over. (APC)JAPAN AIR 123 JAPAN AIR 123. If reading, your radar position 5 miles correction 60 miles northwest of the HAMEBA. Norther ah— 5 mile 50 nautical mile northwest of HAMEBA.	(YOK)TWO THREE JAPAN AIR ONE TWO THREE YOKOTA APPROACH CONTROL on guard, if you hear me (comm. between other aircraft and COM) same as left (YOK)JAPAN AIR ONE TWO THREE JAPAN AIR ONE TWO THREE YOKOTA APPROACH CONTROL on guard, If you hear me, come up 121.5. (STW) keeping communication with eh, besides ... same as left	(same as left) same as left same as left
continue					

1 8 5 6 : 0 0 ～ 1 8 5 6 : 2 8

18"	Alarms. etc.	CVR Area Microphone	Co-pilot Seat(right)= Captain	Captain Seat(left)~ Co-pilot	Flight Engineer Seat
56:00					
01					
02					
03					
04					
05					
06					
07		(CAP)Raise the nose.			
08					
09		(CAP) Raise the nose.			
10	CPWS		(CAP) Power.	same as left	same as left
11		(CAP) Power.			
12					
13		(GPWS)SINK RATE			
14		WHOOPWHOOP			
15		PULL UP			
16		WHOOPWHOOP			
17		PULL UP			
18		WHOOPWHOOP			
19		WHOOPWHOOP			
20		PULL UP (CAP)···			
21		PULL UP <contact sound>	noise	same as left	same as left
22		WHOOPWHOOP·			
23		PULL UP			
24		<contact sound>			
25		<end of recording>			
26					
27					
28					

(Tentative Translation from Original in Japanese)

Recommendation No.1
July 19, 1987

Honorable Ryutaro Hashimoto
Minister for Transport

RECOMMENDTAION ON SECUREMENT OF AIRWORTHINESS OF AIRCRAFT

Aircraft Accident Investigation Commission (AAIC) has completed the accident investigation on JA8119, a Boeing 747 SR—100 of Japan Air Lines Co.,Ltd. which crashed among mountains of Ueno Village, Tano County, Gunma Prefecture, Japan on August 12, 1985.

Based on results of the investigation, AAIC recommends, pursuant to the provision of Paragraph 1 of Article 21 of Aircraft Accident Investigation Commission Establishment Law, that the following actions be taken promptly, because AAIC believes that they should be conducive to prevention of aircraft accidents.

1.   In case where large-scale repairs such as modifications of major structural elements of an aircraft are carried out at a place other than the factory where the said aircraft was manufactured, for recovery from or repair of damage caused by aircraft accident, as much guidance as possible should be provided to the repair agency engaged in the repair work so that the planning and management of the repairs are conducted with special care as individual condition requires.

2.   In case where large-scale repairs such as modifications of major structural elements of an aircraft are carried out for recovery from or repair of damage caused by aircraft accident, as much guidance as possible should be provided to aircraft operator so that special instruction items, if necessary, are established for the portion concerned and continuous monitor is maintained.

3.   In this accident. ruptures of the fuselage tail. vertical fin.
and hydraulical flight control systems were caused as a chain reaction
by flowout of the pressurized air due to rupture of aft pressure
bulkhead. To prevent the recurrence of such situation, a study should
be initiated on the addition to the airworthiness criteria of the
provisions concerning the fail-safe capability of peripheral
structures. functional systems etc. against rupture of pressurized
structural components such as the aft pressure bulkhead on a large
aircraft.

By Aircraft Accident Investigation Commission

/S/   <u>Shun Takeda</u>
      Chairman

/S/   <u>Yoshiomi Enomoto</u>
      Member

/S/   <u>Kiyoshi Nishimura</u>
      Member

/S/   <u>Jiro Koo</u>
      Member

/S/   <u>Akira Azuma</u>
      Member

418

IN THE AFTERMATH...

Delayed rescue operation

United States Airforce controllers at Yokota Air Force base situated near the flight path of Flight 123 had been monitoring the distressed aircraft's calls for help. They maintained contact throughout the ordeal with Japanese flight control officials and made their landing strip available to the airplane. After losing track on radar, a U.S. Air Force C-130 from the 345 TAS was asked to search for the missing plane. The C-130 crew was the first to spot the crash site 20 minutes after impact, while it was still daylight. The crew radioed Yokota Air Base to alert them and directed a USAF Huey helicopter from Yokota to the crash site. Rescue teams were assembled in preparation to lower Marines down for rescues by helicopter tow line. The offers by American forces of help to guide Japanese forces immediately to the crash site and of rescue assistance were rejected by Japanese officials. Instead, Japanese government representatives ordered the U.S. crew to keep away from the crash site and return to Yokota Air Base, stating the Japan Self-Defense Forces (JSDF) were going to handle the entire rescue alone.

Although a JSDF helicopter eventually spotted the wreck during the night, poor visibility and the difficult mountainous terrain prevented it from landing at the site. The pilot of the JSDF helicopter reported from the air that there were no signs of survivors. Based on this report, JSDF ground personnel did not set out to the actual site the night of the crash. Instead, they were dispatched to spend the night at a makeshift village erecting tents, constructing helicopter landing ramps and in other preparations, all some 63 kilometers from the wreck. JSDF did not set out for the actual crash site until the following morning. Medical staff later found a number of passengers' bodies whose injuries indicated that they had survived the crash only to die from shock or exposure overnight in the mountains while awaiting rescue. One doctor said *"If the discovery had come ten hours earlier, we could have found more survivors."*

Yumi Ochiai, one of the four survivors out of 524 passengers and crew, recounted from her hospital bed that she recalled bright lights and the sound of helicopter rotors shortly after she awoke amid the wreckage, and while she could hear screaming and moaning from other survivors, these sounds gradually died away during the night.

Cause

The official cause of the crash according to the report published by Japan's then Aircraft Accidents Investigation Commission is as follows:

1. The aircraft was involved in a tailstrike incident at Osaka International Airport on 2 June 1978, which damaged the aircraft's rear pressure bulkhead.

2. The subsequent repair of the bulkhead did not conform to Boeing's approved repair methods. The Boeing technicians fixing the aircraft used two separate doubler plates, one with two rows of rivets and one with only one row while their procedure calls for one continuous doubler plate with three rows of rivets to reinforce the damaged bulkhead. This reduced the part's resistance to metal fatigue by 70%. According to the Federal Aviation Administration, the one *"doubler plate"* which was specified for the job (the Federal Aviation Administration calls it a "splice plate" - essentially a patch) was cut into two pieces parallel to the stress crack it was intended to reinforce, "to make it fit". This negated the

effectiveness of two of the rows of rivets. During the investigation Boeing calculated that this incorrect installation would fail after approximately 10,000 pressurizations; the aircraft accomplished 12,318 take-offs between the installation of the new plate and the final accident.

3. When the bulkhead gave way, the resulting explosive decompression ruptured the lines of all four hydraulic systems and blew off the vertical stabilizer. With the aircraft's flight controls disabled, the aircraft became uncontrollable.

Aftermath

The Japanese public's confidence in Japan Airlines took a dramatic downturn in the wake of the disaster, with passenger numbers on domestic routes dropping by one-third. Rumors persisted that Boeing had admitted fault to cover up shortcomings in the airline's inspection procedures, thus protecting the reputation of a major customer. In the months after the crash, domestic traffic decreased by as much as 25%. In 1986, for the first time in a decade, fewer passengers boarded JAL's overseas flights during New Years than the previous year. Some of them considered switching to All Nippon Airways as a safer alternative.

Without admitting liability, JAL paid ¥780 million to the victims' relatives in the form of "condolence money". Its president, Yasumoto Takagi, resigned, while a maintenance manager working for the company at Haneda committed suicide to apologize for the accident. Upon discovering the accident, the particular aircraft involved and the cause, the Boeing engineer who supervised the improper repair of the pressure bulkhead, which ruptured at the repair and caused the departure of the vertical stabilizer, also committed suicide.

In the summer of 2009, stairs with a handrail were installed to facilitate visitors' access to the crash site. Japan Transport Minister Seiji Maehara visited the site on August 12, 2010 to pray for the victims. The visit was the first time a transport minister has visited the actual crash site.

Remembrance

The crash also led to the 2006 opening of the Safety Promotion Center. It is located in the Daini Sogo Building on the grounds of Tokyo International Airport. This center was created for training purposes to alert employees of the importance of airline safety and their personal responsibility to ensure safety. The center, which has displays regarding air safety, the history of the crash, and selected pieces of the aircraft and passenger effects (including handwritten farewell notes), is also open to the public by appointment made one day prior to the visit.

Other Air Crash Investigations:

On 23 June 1985, Air India Flight 182, a Boeing 747-237B was on its way from Montreal, Canada, to London when it was blown up while in Irish airspace, and crashed into the Atlantic Ocean. 329 people perished. It was the largest mass murder in modern Canadian history. The explosion and downing of the carrier was related to the Narita Airport Bombing. Investigation and prosecution took 25 years. The suspects were members of the Sikh separatist Babbar Khalsa. Inderjit Singh Reyat, the only person convicted, was sentenced to 15 years in prison.

On April 10, 2010 at 10:41 local time, approaching Runway 26 of Smolensk "Severny" airdrome, a Tupolev-154M aircraft of the State Aviation of the Republic of Poland crashed while conducting a non-regular international flight PLF 101 carrying passengers from Warsaw to Smolensk. The cause of the accident was the failure of the crew to take a timely decision to proceed to an alternate airdrome due to weather conditions at the airport of destination. All 96 persons on board, including Polish President Lech Kaczyński and his wife, died in the crash.

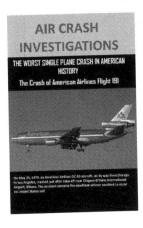

On May 25, 1979, American Airlines Flight 191, a McDonnell-Douglas DC-10-10 aircraft, on its way from Chicago to Los Angeles, crashed just after take-off near Chicago-O'Hare International Airport, Illinois. During the take off the left engine and pylon assembly and about 3 ft of the leading edge of the left wing separated from the aircraft and fell to the runway. Flight 191 crashed killing two hundred and seventy one persons on board and two persons on the ground. The accident remains the deadliest airliner accident to occur on United States soil.

Lauda Air Flight NG 104, a Boeing 767-300 ER of Austrian nationality was on a scheduled passenger flight Hong Kong-Bangkok-Vienna, Austria. NG 104 departed Hong Kong Airport on May 26, 1991, and made an intermediate landing at Bangkok Airport. The flight departed Bangkok Airport at 1602 hours. The airplane disappeared from air traffic radar at 1617 hours, about 94 nautical miles northwest of Bangkok. The probable cause of this accident is attributed to an uncommanded in-flight deployment of the left engine thrust reverser. All 223 people on board died in the accident.

On Tuesday 25 July 2000 Air France Flight AFR 4590, a Concorde registered F-BTSC, took off from Paris Charles de Gaulle, to undertake a charter flight to New York with nine crew members and one hundred passengers on board. During takeoff from runway 26 right at Roissy Charles de Gaulle Airport, a tyre was damaged. A major fire broke out. The aircraft was unable to gain height or speed and crashed onto a hotel, killing all 109 people on board and 4 on the ground. The crash would become the end of the Concorde era.

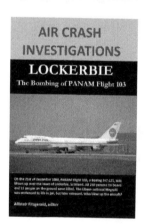

On the 21st of December 1988, PANAM Flight 103, a Boeing 747-121, on its way from London Heathrow to New York, was blown up over the town of Lockerbie, Scotland. All 259 persons on board of the aircraft and 11 residents of the town of Lockerbie were killed. In 2001 the Libyan Megrahi was sentenced to life imprisonment in Scotland. In 2009 Megrahi applied to be released from jail on compassionate grounds. His appeal was granted and on the 20th of August 2009 he was released from prison. But was Megrahi really guilty?

425

On 31 May 2009, flight AF447, an Airbus A330-200, took off from Rio de Janeiro bound for Paris. At 2 h 10, a position message and some maintenance messages were transmitted by the ACARS automatic system. After this nothing was heard of from the aircraft. Six days later bodies and airplane parts were found by the French and Brazilian navies. All 228 passengers and crew members on board are presumed to have perished in the accident. A massive search by air and sea craft for the plane's black boxes failed so far.

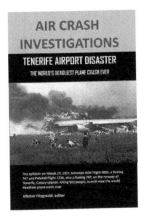

On Sunday, March 27, 1977 KLM Flight 4805 and PANAM Flight 1736 both approached Las Palmas Airport in the Canary Islands, when a terrorist's bomb exploded on the airport. Both flights were diverted to the neighboring island of Tenerife. After Las Palmas Airport reopened first KLM Flight 4805 was cleared for takeoff, a few minutes later PANAM 1736 was cleared. Due to a number of misunderstandings both aircraft collided on the runway of Tenerife Airport during takeoff, killing 583 people.

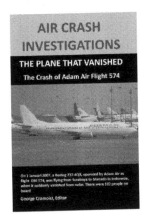

On 1 January 2007, a Boeing 737-4Q8, operated by Adam Air as flight DHI 574, was on a flight from Surabaya, East Java to Manado, Sulawesi, at FL 350 (35,000 feet) when it suddenly disappeared from radar. There were 102 people on board.. Nine days later wreckage was found floating in the sea near the island of Sulawesi. The black boxes revealed that the pilots were so engrossed in trouble shooting the IRS that they forgot to fly the plane, resulting in the crash that cost the lives of all aboard.

426

On February 12, 2009, about 2217 eastern standard time, Colgan Air, Flight 3407, a Bombardier DHC-8-400, on approach to Buffalo-Niagara International Airport, crashed into a residence in Clarence Center, New York, 5 nautical miles northeast of the airport. The 2 pilots, 2 flight attendants, and 45 passengers aboard the airplane were killed, one person on the ground was killed, and the airplane was destroyed. The National Transportation Safety Board determined that the probable cause of this accident was a pilot's error.

On 25 February 2009 a Boeing 737-800, flight TK1951, operated by Turkish Airlines was flying from Istanbul in Turkey to Amsterdam Schiphol Airport. There were 135 people on board. During the approach to the runway at Schiphol airport, the aircraft crashed about 1.5 kilometres from the threshold of the runway. This accident cost the lives of four crew members, and five passengers, 120 people sustained injuries. The crash was caused by a malfunctioning radio altimeter and a failure to implement the stall recovery procedure correctly.

On November 12, 2001, American Airlines flight 587, an Airbus A300-605R, took off from John F. Kennedy International Airport, New York. Flight 587 was a scheduled passenger flight to Santo Domingo, Dominican Republic, with a crew of 9 and 251 passengers aboard the airplane. Shortly after take-off the airplane lost its tail, the engines subsequently separated in flight and the airplane crashed into a residential area of Belle Harbor, New York. All 260 people aboard the airplane and 5 people on the ground were killed, and the airplane was destroyed by impact forces and a post crash fire.

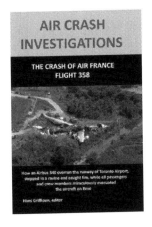

On August 2, 2005 Air France Flight 358, an Airbus A340, departed Paris, on a flight to Toronto, Canada, with 297 passengers and 12 crew members on board. On final approach, the aircraft's weather radar was displaying heavy precipitation. The aircraft touched down 3800 feet down the runway, and was not able to stop before the end of it. The aircraft stopped in a ravine and caught fire. All passengers and crew members were able to evacuate the aircraft on time. Only 2 crew members and 10 passengers were seriously injured during the crash and the evacuation.

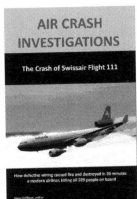

On 2 September 1998, Swissair Flight SR 111 departed New York, flight to Geneva, Switzerland, with 215 passengers and 14 crew members on board. About 53 minutes after departure, the flight crew smelled an abnormal odour in the cockpit. They decided to divert to the Halifax International Airport. They were unaware that a fire was spreading above the ceiling in the front area of the aircraft. They did not make it to Halifax, 20 minutes later the aircraft crashed in the North Atlantic near Peggy's Cove, Nova Scotia, Canada. There were no survivors, 229 people died in the incident.

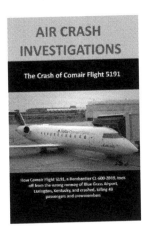

On August 27, 2006, Comair Flight 5191, a Bombardier CL-600-2B19, crashed during takeoff from the wrong runway of Blue Grass Airport, Lexington, Kentucky, killing 49 of the 50 people aboard. From the beginning everything went wrong. First the captain and first officer boarded the wrong airplane, only after starting the auxiliary power unit they found out they were in the wrong aircraft. Taxiing to the takeoff position the captain and first officer were so engaged in a private conversation that they did not realize they took the wrong runway. The air traffic controller did not notice anything.

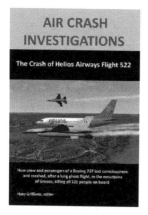

On 14 August 2005, a Boeing 737-300 aircraft departed from Larnaca, Cyprus, for Prague. As the aircraft climbed through 16.000 ft, the Captain contacted the company Operations Centre and reported a problem. Thereafter, there was no response to radio calls to the aircraft. At 07:21 h, the aircraft was intercepted by two F-16 aircraft of the Hellenic Air Force. They observed the aircraft and reported no external damage. The aircraft crashed approximately 33 km northwest of the Athens International Airport. All 121 people on board were killed.

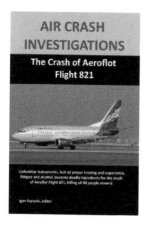

On 14 September 2008 Aeroflot Flight 821, a Boeing 737-505, operated by Aeroflot-Nord, a subsidiary of the Russian airline Aeroflot, crashed on approach to Bolshoye Savino Airport, Perm, Russia. All 82 passengers and 6 crew members were killed. The aircraft was completely destroyed. According to the final investigation report, the main reason of the crash was pilot error. Both pilots had lost spatial orientation, lack of proper training, insufficient knowledge of English and fatigue from lack of adequate rest. Alcohol in the Captain's blood may also have contributed to the accident.

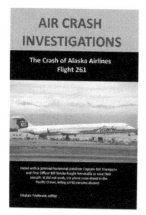

On January 31, 2000, Alaska Airlines, Flight 261, a McDonnell Douglas MD-83, was on its way from Puerto Vallarta, Mexico, to Seattle, Washington, when suddenly the horizontal stabilizer of the plane jammed. Captain Thompson and First officer Tansky tried to make an emergency landing in Los Angeles. The plane suddenly crashed into the Pacific Ocean, killing all 93 people aboard. The NTSB concluded that the crash was caused by insufficient maintenance. The crash of Alaska Airlines Flight 261 could have been avoided.

429

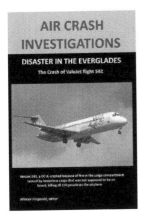

On May 11, 1996, at 1413:42 eastern daylight time, a Douglas DC-9-32 crashed into the Everglades 10 minutes after takeoff from Miami International Airport, Miami, Florida. The airplane was being operated by ValuJet Airlines, Inc., as flight 592 and was on its way to Atlanta, Georgia. Both pilots, the three flight attendants, and all 105 passengers were killed. The NTSB determined that the cause of the accident, was a fire in the airplane's cargo compartment, initiated by the actuation of an oxygen generator being improperly carried as cargo.

On August 24, 2001, Air Transat Flight 236, an Airbus 330, was on its way from Toronto, Canada to Lisbon, Portugal with 306 people on board. Above the Atlantic Ocean, the crew noticed a dangerous fuel imbalance. After flying 100 miles without fuel the crew managed to land the aircraft at the Lajes Airport at 06:45. Only 16 passengers and 2 cabin-crew members received injuries. The investigation uncovered a large crack in the fuel line of the right engine, caused by mistakes during an engine change just before the start of the flight.

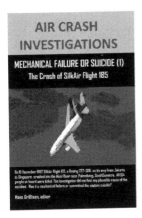

On 19 December 1997 SilkAir Flight 185, a Boeing 737-300, operated by SilkAir, Singapore, on its way from Jakarta to Singapore, crashed at about 16:13 local time into the Musi river near Palembang, South Sumatra. All 97 passengers and seven crew members were killed. Prior to the sudden descent from 35,000 feet, the flight data recorders suddenly stopped recording at different times. There were no mayday calls transmitted from the airplane prior or during the rapid descent. The weather at the time of the crash was fine.

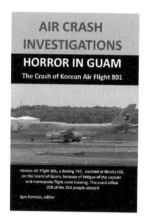

On August 6, 1997, about 0142:26 Guam local time, Korean Air flight 801, a Boeing 747-300, crashed at Nimitz Hill, Guam. The aircraft was on its way from Seoul, Korea to Guam with 237 passengers and a crew of 17 on board. Of the 254 persons on board, 228 were killed. The airplane was destroyed by impact forces and a post-crash fire. The National Transportation Safety Board determined that the probable cause of the accident was captain's fatigue and Korean Air's inadequate flight crew training.

This book explains the accident involving Atlantic Southeast Airlines flight 529, an EMB-120RT airplane, which lost a propeller blade and crashed near Carrollton, Georgia, on August 21, 1995. The accident killed 8 people on board. Safety issues in the report focused on manufacturer engineering practices, propeller blade maintenance repair, propeller testing and inspection procedures, the relaying of emergency information by air traffic controllers, crew resource management training, and the design of crash axes carried in aircraft.

Made in the USA
Middletown, DE
04 October 2023

40120096R00257